BRITISH RAILWAY HISTORY IN COLOUR

Volume 1:
WEST GLOUCESTER
& WYE VALLEY LINES

The attractions of the Gloucester to Hereford route were manifold, with the many scenic locations featuring high on the list. Between Ross and Rotherwas Junction, the River Wye was crossed three times and this Hereford-bound train, with an unidentified 'Manor' Class 4-6-0 at the head, is making the third of those crossings, at Ballingham. It was a scene that was soon to disappear, however. The picture was taken in October 1964 and passenger services were to be withdrawn within a few days, on 2nd November. JOHN STRANGE/NPC

PREVIOUS PAGE: On 23rd January 1963, the coldest day of that bitter winter – the temperature at Ross observatory dropped to a record low of 16.8° F (-8.5° C) – Ben Ashworth ventured out to capture this superb colour shot of No. 7904 *Fountains Hall* approaching Over Junction with what the lamp headcode indicates to be a parcels or perishables train. The Over Junction Down Main Inner Home signal is 'off', as is Over Sidings Signal Box's motor worked Distant signal beneath it. B.J. ASHWORTH

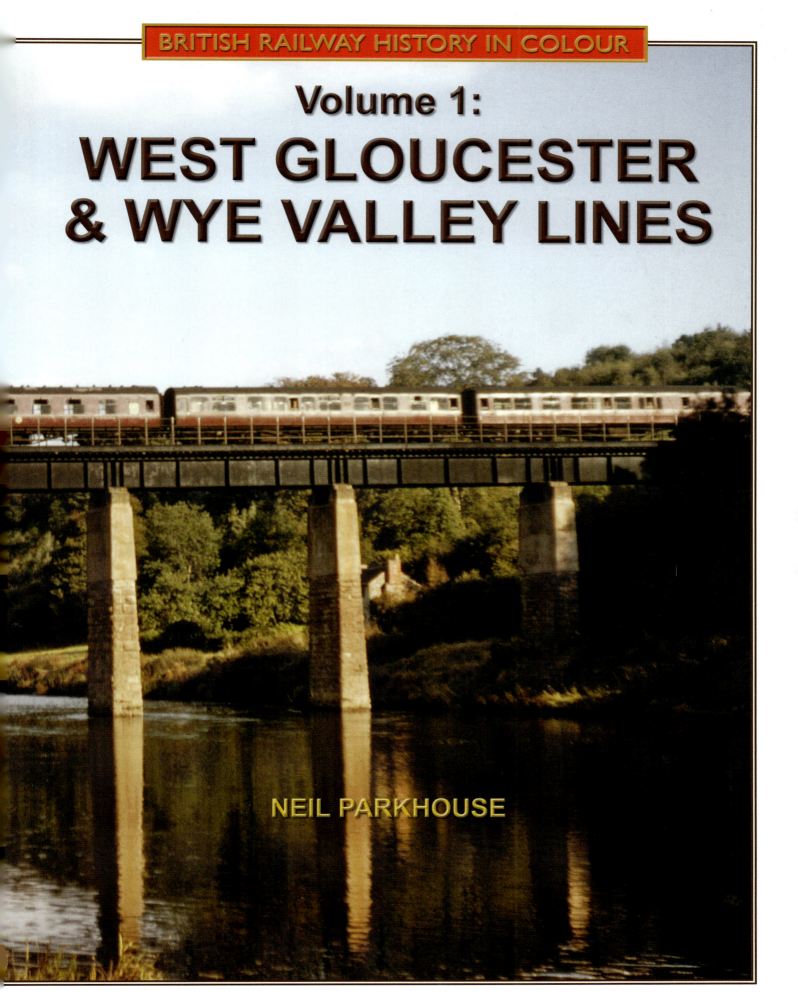

BRITISH RAILWAY HISTORY IN COLOUR

Volume 1: WEST GLOUCESTER & WYE VALLEY LINES

NEIL PARKHOUSE

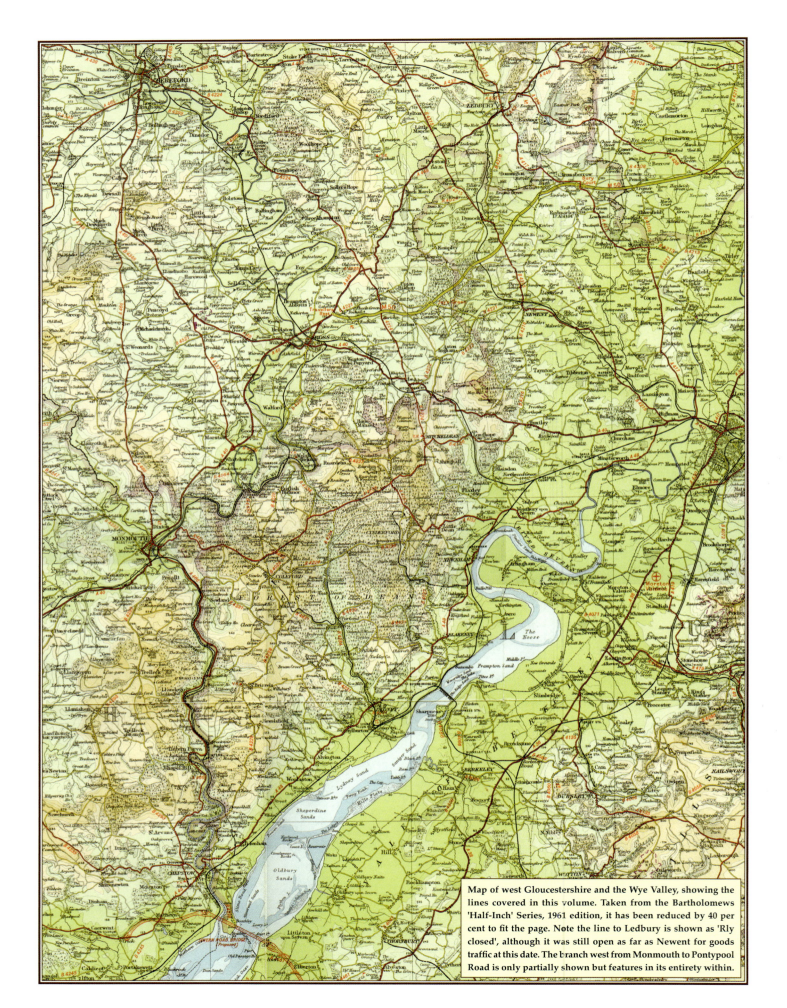

Map of west Gloucestershire and the Wye Valley, showing the lines covered in this volume. Taken from the Bartholomews 'Half-Inch' Series, 1961 edition, it has been reduced by 40 per cent to fit the page. Note the line to Ledbury is shown as 'Rly closed', although it was still open as far as Newent for goods traffic at this date. The branch west from Monmouth to Pontypool Road is only partially shown but features in its entirety within.

CONTENTS

Introduction:	page 7
Acknowledgements	page 11
Sources & Bibliography	page 13
Section 1: Gloucester Central	page 15
Section 2: The Llanthony Docks Branch	page 39
Section 3: The Ledbury Branch	page 49
Section 4: Over Junction to Grange Court Junction	page 79
Section 5: The Hereford, Ross and Gloucester Line	page 95
Section 6: The Ross and Monmouth Railway	page 209
Section 7: Monmouth to Pontypool Road	page 243
Section 8: Monmouth to Chepstow. The Wye Valley Line	page 249
Section 9: Chepstow to Grange Court Junction	page 287

Published by LIGHTMOOR PRESS
© Lightmoor Press & Neil Parkhouse 2013/2018
Reprinted 2014. Enlarged 2nd edition 2018
Designed by Neil Parkhouse

British Library Cataloguing-in-Publication Data.
A catalogue record for this book is available from the British Library

ISBN 13: 9781911038 40 5

All rights reserved. No part of this publication may be reproduced, stored in a retrieval system or transmitted in any form or by any means, electronic, mechanical, photocopying, recording or otherwise, without the written permission of the publisher.

BLACK DWARF LIGHTMOOR PUBLICATIONS LTD
Unit 144B, Harbour Road Trading Estate,
Lydney, Gloucestershire GL15 4EJ
www.lightmoor.co.uk
info@lightmoor.co.uk

Lightmoor Press is an imprint of
Black Dwarf Lightmoor Publications Ltd

Printed in Poland
www.lfbookservices.co.uk

The Wye Valley near Redbrook, circa 1937, from a lantern slide. NPC

Whilst many railway enthusiasts mourned the passing of the steam locomotive from the everyday railway scene, there was perhaps less appreciation at the time of the whole way of life which was also being lost with the closure of many secondary and branch lines, coupled with the modernisation of what was left of our railway system. This scene at Longhope, on the Gloucester to Hereford line looking north towards Ross-on-Wye, typifies that aspect of the railway, as a friend of the photographer lowers one of the oil lamps, an operation which required carrying out every evening when all of the lamps had to be lit by hand and then lowered again to be extinguished when services finished. The stone-built, broad gauge era station building, blue enamelled Great Western Railway notice, corrugated iron goods lock-up, platform barrows and catchpoints sign at the end of the platform all serve to remind us of just how much was lost at a time when many believed the age of the train was coming to an end. JOHN STRANGE/NPC

INTRODUCTION

Like most counties, Gloucestershire's railway system is today but a shadow of its former self. The city of Gloucester has always been the hub of the county's railways and once boasted lines radiating out to all points of the compass – north and east to Worcester, Birmingham, Cheltenham and the Cotswolds; south and east to Swindon and Bristol; and west and south to Ledbury, Hereford and to South Wales. Of the main routes, all survive bar the GWR line to Birmingham via Stratford on Avon, whilst the secondary lines – across country to Hereford and over the Cotswolds, east to Kingham and south to Swindon via Cirencester – have gone. In addition, almost all of the branches and industrial lines have closed, along with over ninety per cent of the stations; there used to be well over a hundred but now there are just nine and three of those are reopenings. Further, at the time of writing, there are only four signal boxes still *in situ* which are not on preserved lines: Awre Junction, which closed in 1976 but was left standing for use as a PW store, the Grade II listed St. Mary's Crossing Signal Box near Stroud (out of use, a cabin adjacent is now used), Moreton-in-Marsh Signal Box (which has not only survived a recent upgrading of the Cotswold Line but has even gained an extra semaphore signal!) and Alstone Crossing in Cheltenham.

Partly due to the perceived dearth of material, railway colour albums have largely kept to a tried and tested formula over the years: landscape format, one shot per page and generally covering quite a large geographic area, with the cost of colour printing dictating the resultant size of most publications. Even the more recent colour books that have been published still seem mainly to adhere to the 'pretty picture' idea, with little concept of telling a story. To date no-one has ever really tried to present an in-depth colour portrait of the railways of a particular area. Thus, what I am attempting to do here is present a colour survey of the railway infrastructure of Gloucestershire (and surrounds) as it existed just before the Beeching Report and the great British Railways modernisation plan decimated decades of railway history.

With a long standing interest in the railways of west Gloucestershire, the idea for a colour book was first stimulated in 2001, when the late Audie Baker, of Kidderminster Railway Museum, made available to me over a hundred scans he had just made of the Forest of Dean branches. These were all from colour slides taken by the late Bill Potter, whose collection had been donated to the museum. However, whilst it was a superb range of pictures, there were many gaps, places which Bill had not photographed and I decided to try and fill these before compiling a book. Gradually, however, the coverage began to spread out across the county. As more contacts were made and more material found, it soon became apparent that enough colour photographs were around to cover the whole of the county – Gloucestershire seems to have been particularly fortunate in the number of railway photographers who were working with colour film from the late 1950s.

The final problem then became one of quantity. So much material was turning up that even fitting it into a couple of books – the initial plan – had to be revised. I eventually decided to split Gloucestershire's railways into six areas, although this involved a certain amount of licence in straying over borders into neighbouring counties to complete particular routes. For instance, this first volume will cross the county boundaries of Herefordshire and Monmouthshire, as we follow the lines serving the Wye Valley and beyond. However, whilst it seemed churlish to cover two of the lines leaving Monmouth and then not the third, to Pontypool Road, perversely perhaps, no attempt has been made to travel south from Chepstow to Severn Tunnel Junction. Subsequent volumes will stray into Oxfordshire (to cover the eastern end of the Banbury to Cheltenham line and the Fairford Branch), Worcestershire (Ashchurch-Upton upon Severn, Ashchurch-Evesham and around Honeybourne), Warwickshire (Stratford upon Avon) and Wiltshire (to Swindon on the ex-GWR main line from Stroud and on the M&SWJR from Andoversford Junction). As a consequence, I made a late decision to deviate from my planned 'Gloucestershire Railways in Colour' series title and have instead renamed it 'British Railway History in Colour', not least because the hope is that others may be stimulated to have a go at covering further regions in such detail.

For anyone else tempted to study another region in this sort of detail, it is my belief, from the colour material that I have been made aware of over the last ten years or so, that there is plenty of scope. The railways of Cornwall, Devon and Somerset could easily be covered in depth, and Dorset, Hampshire and Wiltshire probably would not be too difficult either. The lines, particularly many of the branches, of Herefordshire, Worcestershire and Shropshire were also well photographed and would make for very interesting volumes. The railways serving the beautiful and often remote stretches of Mid Wales seem to have been another magnet, whilst the ex-Cambrian Railways lines were always popular. And these are just the regions with which I am familiar; I am sure that there are others.

Most enthusiasts understandably lament the passing of the steam locomotive and thousands flock to see them when occasionally a preserved example ventures out onto the main line. However, for many others, the mourning is for the loss of the stations and particularly the 'look' of the steam age railway – the hugely varied architecture of the buildings (and yet always managing to look like a station), signal boxes, goods yards and engine sheds, semaphore signals, lamps, signs, totems, nameboards – in short, the paraphernalia that went to make up the steam age railway. As a result, many of these items are now highly sought after by collectors, whilst today's railway has an anodine corporate appearance. However, times have to be moved with and these volumes will be a document, not a peon for moving backwards. Progress is inevitable, although some of the decisions taken back then – the destruction of the Severn Railway Bridge for instance – now look very short sighted.

The motor age has also drastically changed the nature of the landscape. Roads now are festooned with signs, mostly large and obtrusive so as to be readable to the speeding motorist, whilst cameras, white lines and heavy lorries all serve to slow him down again. Towns and villages are now divided by their roads, whilst shoppers drift away to large out of town arcades with ready parking and, with few exceptions, every town centre has the same uninviting look. On Bank Holiday weekends, tourists now drive around the Cotswolds, the Forest of Dean and the Wye Valley, whilst the railway lines which could have taken them around these picturesque areas in peace and safety have almost all been taken up, and the track beds turned into walkways and cyclepaths. But might some of them one day make a comeback, as worldwide we reach the state of 'peak oil'? Or will a new, efficient, practical means of powering motor cars finally be achieved? We have become used to the individuality the car affords us and most will not give that up lightly.

Thus, as well as showing the railways, the heavy industry and the docks which were all still at work in the region in the 1960s, these photographs also portray Gloucestershire at the end of an era, when it was safe to cross the road, when the landscape was still maintained and before the post-war expansion in population created such a demand for new housing, roads and services. There is still, just, a discernable air of innocence prevalent in these photographs, of the simple life many led before the wholesale advent of motor cars, television and the consumer society. In 1960, under half the population had access to a motor car.

Indeed, this is perhaps the most difficult aspect for the vast majority of people who will peruse these pages to take in. Almost all the pictures contained herein were taken within the last fifty years, or in other words, well within living memory. We live today in a world of computers and scanners, digital cameras, high definition colour TV which can be paused in mid live coverage, and DVD recorders and players – a world of vision, filled with colour. Fifty years ago, colour photography was still a novelty. Most photographers, not just of railways, worked mainly or solely in black and white. There were several reasons for this, such as the cost of colour film and the very low film speed (10ASA) then available, as well as the variable quality of the colour and the difficulty of processing and printing your own film, which many did with their black and white negatives. Also, with railway photographers, it may in part have been because many of them believed that black and white WAS the medium for photographing trains and that colour did not produce such dramatic results. I remember that lovely gentleman Bill Potter telling me many years ago that he never regarded colour photography seriously – "*It was just a bit of fun*" – and yet over 4,000 of his colour slides now reside in the collection at Kidderminster Railway Museum. Many are reproduced herein and more will appear in future volumes, so you can all judge for yourselves as to how good they are.

However, I did wonder when scanning the many slides I have collected or been given access to if, perhaps, it was the end result that often disappointed the likes of Bill and his fellow 'photters'. As mentioned above, the low speed and variable quality/colour reproduction of early colour film meant the end result, even for an experienced photographer, was often something of a lottery. Even Bill's slides have a proportion of poorer results, for all sorts of reasons, which may explain his remark. What he did not have the benefit of access to back then though was a computer, scanner and image manipulation technology. Many of the perceived faults can today be corrected, with colours adjusted, shadows highlighted and paler areas darkened, thanks to the sophisticated software now available. I'm sure Bill would be amazed at what can now be achieved, as Ben Ashworth was when I showed him the results of hours spent working on his slides, sadly way too few in number. Additionally, many photographers liked to show their work at enthusiasts evenings, giving slide shows. Unfortunately, this invariably gradually gave most of the slides used a coating of dirt and dust, much of which can now only be cleaned off 'on screen'.

Despite all these codicils, many of the photographs featured within these pages will go some way to disproving the view that colour was for amateurs, for holidaymakers or just for when the sun was shining. Having said that, the criteria on which I have based the choice of images has not been dictated by their quality as an overriding factor. The principle aim has been to provide colour views of as many locations as possible, illustrating the infrastructure that has been lost as much as the trains. The composition of the picture has been of secondary consideration and, in some instances, so has the quality. Whilst modern computer software can work wonders on many images, it cannot completely solve some of the problems encountered, such as softness or blurring. Some pictures have been chosen for their rarity, simply because nothing better has been located and this may therefore represent the best colour image which was taken. The slow film speeds I mentioned earlier meant that photography in all but the most optimum conditions was fraught with difficulties; poor weather, with bad light was almost impossible, very bright sunlight brought a different range of problems and snow could cause glare. Nevertheless, if the occasion was important – the running of a special for instance, or the last train on a particular line – the photographer had little choice. As you will find within these pages, the Wye Valley lines to Monmouth were closed with the running of a special on 5th January 1959, when there was deep snow on the ground but the sun shone very brightly, conditions for colour photography at that time which it would perhaps have been more difficult to encounter.

Indeed, many colour photographs were taken on rail tours, of a particular area, along goods lines or on last day runs. I have taken the decision, throughout the series, to include those which show something of interest, rather than just restricting the choice to views of regular service trains and stations when open. This is also partly because of the interest which has now built up in the history of railtours themselves, fueled in no small part by the excellent Sixbellsjunction website. However, where ordinary working trains feature, I have also attempted to show as great a variety as possible, of trains as well as locomotives, sometimes staying at a particular location for several pages, to give the reader a feel of some of the lineside locations favoured by photographers back then. Gloucester, as a major railway centre with two large stations, was a real magnet for railway photographers. However, away from there, there were several other places in the county which could provide a busy and immensely varied day's trainspotting; Standish Junction, for instance, where the four tracks from Gloucester split to run to Swindon and Bristol, or Grange Court Junction, where the line to Hereford diverged from the main line to South Wales. The less busy locations often had their own attractions though, drawing photographers back time and time again. Within these pages Longhope, a little way up the line to Hereford, is somewhere we linger for several pages (and could have stayed longer) simply because of the number of superb photographs from which I had to choose of this delightful station. Other locations were simply superbly picturesque, such as up the Golden Valley from Stroud to Chalford or the Forest of Dean.

The area west of the River Severn is rich in railway and industrial history. Here, on the borders of England and Wales, in one of the most beautiful and picturesque corners of the United Kingdom, is where the counties of Gloucestershire, Herefordshire and Monmouthshire meet. The landscape of alternating hills and valleys, veering from dramatic cliffs to alluvial flood plains, is clothed for the most part by the Forest of Dean and bordered by the meandering Wye and the tidal Severn. Beneath its topsoil, the richness of which has seen parts of the area farmed for at least a millenia, lies untold mineral wealth, coal and iron ore, which has attracted the attention of man since Roman times. With the coming of the Industrial Age, it was to attract the attention too, from the very earliest years, of the railway builders.

The history of the individual routes depicted within these pages will be covered briefly at the beginning of each chapter. A network of lines encircled the Forest of Dean, linking Gloucester with Hereford and South Wales, and serving the market towns of Ross-on-Wye, Monmouth and Chepstow. Although conceived and built as separate lines, their services were all interlinked and they mostly shared an affinity with the River Wye, at times bordering it, whilst at other times criss-crossing it in seemingly playful fashion. A journey from Hereford to Chepstow for instance, a distance of about 36 miles and which involved changing trains at both Ross-on-Wye and Monmouth, would also have seen the softly flowing waters of the Wye crossed no less than eleven times.

Perhaps this partly explains why Gloucestershire, as a county, proved popular with railway photographers, especially those using colour film. The breadth of images from which I have been able to choose has, at times, been astonishing and I know there are any number of talented photographers, whose work has appeared elsewhere, who I have not been in touch with. Indeed, some of them may wish to contact me in regard to future volumes, for my search for good colour images of Gloucestershire's railways never ceases.

Gloucester itself had been a mecca for railway photographers for many years, with its plethora of lines, many of which were grouped into quite a small area. The two stations were only around 500 yards apart, joined by a long covered wooden footbridge, and boasted their own separate engine sheds – Horton Road for the GWR and Barnwood for the Midland. Add in the lengthy mileage of lines and sidings serving the docks and various local industries, along with the Gloucester Railway Carriage & Wagon Company which was responsible for building items of rolling stock for home and abroad in huge numbers, and the city's attractions as far as the railway enthusiast was concerned are all too apparent. However, rather than devote one volume simply to the railways of Gloucester, coverage of the city's railway network will be split across various titles in this series. In this first volume, we look at Central station, its western approaches, and services to and from the west, along with the Llanthony Docks Branch. The Midland station, Tuffley Loop, Barnwood shed and the High Orchard and Hempsted Sidings docks branches will be covered in the volume looking at the Midland lines in Gloucestershire. The ex-GWR yards and Horton Road shed will all be covered in the volume which then goes on to follow the main line through Stroud to Swindon, along with the passenger train services for this route, such as the Chalford auto trains. Finally, the four track main line east from Gloucester through Churchdown and the services along it will feature in both the Midland and Cheltenham volumes. This is partly because of the way many services were worked between these two places. It seems astonishing now but in steam days, many London expresses were hauled the few miles between Gloucester and Cheltenham by tank engines. The ex-GWR 4-6-0s which covered the bulk of the mileage were detached at Gloucester and usually a '61XX' 'Prairie' tank attached instead but it was not unknown for a '94XX' Class pannier tank to be rostered if that was all Horton Road had available, which would then scurry off towards Cheltenham with ten or more coaches behind it.

The period covered within these pages is also largely dictated by the medium. Anything pre-WW2 in colour is astonishingly rare, although I have managed to collect some courtesy of a certain internet auction site. The Wye Valley has long been a mecca for tourists of all descriptions and walks of life but, from the late 18th century, attracted the more well to do to take the 'Wye Valley Tour'. Upper class tourists during the first half of the 20th century came with their cameras, some equipped with colour film, so a number of pre-war views feature within; the Dufaycolor slides of Tintern station in the 1930s will surely take the breath away, as they did mine when I first glimpsed them.

Wartime privations, which lasted well into the 1950s, means that anything pre-1955 is equally rare. It is not until you reach 1958 that colour slides start to be found in any quantity, whilst the Western Region, in its infinite wisdom and race to be ahead of the game, had dispensed with steam completely by the end of 1965. Many of the photographs within these pages do not, therefore, show ex-GWR engines at their finest, as they were run down prior to withdrawal and photographers understandably snapped anything that passed as a final record. I have not, however, used 1965 as the cut-off point but have extended this forward another decade, to the mid 1970s, when the railways of Gloucestershire underwent more great change. In 1975, Gloucester Central station building was demolished, to be replaced by a modern design of little architectural merit, whilst the old Eastgate station was closed completely, along with the Midland's loop line through the suburbs. The ex-MR High Orchard and Hempsted Sidings docks branches had already gone, shut in 1971 but the GWR Llanthony Dock Branch soldiered on until 1985. Also, although most of the branch lines to the west had been closed in the 1960s, the old Severn & Wye line remained in use from Lydney as far as Parkend Wharf for stone traffic, as did a stub of the Wye Valley line, serving quarries at Tintern and Tidenham. The Parkend Branch closed in 1976 and the line is now operated as the preserved Dean Forest Railway, whilst stone traffic from Tidenham ceased in 1990. With the disappearance of much of what was interesting about the railway by the late 1970s, as BR gradually imposed its modern corporate image, this seemed a more sensible period to use as the cut off date.

Using this later date also allows us to study the first decade or so of the diesel era, from the green livery of the early 1960s, through the introduction of BR's corporate blue image and the TOPS renumbering of 1973. This in itself is now an important and historic era on the Western Region, which once again struck out on a tangent all of its own with the promotion of the diesel-hydraulic classes. By the end of the period we cover here, all of these, the 'Hymeks', 'Westerns', 'Warships' and even the little 'D95XX' shunters, had been withdrawn but not before they had managed to find a place in the hearts of many railway enthusiasts, some of whom had been looking for something to replace steam in their affections, only to find it snatched away a second time.

I have also not strayed too far into the politics, both then and now, of the closing and mooted reopening of certain lines. If one fails to don the rose tinted specs favoured by many railway enthusiasts, it is quite obvious that, of the lines featured in this first volume, most deserved to go. Newent and Dymock lost their passenger trains three years before

From Ballingham to Holme Lacy was a distance of three miles, the biggest gap between intermediate stops on the line between Hereford and Gloucester. This view is looking east from the bridge at the east end of Holme Lacy station. Taken on on 8th August 1962, '63XX' Class No. 6381 is seen arriving with a three-coach train from Gloucester. Moments after taking this picture, the photographer turned to take a second view as the train pulled in to the station, which can be found on page 194. In the left background is the village of Fownhope, which is situated on the far bank of the wildly meandering River Wye. Capler Woods clothe the hill in the background, on top of which is Capler Camp, an Iron Age hill fort. T.B. Owen/Colour-Rail

Beeching, the bus services being far more convenient, whilst despite Monmouth's total isolation from the railway network today, it too succumbed before the good doctor began drafting his report. A strong case could be made for the Wye Valley lines to have been retained as a tourist operation but this ignores the fact that railway preservation was in its infancy when they shut to passengers at the end of 1958. Despite repeated calls to reopen the Chepstow to Tintern section, it seems unlikely that either the will or the money to achieve this will be found in the foreseeable future. The one line that perhaps should not have closed is Gloucester to Hereford, which will forever remain a tortuous journey by road. However, even on that route, it is likely that only Ross would have retained a station if rationalisation had prevailed in 1964, instead of closure. Longhope would probably have been reopened again since, to provide a rail outlet at the northern end of the Forest of Dean for commuters into Gloucester.

On the main line, the stations that remained were those that saw good usage – Chepstow and Lydney. A strong case could and indeed, on occasion, has been made for a new intermediate station near Newnham (the old one was poorly sited for car users), again to alleviate rush hour

A fine study of ex-GWR Class '43XX' 2-6-0 No. 4358 outside Gloucester Horton Road shed on 8th June 1958, with the 85B shedplate visible on the smokebox door. Coaled and watered, the 'Mogul' and her cheerful footplate crew pose for the photographer prior to heading down to the station to take out a train for Hereford via Ross-on-Wye. Some one has bothered to give the BR lion emblem on the tender a clean but the rest of the engine's green livery is also in need of a polish with some oily rags. No. 4358 was quite an elderly lady by this date, having been built in April 1914 and, at the date of this view, she had just over a year left in service, being withdrawn from Gloucester on 11th August 1959. Ex-WD 2-8-0 No. 90095 in the left background was a Woodford Halse-based engine. With the breadth of coverage of the west Gloucestershire lines in this volume eating up the space we only have room for this brief glimpse of Horton Road shed here but we will return for a detailed tour of 85B and a look at many of its locomotives in a future volume. BILL POTTER/KRM

queues on the A48 but once more neither the political will to make it happen, nor the money, has been forthcoming. As such, what we currently have in terms of railway lines and stations in west Gloucestershire and surrounds is likely to remain the *status quo* for the next decade at least.

This, therefore, was an essay in nostalgia and a labour of love, as I attempted to compile as complete a picture of the lines traversed as I could and to cover their history in reasonable detail along the way. It is the pictures which are important, the fact they are all in colour, tugging at the heartstrings of those who knew and loved this beautiful corner of the world then. But why the obsession with colour on my part, for that is what it has become. The primary answer to that goes to the very heart of our being. We see the world in which we live in colour and therefore black and white photographs, dramatic though many of them undoubtedly are, will always be lacking something. A good colour image, however, can bring a long forgotten scene to life in a way that black and white prints never can. Colour brings immediacy, relevance and a sense of time travel that still retains a strong link to the present. With colour also comes warmth from the sun, damp from the rain, sound from everywhere and the scent of steam, as the visual richness of the picture stimulates all the senses.

Lastly, the pictures herein also form an important resource for railway modellers, amongst whom I count myself as one, because without images such as these, getting the colour right is very difficult. We all know or think we know the colour things were painted but these did not stay the same for very long once in use. Consequently, the effects of UV rays, weather, soot, dirt and so forth on paint shades can only be accurately determined from colour pictures. And this works despite the colour variations given by the different makes of film then available – and almost without exception, all of the photographers using colour film experimented with many of them. Surprisingly, the pictures still generally all retain a sense of authenticity, despite the fact that, even with the best software, it is impossible to get pictures shot on different makes of film to colour match, which will be clear throughout these pages. And yet such is the capacity of the brain to adjust that nearly all of these pictures all look 'right' in terms of colour, even when side by side on the page it is clear that different films were used. Incidentally, it is generally recognised nowadays that Kodak film produced the best results, such that the card mounts with the yellow corners are the slides after by collectors. Nevertheless, many fine colour views w other types of film, particularly if it had been used in conj a more expensive camera.

The railway we knew and loved, the steam railway of the first half of the 20th century, has now gone forever and these colour images also serve to remind us of just how recent is this brave new world of ours. Today's railway likes to portray itself as sleek, modern and fast, whilst passenger usage today is at levels not seen since the 1920s, despite over a third of the system having gone. But for nostalgists like myself, the look of a British steam age railway station, with all its quirky accoutrements and paraphernalia, is as great a loss as all the steam locomotives. And I write that fully recognising that things change because they have too and that we can now only go back to that age courtesy of the railway preservationists and the lines around the country that they have reopened.

The pace of change since the late 1950s/early 1960s has been phenomenal, which is why the pictures within these pages are so nostalgic. Wouldn't it be great to go back then, to a time when the sun shone, the clock ticked more slowly and we all had less responsibilities. But would we want to stay there? Or have we all got too used to our 21st century gadgets and creature comforts? *Neil Parkhouse, Lydney, 2013*

INTRODUCTION TO THE SECOND EDITION: With some important new colour images having come to light in the five years since this book was first published, it was felt that the time was right for an enlarged new edition. Many of them fill what I felt were significant gaps in the original coverage, whilst others are just superb images that merit a wider audience and I have endeavoured to place all of them through the book in context and in order. The opportunity has also been taken to correct a number of the more serious errors kindly pointed out by interested readers and to move a few pictures, the locations of which were miss-identified in the first edition. Finally, in fairness to those who already own a first edition and thus would not wish to buy the whole book again, the additional pages/images have also been published as a separate supplement.

Thanks and acknowledgements are now also due to the following: Roy Denison, Nick Freezer, John Hill, John Jenkins, Brian Mills, John Prytherch, Tim Stephens and Chris Walker. *Neil Parkhouse, Lydney, 2018*

ACKNOWLEDGEMENTS

As already indicated in the Introduction, the whole concept of this series of colour books was stimulated by my friends at Kidderminster Railway Museum, who first provided me with scans of Bill Potter's colour transparencies of the Forest of Dean branches. The late Audie Baker, for many years KRM's photograph archivist, was most helpful in this respect, whilst David Postle has since generously given me full access to the museum's database of colour images, which has enabled me to make more rapid progress with the project. So to them must go much of the credit for this series, along with Bill himself, sadly also no longer with us but whom I got to know quite well in the late 1970s. A gentle unassuming man, his love of the railways of his adopted county – he was a Lancastrian by birth – shines through in his photographs. Incidentally, KRM is one of the best repositeries for photographic collections, as they have a team of trusty volunteers busily scanning and cataloguing everything that is deposited with them.

Following on from that, a number of photographers have been most generous and helpful in allowing me access to their collections. The first was John Ryan, a friend for many years, who has also helped out with the distribution of Lightmoor Press publications since we began publishing way back in 1994. On the advice of Ron Wight of Colour-Rail, I then wrote to Trevor Owen to inquire as to what he may have taken around the Wye Valley and the Forest of Dean. Trevor didn't know me at all but, two days later, a package arrived in the post containing 160-plus colour slides. Such generosity was astounding and I repaid his trust by making sure they were safely back in the post 48 hours later. I was fortunate, also, to get to know both Alan Jarvis and Derek Chaplin, friends who often travelled around together with their cameras and both very talented photographers, who mastered the art of taking colour transparencies right from the start. Their work does indeed grace these pages. All of these gentlemen were kind enough to loan me their slides for copying but, since that time, I have also managed to acquire a great many original slides of Gloucestershire. Sadly, this is usually as a result of someone having passed away and their collection then being disposed of but at least it ensures that some of their photographs will eventually see publication.

A major asset in this modern age for the collector of anything but particularly of railway images has been the internet and, in particular, a certain well known auction site. This has enabled me to fill quite a few gaps in my coverage of the county. A determined bid to acquire an original slide of a pannier tank shunting at Monmouth Troy several years ago led to my fortunate acquaintance with Alan Sainty, whose ability to discover and acquire collections of original colour slides is legendary. I was lucky enough to purchase from him many slides taken by the late John Strange and getting to know Alan has greatly increased the scope of this series of books as a result. A lot of the slides I have acquired are now of unknown provenance as regards who took them. With those

I do know, I have cited the photographer as well as my collection but many will now be forever uncredited. Fortuitously, the identity of the photographer who took the magnificent slide of the frontage of Ross-on-Wye station, purchased via the internet, was provided to me just two weeks beofre the book went to the printers.

I was also fortunate that Ben Ashworth, an artist with a camera if ever there was one, lives quite locally. A generous but modest man of the countryside, who still cycles everywhere and is never happier than when up a tree, Ben's colour output was not prolific, only around a hundred slides in fact, but nearly every one a gem as we shall see. The late David Bick, another good friend, well known as a publisher in his own right in the field of industrial archaeology, also turned out to have fielded a camera loaded with colour film in the late 1950s and 1960s. Whilst not a railway enthusiast as such, he nevertheless turned his attention to what was happening on our railways at this period and took a number of most unusual shots which will appear throughout this series. I have not yet found any other colour photographs of regular passenger trains on the Forest of Dean Branch, which were withdrawn in late 1958 – but David took two, along with a couple of service trains between Ross and Monmouth and some very unusual shots at Ledbury in the late 1950s. Admittedly, their quality was not of the highest but their rarity served to override any other considerations.

Oddly, perhaps, contact with Paul Chancellor, who took over Colour-Rail from Ron White, was only made quite late on but this was partly because I wanted to use images that had not been seen before and partly because I felt that the CR archive was generally quite locomotive orientated. In the event, I realised that it was a contact I should have made much sooner. Paul was extremely helpful and came up with a number of colour views that I had never seen before, one or two of which filled significant gaps. This archive continues to grow from strength to strength under its new owner and the fact that much of it is now available for search online has made it even more useful

Thanks should also go to a few others others who have lent me pictures for this particular book. Stanley C. Jenkins provided further images taken by his friend, the late John Strange. Hugh Ballantyne, who sadly passed away in May 2013, kindly sourced various images from his collection. Sadly, he did not take as many colour views on this side of the county as he did elsewhere but hopefully more of this talented photographer's work will appear in future volumes. The late Michael Hale also allowed me to copy the slides that he had taken on the west side of the Severn. His *forté* was as a documenter of stations and he filled in several very important gaps, not least in providing the only colour image I have seen to date of Newnham station. John Jennison sent me a selection of images of Gloucester Central from which to choose, which come from the www.rail-online.co.uk collection.

Peter Barnfield, better known as the artist behind the Railways of Whimshire series of paintings, an eccentric, whimsical, Heath Robinson-esque system based on an imaginary island, was another acquaintance who came up trumps in terms of colour slides. I count myself fortunate indeed to own three of Peter's original Whimshire paintings, a constant source of amusement, but his colour photographs of the Wye Valley, taken on the occasion of an obscure brake van trip with a Chepstow to Monmouth goods working in 1963, proved every bit as valuable in their own way. John Thorn's view of the ballast train at Tintern was found on a Forest of Dean history website and he very kindly responded to an email request to use it, also producing a couple of other useable views. There is also one picture taken by the late David Norton, a Birmingham man who moved to Ledbury and died of an asthma attack in 1965 at a tragically early age. Many of his black & white railway photographs of the Birmingham area have been published in three volumes by Wild Swan but he also took quite a number of colour pictures and his output is now available to study on line, courtesy of his son Mark, at www.photobydjnorton.com. It was here that I found his delightful study of Bye Street, Ledbury, looking down the road and over the bridge spanning the branch from Gloucester, which Mark has kindly allowed me to use.

A number of views were also sourced quite late on as a result of appearing in other publications. Whilst some may question my using images which have only recently appeared elsewhere, my counter would be completeness and the fact that whilst many local people will hopefully buy this book because of its coverage, someone with only a passing interest in railways is most unlikely to have bought a West Country branch line album for one or two pictures of the Wye Valley for instance. The four images kindly provided by Michael Clemens of Kerne Bridge and Lydbrook, taken by the late Alan Maund, fall in to this category. Published in early 2013, in a book compiled by Michael of the last years of Midlands steam, I venture to suggest that few Wye Valley residents will know about them unless they have a deep interest in railways. Far more will see them here because of what else besides the railway is illustrated in the pictures within this book.

In a similar vein are the five photographs taken by David Soggee and here there is a tale to tell. David took several photographs of interest in the Wye Valley and between Ross and Hereford, which appeared in a book published in 2012. A couple of them were reproduced in our local advertising newspaper, the *Forest of Dean & Wye Valley Review*, as promotion for the book but few copies were bought locally by non railway folk, because the coverage was West Country-wide. The excitement for me was in the slide of Brockweir Halt, of which I had not previously seen a colour view. Initial attempts to track David down met with no success and none of my contacts knew of him. With completion date starting to draw near, the gap in coverage at Brockweir started to bother me more and more, knowing that there was a picture out there. Eventually, another internet search (I had tried one when I had first bought his book) came up with contact details for a David Soggee in Ingatestone, Essex, so I phoned, thinking the name is not a common one, there must be a fair chance of success. Bingo! But then logistics kicked in. David was, understandably, unwilling to entrust his slides to the post, so I was faced with the prospect of a 350 mile round trip to borrow them and get them scanned. He did not have scans himself and a friend who did do some scanning for him lived even further away, in Devon. At a loss, I tried another internet search for a local shop where he could get them scanned, whilst bearing in mind that David is now quite elderly so I could not possibly put him to any trouble. There was nothing very local to him in the way of photographic shops that looked as though they might be able to help but the search did also bring up the details of Ingatestone & District Camera Club and the contact details of their Chairman, Max Carter.

An author's desperation now took over, so I phoned Max to see whether the club would be able to assist. Although he was out when I first phoned, his wife sounded quite positive about the prospects of him being able to help and took my number. Max phoned me back the next day and, to cut a long story short, took David's details (he lived about 5 miles away), made contact, popped round a few days later when he had dug out the slides, took them back home and scanned them, and then returned them to David. Five large files subsequently arrived on my desktop via a file transfer website, superb scans and just what I needed. My grateful thanks to him for going out of his way to help with this, which all goes to prove that there are still far more real human beings out there than the other sort. My thanks to David also for searching out the slides and allowing me to use the pictures.

Having thought the book was now complete, Gerry Nicholls then showed me some of the colour slides he had scanned which were taken by the late Mark B. Warburton. Gerry is handling the collection on behalf of Mark's widow, Margaret, facilitating the publication of as much of it as possible. Having clearly sought out different viewpoints to others whose material I was using, there was no question that I would have to add in some more pages to include as many of these superb slides as possible. Mark's pictures of Dymock, Newent, along the Gloucester to Hereford line and particularly of Chepstow station, showing it in all its GWR/WR glory, can now be enjoyed and appreciated by a much wider audience. In similar vein, Ian Pope also facilitated the use of some lovely colour views of the Gloucester to Hereford line taken by John

Dagley-Morris, including several on the line north of Holme Lacy.

I am always on the look out for further pictures, so I would also now like to take the opportunity to invite anyone who took colour slides in Gloucestershire or who has acquired slides of the area, who would like to contribute to this series to get in touch. I can be contacted direct by email on neil@lightmoor.co.uk or by ordinary mail via the address on the contents page. Obviously, I am mainly interested in the railways but I would also like to see any views taken in the late 1950s/1960s/early 1970s of town scenes, particularly including vehicles, or of local industries, docks or anything else that might be considered of interest. I have included some in this volume, street views in Ross and Monmouth, and some 1930s colour photographs around the Wye Valley, because they help to paint a broader picture of the way things were.

I need also to pay credit for other assistance provided. Firstly, to Ian Pope, my business partner in Black Dwarf Lightmoor Publications, who gave me access to colour images he has collected, including those taken by John Dagley-Morris, many more of which will feature in the next volume; Ian has also checked the manuscript utilising his local knowledge. Mike Christensen emailed details for some of the signal boxes and Malcolm Bobbitt identified the vehicles on pages 203 and 228. Andrew Neale kindly provided me with details of the demolition contractor's locomotive on page 226. The excellent www.sixbellsjunction.co.uk website has also been used to check details of rail tours. And whilst you cannot beat getting out on the ground when researching long closed routes, Google Earth is now a powerful research tool at times when deskbound.

Many of the captions to pictures of identified locomotives contain details of their disposal. For some years now, the HSBT Project, or What Really Happened To Steam (www.whatreallyhappenedtosteam.co.uk), have been collating information on the disposal of British Railway's steam fleet, in order to compile what will hopefully be a definitive listing. This project was commenced as a result of the discreditation of the Peter Hands volumes, when it was discovered that one of the major contributors to that series (not Peter Hands himself) had falsified the information that he provided. As a result, in many instances, what has been written since on locomotive withdrawals and disposals can not now be relied upon because it was sourced from these volumes. We first came into contact with the HSBT Project as a result of the 'Norman Lockett Archive' volumes, author Mike Arlett having checked all his 'loco gen' with Roger Butcher prior to publication in return for which we placed an 'advert' for the Project in each book. I must therefore thank both Roger and particularly Keith Gunner of the HSBT team, for checking all such information in this volume. Undertaken at quite short notice, Keith did most of the checking because Roger was busy with another project, so my grateful thanks to him for his prompt attention to this.

Finally, to my father, Dennis Parkhouse, who sadly died in 2006 and therefore never lived to see the project I started back in 2001 come to fruition. My parents retired to a bungalow they had bought in the Forest of Dean in the 1970s and although neither of them were local to the area, Dad loved the Forest of Dean and the Wye Valley with a passion. I have paid him the honour of including a couple of his slides within these pages; he only got to know the area after the period covered, so most of his slides were only of remains, not of a working railway. He would have loved to have seen the finished book and would be thrilled that his name appears in it, so it is to him that I dedicate this first volume.

A Note on the Tickets

From the outset I felt that it was important to further illustrate these volumes with relevant ephemera and tickets, so the pages are liberally sprinkled with working time table excerpts, passenger time table extracts, handbills, leaflets and other items, all of which I have spent some considerable time (and money!) collecting over the last few years. They are important in building up a picture of the railway of the period and the inclusion of just a small selection adds further flavour to the book. Most numerous of all, however, are the tickets. Most I have collected myself but some have been loaned to me by a good friend of Lightmoor, Tony Dyer, who has loyally supported our endeavours for many years. Probably longer ago than he cares to remember now, Tony also worked with Alec Pope (Ian's Dad) at Fielding & Platt's works in Gloucester, so his interest in our well-being has a paternal air to it. The tickets, being so numerous, are not individually credited, so I have not distinguished Tony's tickets from those I have collected but he will recognise those which are his.

Having decided that relevant tickets would form an integral part of the series, I have now built up rather a nice collection of Gloucestershire railway station tickets of my own. I have generally tried to keep those that I have used here within period, as it were, although the collection is starting to go back much earlier. However, the use of pre-BR tickets in most instances is entirely justified because, in many places, GWR tickets were still being used long into the BR era, often right up until closure, as the stock of tickets printed by the GWR had never been exhausted. I decided, however, that they did not need captions and therefore they speak for themselves where they sit within these pages. It should also be noted that they have all been reduced in size by 25%, as they would otherwise appear too large and dominating. Similarly, the ephemera and time table extracts have all been reduced, by varying amounts, to fit the space available.

SOURCES & BIBLIOGRAPHY

Bridges on the River Wye, Alan Crow, Lapridge Publications 1995
British Railway Journal No. 8, Wild Swan Publications, 1985
British Railways First Generation DMUs, Hugh Longworth, Oxford Publishing Co., 2011
Camp Coach Holidays on the GWR, Mike Fenton, Wild Swan Publications 1999
From Ledbury to Gloucester by Rail, David Postle, Amber Graphics, 1985
Great Western Auto Trailers Part 1, John Lewis, Wild Swan Publications 1991
Great Western Railway Halts Vol. 1, Kevin Robertson, Irwell Press 1990
Great Western Railway Halts Vol. 2, Kevin Robertson, KRB Publications 2002
Great Western Railway Journal, Wild Swan Publications, various issues
Peto's Register of GWR Locomotives Vol. 2, Manor 4-6-0s, Irwell Press 1996
Peto's Register of GWR Locomotives Vol. 3, 14XX and 58XX 0-4-2Ts, Irwell Press 1996
Railway Passenger Stations in England, Scotland & Wales, M.E. Quick, Railway & Canal Historical Society, 2003
Severn & Wye Railway Vol. 1, Ian Pope, Bob How & Paul Karau, Wild Swan Publications 1983
The Forest of Dean Branch Vol. 1, Ian Pope & Paul Karau, Wild Swan Publications 1992
The Locomotives of the Great Western Railway, RC&TS, various vols
The Place Names of Gloucestershire Part III: The Lower Severn Valley, The Forest of Dean, A.H. Smith, Cambridge University Press 1964
The Ross, Monmouth and Pontypool Road Line, Stanley C. Jenkins, Oakwood Press 2002
The Wye Valley Railway and the Coleford Branch, B.M. Handley & R. Dingwall, Oakwood Press 1998
Track Layout Diagrams of the GWR & BR (WR), Sec. 33 Worcestershire, R.A. Cooke, 1976
Track Layout Diagrams of the GWR & BR (WR), Sec. 35 Gloucester and Cheltenham, R.A. Cooke, 1978
Track Layout Diagrams of the GWR & BR (WR), Sec. 36 Ross, Monmouth & Chepstow, R.A. Cooke, 1998
Wartime Standard Ships Vol. 3, British Standard Ships of WW1, W.H. Mitchell & L.A. Sawyer, The Journal of Commerce & Shipping Telegraph Ltd 1968
Various Public and Working Time Tables (WTT), Appendices and other official railway publications in my own collection
www.sixbellsjunction.co.uk

CREDITS: **KRM**: Kidderminster Railway Museum; **NPC**: Neil Parkhouse Collection

GLOUCESTER CENTRAL

Although in effect the 'quieter' end, because the locomotive sheds and goods yards were all situated either side of its eastern approaches, the west end of Gloucester Central station could also have its busy moments. Here, in October 1964, 2-6-2T No. 4161 departs with a train for Ross-on-Wye and Hereford. On the right, a 3-car DMU sits in the bay waiting to depart along the main line to Cardiff, via Severn Tunnel Junction, whilst in the background 'Hall' Class 4-6-0 No. 6957 *Norcliffe Hall* is either depositing stock in the Up platform or collecting it to move over to the Down side, a station pilot duty that would more commonly have been carried out by a tank engine. The locomotive looks to be a 'good cop' for the young trainspotters standing in front of it. No. 4161 was a member of the '51XX' Class, built from 1929, although in effect they were a perpetuation of a Churchward design, the '31XX' Class built over twenty years earlier. The '51XX' series were built between 1929 and 1934, and then a further number batch were ordered, the '41XX' series, construction of which began in 1935. However, the Second World War intervened before the order was completed, so the final forty engines were all built in the later 1940s, half of them after Nationalisation. No. 4161 was one of these latter, emerging from Swindon Works at the end of September 1948. It was withdrawn from Worcester shed on 18th November 1965 and cut up by Cashmores of Newport the following year. DEREK CHAPLIN

SECTION 1
GLOUCESTER CENTRAL

'Prairie' tank No. 4157 stands beneath the covered footbridge at Gloucester Central after arrival with a service from Hereford on 27th June 1964. Another member of the '51XX' Class, this engine only just qualified for the soubriquet 'ex-GWR', having been built in August 1947. It had just a year left in service when seen here, being withdrawn from Severn Tunnel Junction shed during the week ending 12th June 1965. It was one of the unfortunate few to arrive at Woodhams of Barry before they stopped cutting locomotives and was scrapped later that year. BILL POTTER/KRM

The railway at Gloucester in the 21st century is much simplified from its heyday in the first half of the 20th century but, nevertheless, still shows some of the distinctive features which derive from its origins. Trains not heading to or from South Wales still have to reverse here and most services still use the long Up platform, which is split in two for operational flexibility, much as both platforms were in steam days. The Down platform was reopened to passengers in 1984, having been used for parcels traffic only since 1968, whilst the bay at the west end is still in use for stopping trains originating here and bound for Cardiff. There is much about the station, its layout and the approach to it from the west that Brunel would still recognise.

The Birmingham & Gloucester Railway (B&GR) was the first railway to reach the city, with a terminus station (on the site of the later Midland goods yard) opened on 4th November 1840. The financially straitened B&GR built what they considered to be a temporary facility but which was in fact to last for another fifty-six years, until eventually replaced by a new station, Gloucester (Midland) – or Eastgate as it became under BR, in 1896. The broad gauge Bristol & Gloucester Railway (Br&GR) came next, when it also began running trains to the B&GR's station on 8th July 1844. The GWR finally arrived in 1845, when they were given permission to run trains into the station following the completion of their line from Standish Junction to Kemble on 12th May, pending the construction of their own station. By this date, the embryonic Midland Railway had its eyes set on the B&GR and Br&GR, leasing both concerns from July 1845 and finally absorbing them completely the following year. The GWR were now working into a Midland station and the broad gauge line to Bristol was soon to be converted to mixed gauge by its new owners.

Having lost the so called 'Battle of the Gauges' at this point, the GWR now set its sights on a different strategy. It had the prospect of extending west from Gloucester, across the River Severn and on into south and ultimately west Wales via the projected South Wales Railway (SWR). This was formed by Act of Parliament in 1845 and supported by the GWR as part of a grand plan to connect directly with Ireland. The GWR still held running rights over the line to Cheltenham and, with the anticipated arrival of the railway from South Wales into the city, the development of a station of their own became paramount. Running via Swindon, Gloucester and Chepstow, this would give them a seamless connection between Paddington and South Wales, with the ports at Pembroke Dock and Neyland the ultimate intended destinations to connect with the boats to Ireland. The South Wales Railway was duly incorporated by Act of 4th August 1845.

Meanwhile, another company, the Gloucester & Dean Forest Railway (G&FDR) was authorised in 1846, with GWR support, to build a line running west from Gloucester, to join with the Great Western's proposed Monmouth & Hereford Railway of 1844 at Grange Court. When tentative SWR proposals for crossing the Severn below Gloucester at Fretherne failed, the GWR negotiated an extension south of the G&DFR line, to connect with the SWR at Awre, which meant trains would run via Gloucester. It also blocked a proposal to take the SWR line through Monmouth to Newport, in preference to the shorter and far more easily graded coast route via Chepstow.

However, due to a lack of finance, despite the SWR having subscribed £100,000 towards its construction, the G&DFR were unable to proceed with construction of the line south from Grange Court. The SWR now took over the project and built it themselves, with the result that Grange Court effectively became the western terminus of their line. The first section of the SWR, between Swansea and Chepstow, was opened for traffic on 18th June 1850. Gloucester to Chepstow opened on 19th September 1851, to a temporary station called Chepstow East on the north side of the Wye, whilst completion of Brunel's tubular bridge spanning the river was awaited. A single line over the bridge was opened on 19th July 1852, finally bringing Paddington and Swansea in direct contact by iron rails, running via a new station at Gloucester. Also in 1851, the broad gauge Hereford, Ross & Gloucester Railway was incorporated, with the first section of line, from a new junction at the west end of Grange Court station to a temporary terminus at Hopesbrook, opening in 1853. This was another line built with the support of the GWR, who, having converted their 1846 lease of the SWR into an outright purchase of it in 1863, then enjoyed a monopoly on the lines heading west out of Gloucester.

The GW and Midland railways operated alongside each other at the terminus station in Gloucester for six years, from May 1845. This situation finally came to an end on 19th September 1851, when the new station was brought in to use with the opening of the SWR to Chepstow. It comprised two short platforms with a wooden covered roof or train shed spanning them. However, the GWR quickly decided the layout was too restricted and rebuilt the station completely. The train shed and the northernmost platform were swept away, whilst the surviving platform, backing on to the Midland station, was lengthened by 280 yards. The rebuilding work was completed in 1855 and the station operated with this single platform layout for the next thirty years, until a new Up platform was finally built in 1885. In that same year, the cross-country branch from Over Junction to Ledbury opened, further increasing traffic to and from the west, as up until the early years of the 20th century, this line was used as the GWR's route for goods traffic between Gloucester and Worcester.

The new layout provided lengthy Up and Down platforms which were both signalled for working in either direction, required not only because of the number of destinations served but also because GWR services running to or from Cheltenham had to reverse here (as trains still do today). There were two central through lines, used both for goods trains and to allow, via double crossovers on both Up and Down sides, for both platforms to be split effectively into two. A bay on the south side at the west end was used by stopping trains to South Wales as well as branch services to Ledbury and to Hereford, whilst another bay on the north side at the east end was used mainly by Stroud Valley trains. With the relocation of the Midland station to a new site in 1896, some distance further away (the two stations having up to that date been side by side), they were to be linked by a covered wooden footbridge some 250 yards in length which became a noted local landmark.

With its proliferation of lines and two major stations in close proximity, plus all their attendant facilities, Gloucester unsurprisingly became something of a mecca for railway photographers. To stand on the platforms at the east end of Central station in particular was to be faced with a scene of almost total railway interest, with Horton Road shed to the left, Barnwood shed and Eastgate station to the right, goods yards to both sides, several signal boxes in view and a forest of semaphore signals. London Midland Region trains would be swinging past into and out of Eastgate station, whilst services to and from Swindon and London, the Stroud Valleys and Cheltenham, and to and from South Wales would be heading in and out of Central. This could be intensified with the occasional weekend closures for maintenance of the Severn Tunnel, which would see services then diverted via Gloucester. As a consequence of all this, the range of motive power on view was a major attraction. Apart from the heavily weight restricted 'King' Class 4-6-0s and '47XX' 2-8-0s, almost every class of ex-GWR engine could be seen at some stage on the Western Region side. Meanwhile, there was also an extensive list of ex-Midland and LM&SR types to be seen on the Midland Region side. From the mid 1950s, the BR 'Standard' Classes were well represented, along with the 'Austerity' locomotives inherited from the War Department. From the early 1960s, there followed a similarly wide range of the new diesel classes and so, as a consequence of all this, we shall dally here for a while to watch the trains come and go.

Gloucester truly was a railway enthusiasts paradise in the 1950s and '60s but all this changed in the 1970s, with the closure of Eastgate station and the Loop line, the rebuilding of Central, the closure of the docks lines, and the gradual loss of the yards and the sheds. The railway at Gloucester today is but a shadow of what it once was, although the station still boasts the longest platform in the UK.

After the formation of British Railways in 1948, ex-LM&SR locomotives were regularly to be seen at Central and, indeed, venturing south-westwards along the banks of the River Severn heading to South Wales. Here, two 'Black 5' 4-6-0s, No. 44831 and an unidentified sister behind, stand light engine on the Up through road. With tenders coaled up, they may be waiting for an incoming goods from South Wales to take on northwards to Birmingham, although double heading from Gloucester was not common. No. 44831 was a wartime build, emerging from Crewe Works in August 1944. With the later withdrawal of LMR steam, it was to have another three years in traffic after being photographed here, being retired from Wigan Springs Bank shed on 2nd December 1967. BILL POTTER/KRM

A filthy Class '28XX' 2-8-0, No. 2832, clatters past Gloucester West Signal Box with a coal train from South Wales, which comprises a motley selection of coal wagons, on 12th April 1958. Built in April 1911, No. 2832 had 18 months left in traffic, being withdrawn from Severn Tunnel Junction shed on 18th November 1959 and cut up at Swindon in 1961. Note the ash ballast on the track at this end of the station. BILL POTTER/KRM

Towards the end of steam on the Western Region, many of the locomotives presented a sorry sight. Here, on 6th March 1964, 'Mogul' No. 7307, in poor condition and minus its numberplates, stands on the Down through road. It was probably about to back on to the coaches forming a Hereford train. Built in 1921, the engine was to be withdrawn from Gloucester Horton Road shed less than three months later, on 1st June 1964. BILL POTTER/KRM

LEFT: 'Hall' Class 4-6-0 No. 5939 *Tangley Hall* breasts the distinct 'hump' on the main line at the west end of Gloucester station, with a train of 20-ton BR coke hoppers from South Wales on 24th August 1964. A Newport Ebbw Junction engine and seen here in appallingly filthy condition, No. 5939 had less than ten weeks left in service, being withdrawn on 23rd October. A.B. JEFFREY/COLOUR-RAIL

ABOVE: By contrast, ex-GWR heavyweight 2-8-0 No. 3866 looks much better cared for here in April 1962, as it heads into the station with another long train, mostly of laden coal wagons but with three vans at the front. The bracket signal in the left background shows that the train is signalled onto the Up middle road. All of both East and West boxes Distant signals were fixed at caution, as most trains would have business here, either to platforms or middle lines goods trains changing crews. No. 3866's final allocation was to Southall shed, from where it was withdrawn on 2nd July 1965. JOHN CHAMPION/COLOUR-RAIL

RIGHT: Having breasted the 'hump' at the west end of the station, 'Mogul' No. 6365 rumbles through on the centre road with a mixed freight heading for Gloucester yard, on 13th May 1961. Based here at 85B, No. 6365 has fresh black paint around the smokebox, in contrast to the rest of her appearance, so had probably recently been in works for a minor repair. The engine was withdrawn from Gloucester shed on 21st October 1963 and cut up by Cooper's Metals at Sharpness the following year. NPC

RIGHT: Churchward's '42XX' 2-8-0 tanks were another class built over a long period of time, with the first, No. 4201, emerging from Swindon in 1910, whilst the last batch, No's 5255-64, were completed in early 1940. No. 5263, seen here running light engine through the Up centre road at the west end of the station sometime in the early 1960s, was thus the penultimate member of the class. Shedded at Aberdare, the engine may have brought a freight up from South Wales as far as the sidings at Over Junction and was then photographed heading for Gloucester shed for servicing and perhaps turning before waiting for a train back. No. 5263 was withdrawn from Aberdare shed during the week ending 14th December 1963. BILL POTTER/KRM

LEFT: 'Austerity' Class 2-8-0 No. 90719 waits patiently on the Up centre road with another long mixed freight from South Wales in April 1964. Built by Vulcan Foundry in March 1945 and originally WD No. 79282, the engine was taken into BR stock in September 1949 and renumbered as seen here. At the time of this view it was based at Canklow, near Rotherham, so it was probably on a lengthy cross-country journey back home. No. 90719 was withdrawn from Langwith Junction shed on 6th February 1966. JOHN CHAMPION/COLOUR-RAIL

BELOW: Come down for a 'Castle'! No. 7011 *Banbury Castle* waits for a clear road with a train of ballast wagons in June 1964. Despite its tidy condition, No. 7011 had only eight months of service remaining, being withdrawn from Wolverhampton Oxley shed on 9th February 1965. The flat-sided Hawksworth tender does not add to the engine's visual appeal. The Swindon 'Cross-Country' DMU behind, on a Swansea or Cardiff to Birmingham service includes a van as tail traffic. J. HARRISON/COLOUR-RAIL

Whilst ex-GWR 'Mogul' No. 7318 appears quite regularly over the coming pages, in no way could it be said to grace them. It is invariably seen in this awful condition, covered in dirt, soot and limescale and all the more distressing here on 31st October 1964 perhaps, because this is the condition in which the engine was sent out to work one of the last day services on the line to Hereford. It was photographed back at Gloucester Central, gently leaking steam and it is, therefore, not surprising to learn that this was also No. 7318's final duty, as it was officially withdrawn from service on its return to Gloucester shed. J.L. LEAN/COLOUR-RAIL

Collett '22XX' 0-6-0 No. 2295 waits to depart Gloucester with a train for Hereford on 11th July 1959. These versatile engines were built as a replacement for the 'Dean Goods' 0-6-0s, over a period of 18 years from 1930 to 1948, although their 'yellow' route availability meant they were not quite so widespread as their ancestors, which were classified as 'uncoloured'. No. 2295 was new into GWR stock at the end of February 1938 and was to be withdrawn from Hereford shed on 31st July 1962. It is seen here in work stained condition, beneath which lies British Railways Western Region's attractive lined green passenger livery. BILL POTTER/KRM

Another of these well proportioned locomotives, No. 3203 from the final batch, lot No. 360, rests alongside the Up platform at Gloucester, after arrival with a service from Hereford, also on 11th July 1959. No. 3203 had previously spent time in North Wales, working from Croes Newydd shed near Wrexham but by this date was allocated to 85B Gloucester. It was to be withdrawn from here on the final day of 1963 and was cut up by Kings of Norwich in April 1964. Sister engine No. 3205 is the only one of these versatile engines to have survived into preservation. BILL POTTER/KRM

ABOVE: Gloucester Central was certainly a railway photographer's paradise in the days when all the branch and local services were in operation. In this July 1959 view, 'Large Prairie' No. 6159, on the right has brought in a four-coach train from Hereford, whilst a 'Mogul' 2-6-0 waits to depart from the Down platform with a return working. Behind it, the ex-GWR railcar working the Newent passenger service also waits to depart. Meanwhile, just glimpsed through the canopy beyond it, an all stations train to Cardiff stands in the bay platfrom. No. 6159 finished up at Didcot, from where it was withdrawn during the week ending 12th June 1965.
BELOW: On 27th June 1964, '57XX' Class 0-6-0PT No. 3693 is most likely on station pilot duties and is coupled to a maroon liveried, ex-GWR Brake Composite. Beyond, '4101' Class 2-6-2T No. 4107 stands with a train from Hereford, whilst on the left, the new order is represented by an unidentified Beyer, Peacock-built 'Hymek' diesel-hydraulic and a DMU in the bay on an all stations to Cardiff 'stopper'. BOTH BILL POTTER/KRM

A fine view beneath the canopy on Gloucester Central's Platform 1, looking west towards Hereford and South Wales during a quiet period on Monday 7th June 1965. With the closure from early November 1964 of the line to Hereford, the Sharpness Branch, many of the local stations on the main lines radiating out from Gloucester and the cessation of the Chalford auto trains, the station lost much of the hustle and bustle evident from earlier pictures. The diesel shunter just visible in the centre distance was a harbinger of the future, with the end of steam just over six months away. The array of hanging enamelled signs, for the various rooms and offices, lead down to the entrance/exit just before the bookstall. The soulless mid-1970s rebuilding of the station moved the main entrance on to the platform nearer to where the photographer was standing. ROY DENISON

RIGHT: The east end of the station, with a rake of 'Herring' hoppers loaded with ballast stone from Whitecliff Quarry near Coleford in the Forest of Dean, standing on the Up main line circa 1963. The grey painted 'Shark' brake van bringing up the rear was lettered 'C.O. RETURN TO LYDNEY. W.R.'. NPC

BELOW: The Berry Wiggins tank wagon at the head of this freight marks it as another from the Forest of Dean, off the Cinderford Branch. Class '57XX' No. 4689 had been allocated to Horton Road shed in March 1965, which would thus date this view as the summer of that year. NPC

LEFT: BR 'Standard' Class '5' 4-6-0s were not common motive power on Hereford line services, so this view of No. 73070 waiting to depart from the bay on 31st August 1964 merits inclusion on that basis alone. No. 73070 came new from Crewe Works in November 1954 and was based at Shrewsbury at the time of this picture, so was being worked back home via Hereford. It was withdrawn from Bolton shed in April 1967. The two boys, 6-year old Eric and 8-year old John Jenkins were about to enjoy a ride over the line in the company of their father, holding the camera. John, in the red pullover, went on to enjoy a 43-year career on the railway, starting as a Signal Engineer Trainee at Gloucester in 1972 and ending in 2015 as Principal Assistant to the Western Route Signal Engineer, specialising in manual signalling and level crossing control systems.
G.H.C. JENKINS, COURTESY JOHN JENKINS

LEFT: Class '5101' No. 4100, in smart plain green livery, with a four-coach train from Hereford at the Up platfrom on 13th April 1962. New in August 1935, the '5101' Class were a later build of Churchward's '31XX' Class 'Large Prairie' tanks, with the last ten actually coming out of Swindon in early BR days, a testament to the success of the original design. A Gloucester Horton Road engine, No. 4100 failed by a few weeks to make it to the end of WR steam, being withdrawn during the two week period ending 23rd October 1965. COLOUR-RAIL

BELOW: Tidy looking No. 7928 *Wolf Hall* stands at the Up platform with a local passenger service, on 6th March 1964. This engine was the penultimate member of Hawksworth's 'Modified Hall' Class, built between 1944-50, so is thus one of the BR-built 'Hall's. No. 7928 spent most of its career as a Worcester-based engine, which may well be where it was bound with this working, and was withdrawn from there during the week ending 6th March 1965. BILL POTTER/KRM

OPPOSITE PAGE BOTTOM: Immaculate 'Modified Hall' Class 4-6-0 No. 6986 *Rydal Hall* at the west end of Gloucester Central on 12th August 1961. The locomotive's condition suggests ex-works, possibly here on a running in turn from Swindon. However, the full tender would point to it being fresh off Gloucester shed and therefore perhaps about to work a special to South Wales. No. 6986 was a 'BR Hall', being new in to stock in March 1948. The 'Modified Halls', considered as a separate class, incorporated a number of design changes by Hawksworth and commenced with No. 6959 *Peatling Hall* in March 1944. *Rydal Hall* was sent first by British Railways to Tyseley shed but, by 1959, was allocated to Bristol, St. Philip's Marsh. It was withdrawn from Didcot during the week ending 24th April 1965 and scrapped by Bird's of Bridgend later the same year. With the writing on the wall for steam by the early 1960s, this is a nice reminder of just how good the BR(WR) lined green passenger livery could look; probably an improvement, in fact, on the old GWR. Note the short tubular post gantry signal spanning the line running in to the bay platform; all of the signals seen here have small calling on or shunt arms lower down the post, whilst the main arm on the farther post on the gantry is also lettered 'BAY'. In the background, the lofty spire of St. Peter's RC church, looks down on the railway. Construction of this church began in 1859 and it was consecrated in 1868. Prior to that, when the railway first arrived here in 1851, a smaller chapel building dating from the 1790s had occupied the site. NPC

Following the closure of the Severn Bridge after the October 1960 disaster, one new working through Gloucester was the Sharpness to Lydney and return school train, carrying Sharpness children to Lydney grammar school. This was run for another two years after the loss of the bridge, to allow those children who had commenced their exam courses to complete them. After that, all Sharpness children were educated on that side of the river and the decades long social connections between the two communities – Sharpness folk crossed the river for the Lydney shops, for dances and the cinema – were lost. Here, ex-GWR Class 64XX 0-6-0PT No. 6437 arrives at Gloucester Central, with a return working to Sharpness on 5th June 1962. The service was booked to work non-stop through Gloucester, although the locomotive often halted on one of the centre roads to take on water. Gloucester West Signal Box, built of blue engineering brick, is behind the locomotive. The pannier tank was withdrawn from Gloucester shed on 2nd July 1963. ALAN JARVIS

ABOVE: No. 82002 again, with a train from Hereford on 6th April 1963 that includes a 'Fruit D' van on the rear. Although built, as the name indicates, by the GWR for perishables traffic and equipped to run in passenger trains, these vehicles were also used to convey general parcels and other goods. Introduced in 1939, later batches were also built under BR. The Class '82XXX' were a Swindon product and No. 82002 was new in 1952. First allocated to Tyseley, by 1959 it was at Chester West. No. 82002 was then transferred to Exmouth Junction shed after its spell here at Gloucester, from where it was withdrawn on 7th February 1964 MARK B. WARBURTON

OPPOSITE PAGE TOP: A superb study of Class '9F' No. 92247, blowing off steam as the crew get the road to proceed towards South Wales from Gloucester on 20th October 1962. The lime stained 2-10-0 has obviously suffered priming problems, caused by impurities in the water in the boiler. The engine was less than four years old when seen here, emerging from Crewe Works and entering BR stock on the last day of 1958, its first allocation being to Old Oak Common shed. Its career came to an end on 8th October 1966, when it was withdrawn from Newton Heath shed in Manchester. In the background, BR 'Standard Class '3' 2-6-2T No. 82002 is seen arriving with a train from Hereford, the usual three-coach consist being supplemented by the addition of a parcels van. MARK B. WARBURTON

RIGHT: The '5205' Class of 2-8-0 tanks were a later development of the Churchward '42XX' Class, given larger cylinders and introduced in to service from 1923. No. 5252, seen here waiting on the Up centre road for a clear route through the station with a train of laden ballast hoppers, was new in to stock on the final day of 1925, so did not quite complete forty years in service when withdrawn on 7th May 1965. The engine spent much of its life working from Newport, latterly from Ebbw Junction shed. As can be seen, their weight restricted their availability to red routes and they were principally used on the heavy coal, steel and minerals traffic from and around South Wales. MARK B. WARBURTON

ABOVE: Soot-covered No. 7319 has just arrived with a service from Hereford on 22nd August 1964, as a corresponding northbound working waits for the 'off' from the Down platform. These three-coach 'sets', often comprised of ex-GWR Collett or Hawksworth stock, were the mainstay of Gloucester-Hereford services, although supplemented when required by a Brake or GUV for parcels traffic, or by an extra coach at busy times. MARK B. WARBURTON

RIGHT: Collett Class '22XX' No. 2241 stands on the centre Up road with a short train of vans on 13th April 1962, sporting the BR lined green passenger livery which a few of these engines got to wear. The 0-6-0 was a Hereford-based engine, so this is likely to be a pick-up goods working from there to Gloucester via Ross-on-Wye. No doubt once the crew have been given the 'road clear' signal, the train will be worked into one of Gloucester's yards. Note the green-whiskered railcar in the background, which is probably heading to the west end bay platform. No. 2241 was withdrawn from Hereford on 14th February 1964. COLOUR-RAIL.

ABOVE: 'Black 5' No. 44815 waits on the Down centre road with a train of empty mineral wagons returning to South Wales on 10th June 1965. This locomotive was a wartime build, emerging from Derby Works in late November 1944 and it finished its career far away from here, being withdrawn from Trafford Park shed, in Manchester, on 24th February 1968, just months before steam on BR finished completely. WWW.RAIL-ONLINE.CO.UK

LEFT: Work stained 2-8-0T No. 5220 has arrived with a mixed freight from South Wales and now waits on one of the centre roads for a clear path to proceed in mid 1963. The locomotive was to be withdrawn at the end of that year, from Cardiff East Dock shed on 28th December. The leading wagon is a Blue Circle Cement covered hopper and there are a number of sheeted open wagons behind. The covered footbridge linked the Up and Down platforms at Central. JOHN RYAN

LEFT: Ex-GWR Class '28XX' 2-8-0 No. 2852 with a mixed freight on the Up centre road circa 1962. Although not of great quality, the picture is interesting for the train consist, with Class 3/1 (later 08) diesel shunter No. D3106 tucked in behind No. 2852. Quite why is a mystery; the diesel, new in 1955, was allocated to Banbury at this time, so presumably it was being returned home but where had it been? Behind the shunter can be seen a couple of container wagons and several oil tank wagons. No. 2852 ended its working career at Didcot, from where it was withdrawn on 5th October 1963. D3106 spent time at several different sheds in the Midlands after Banbury, then went south to London before finally migrating north to Gateshead; it was withdrawn in 1980. J.L. CHAMPION/COLOUR-RAIL

ABOVE: With plenty of freight transferring between South Wales, the Midlands and beyond, the centre through roads at Gloucester were well used and provided plenty of opportunity for photographers. Here, grimy No. 7318 has arrived with a passenger service from Hereford, whilst gleaming Class '9F' No. 92227 clanks slowly by with a mixed freight on 4th July 1964. The 2-10-0 was new into service at the end of July 1958, so was just approaching its sixth birthday; it was to enjoy three more before being withdrawn during the week ending 4th November 1967 from Speke Junction shed, in Liverpool. WWW.RAIL-ONLINE.CO.UK

RIGHT: What a sad sight to behold and what a comedown. Built in April 1951 as a top link express engine, this is 'Britannia' No. 70008 *Black Prince* on 16th June 1965, having just gained the road east with what could be a train of iron ore empties returning to Northamptonshire via Stratford on Avon and Woodford Halse. Covered in dirt and limescale, and with its nameplates removed, No. 70008 still had eighteen months of service left, being withdrawn from Carlisle Kingmoor shed on 14th January 1967. WWW.RAIL-ONLINE.CO.UK

RIGHT: Auto-fitted '64XX' 0-6-0PT No. 6424 gets ready to depart Gloucester Central at 1.30pm on 23rd June 1962 with a Gloucestershire Railway Society tour of the branch lines in the Forest of Dean. Members of the '64XX' Class had regularly featured on Cinderford Branch trains, up until the cessation of services in November 1958. No. 6424 was soon to migrate up to the West Midlands, where it was withdrawn from Stourbridge Junction shed during the week ending 5th September 1964. BILL POTTER/KRM

LEFT: In the warm sunshine of the early evening of 13th May 1961, No. 6437 arrives back in the bay platform with the Stephenson Locomotive Society's Severn & Wye District rail tour, which again explored the lines in the Forest of Dean. This is another special that we shall see more of in the next volume. JOHN RYAN

RIGHT: An unusual aspect of Gloucester's Down bay platform, with the Railway Enthusiast Club's 'The Severn Bore' brake van tour of Forest of Dean branch lines alongside the south side platform, which was rarely used for passengers. As the loading gauge at the end of the siding indicates, this side of the bay was normally used for goods traffic. We shall meet this tour again later on in these pages (as well as in the next volume); it ran on two dates and this is the later tour, which took place on 20th June 1964, two weeks after the first run. COLOUR-RAIL

LEFT: As we shall see as we move through these pages, the Gloucester-Hereford services were worked by the full gamut of mid power ex-GWR types in the BR years, which is one reason why the line proved popular with many photographers. Regular performers on the route included various of the 'Large Prairie' types, 'Manors' and Collett '22XX' engines, along with Churchward 'Mogul' 2-6-0s. This large and successful class, eventually totalling 242 members, was built over an extended period from 1911 to 1932. No. 7319 was new from Swindon in January 1922 but was obviously on its last legs when photographed here in the west end bay at Gloucester on 27th June 1964; battered and grimey, with rusting cylinder covers and missing its smokebox numberplate, the engine was withdrawn from Gloucester three and a half months later, during the week ending 10th October. BILL POTTER/KRM

LEFT: There is no doubt the the Western Region's lined Brunswick Green passenger livery suited the ex-GWR locomotives to which it was widely applied, to the extent that many now believe this to be their 'Golden Era' in terms of appearance, above their Great Western days. 'Mogul' No. 7312 certainly looks resplendent here, whilst waiting to depart the bay platform with a Hereford train in late 1958. There were twelve stops to be made *en route* and the time allowed to make the journey averaged around an hour and a quarter; today, you would be hard-pressed to match that by main road between the two cities. Such is progress! No. 7312's working life, which had begun on the last day of 1921 and which had included many years as a Gloucester-based engine, ended with withdrawal from Severn Tunnel Junction shed exactly 42 years later, on 28th December 1963. NPC

RIGHT: As can be seen from the 85B shedplate on its smokebox door, No. 6993 *Arthog Hall* was a Gloucester based engine when this photograph was taken on 13th April 1962. Gleaming after a polish by the shed cleaners with oily rags and with its tender filled with coal, *Arthog Hall* is presumably waiting here in the bay to take over a South Wales express. Note the parcels traffic on the Down platform waiting to be loaded, including the bicycle beside the bench, with all its important bits wrapped. One of Hawksworth's 'Modified Hall' Class, No. 6993 was a BR build, emerging from Swindon on the last day of 1948. Its final allocation was to Oxford, from where it was withdrawn on 18th December 1965. COLOUR-RAIL

LEFT: Enjoy the picture of No. 7312 at the top of the page; this view of sister '43XX' No. 6346 in the bay in November 1962 is unfortunately far more representative of the condition in which we shall find most of the 'Mogul's featured throughout these pages. This is likely to be a Hereford train waiting to depart, with No. 6346 again being a Gloucester Horton Road engine, as the shedplate shows. New in 1923, the engine finished its career at 85B, being withdrawn during the week ending 5th September 1964. JOHN CHAMPION/COLOUR-RAIL

ABOVE: Collett 0-6-0 No. 2241, in WR lined green passenger livery, blows off gently in the bay platform whilst waiting to depart with a train for Hereford in the summer of 1962. A lengthy allocation to Hereford shed (86C), from May 1958 to withdrawal in February 1964, was interrrupted by a brief sojourn down to Exmouth Junction in the late summer of 1963. Note the Parcels Train Brake Van on the left, lettered for 'WOLVERHAMPTON SWINDON AND SWANSEA'. ALAN JARVIS

BELOW: Consecutively numbered Collett No. 2242, also of Hereford shed and again wearing lined green, has just been given the right away with another Ross line train but this time departing from the main platform in 1962. New in April 1945, No. 2242's time at Hereford lasted from July 1957 to early November 1964, when it was transferred to Horton Road for its final six months of service. ALAN JARVIS

LEFT: Red & cream liveried ex-GWR railcar No. W16W alongside the Up platform at Gloucester on 17th March 1957. The unit was on a joint Imperial College Railway Society/City & Guilds Engineering Society railtour, which visited the Sudbrook Branch and the Severn Tunnel pumping station. The tour had started out from Paddington, with the group changing into No. W16W here at Gloucester for the trip down to Portskewett, the junction for the Sudbrook Branch. The return journey may have been made via Severn Tunnel Junction and then through the Severn Tunnel. New into stock in April 1936 as No. 16, the railcar had strong local connections, being from the batch whose bodies were supplied by the Gloucester Railway Carriage & Wagon Co. Its service came to an end six months after this railtour, in late October 1957. COLOUR-RAIL

RIGHT: Not the best composed of photographs perhaps but colour views of first generation DMUs, in the distinctive green livery with cream body bands and whiskers, at Gloucester or anywhere else within these pages, have proved decidedly elusive. These Inter-City units were built at Swindon with W79092, seen here in September 1958, having emerged from the works in June 1957. Designed for semi-fast Birmingham to Swansea services, they were generally run in six car formations. R. SHENTON/COLOUR-RAIL

BELOW: In rail blue livery, 'Western' Class diesel-hydraulic No. D1023 *Western Fusilier* is seen at Gloucester in 1976. With Eastgate station having closed by this date, this could be a Cheltenham-London train or vice versa, the call at Gloucester neccesitating a change of end for the locomotive. With the advent of HST sets and other multiple unit type trains, reversal at Gloucester today only requires a change of ends by the driver. D1023 was new from Swindon Works in September 1963. Although redesignated as Class '52' under TOPS, none of the 'Westerns' were ever given TOPS numbers. No. D1023 was withdrawn at the end of February 1977 but happily was preserved and is today part of the National Collection, residing in the NRM at York. WWW.RAIL-ONLINE.CO.UK

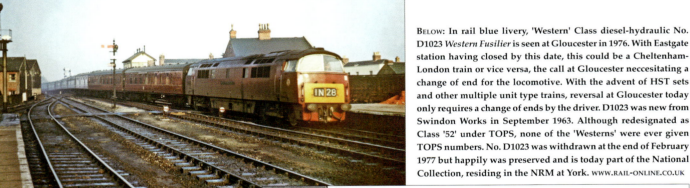

ABOVE: In 1906, the GWR, in conjunction with the North Eastern, Great Central and Barry railway companies, started an express train service between Barry and Newcastle. This train, which comprised a single service in each direction every day utilising one set of stock each from the GWR and the GCR, was run to facilitate the transfer of merchant seamen between the two large ports and, as such, it gained the unofficial title of the 'Ports to Ports Express'. It ran via the Banbury to Cheltenham route, for which a new direct avoiding line and bridge was built over the GWR Oxford-Worcester main line at Kingham. The service was later extended to Swansea and, at its other end, also included a through coach to/from Hull. After WW2, the train was diverted to run via the Honeybourne line, by which time it had lost some its 'seafaring' connections and become more of a general long distance cross-country service. Here, on 31st October 1964, No. D1032 *Western Marksman* climbs up the short rise into Gloucester station with the northbound working of the erstwhile 'Ports to Ports Express'. Maroon liveried No. D1032 had been new into service at the beginning of the year and its short career was to come to an end on 6th May 1973. BILL POTTER/KRM

In this first volume, we restrict our study of the railway at Gloucester to the east end of the station and those services travelling to or from locations to the west of the city. The locomotive sheds, goods yard and the Midland station at Eastgate will therefore be covered in future volumes in the series. However, this view of Brush Type 4 (later Class '47') No. D1727 at Central on 4th February 1967, again on a Cardiff to Newcastle working, provides a tantalising glimpse of the extensive amount of railway to be explored at the west end of the station. Gloucester East Signal Box is visible to the right, with Horton Road shed (85B) in the centre distance, still in use although having lost its steam allocation thirteen months previously. BILL POTTER/KRM

RIGHT: As a contrast to the picture above, this November 1975 view chronicles the end of an era at Gloucester Central, with the old GWR station building having been demolished to make way for the bland new building which would take its place. The bay canopy remains, as it still does today, whilst the Up platform on the left also survives much as seen here. The buildings in the background on the right have been cleared, whilst the demolition of the covered footbridge linking the two stations was completed following closure of Eastgate on 1st December 1975. NPC

LEFT: A series of brick-built arches carries the South Wales main line across the River Severn flood plain just to the west of Gloucester. As this 13th February 1977 view shows, the land here floods regularly, so they were a vital requirement in preventing the line from being damaged or washed away. The train, with D1010 *Western Campaigner* at the head, was the Railway Pictorial Publications Railtours 'Western Requiem Relief' trip from Paddington to Treherbert, Pontypridd, Aberdare and Merthyr. This was run a week in advance of the 'Western Requiem' tour, which had presumably sold out, and was one of several 'end of the Westerns' tours run in February 1977. BILL POTTER/KRM

ABOVE: A Collett 0-6-0 heads towards Gloucester with a pick-up goods from Hereford on 3rd February 1961. The train is on the low embankment passing the Little Meadow playing fields, leading from the brick arches of St. Catherine's Viaduct in the middle distance. Beyond that can just be seen Black Bridge (the OS refers to it as Pump House Bridge) over the East Channel of the River Severn, which had been rebuilt as a single span by British Railways in 1957. This replaced the original 125ft long, iron swing bridge designed by Brunel, the Gloucester & Dean Forest Railway which built this section of line being required by its Act to keep the channel clear for the passage of sailing vessels. To its left can also be seen the brick-built pump house for the pumping engines that operated the bridge, which swung on a central pier. The pump house still stands, albeit now in a derelict state. ROY DENISON

RIGHT: Gloucester Horton Road shed's Collett 0-6-0 No. 3203 pilots an unidentified 'Large Prairie' heading west away from Gloucester and just coming off Black Bridge, circa 1963. No details were recorded by the photographer, so we don't know whether this is a train for Hereford or a Cardiff 'stopper'. CHRIS WALKER

On 10th August 1963, an unidentified ex-GWR 'Mogul' is seen at the start of its journey to Hereford with a Saturday service loaded to four coaches. Just visible in the left distance above the roof of the rear carriage is Ham Viaduct, similar in design to St. Catherine's Viaduct and in common with that structure provided to assist the passage of flood water, the fields here being part of the Gloucester flood plain. The blue brick arches in the foreground performed a similar task but were not of a sufficient size to be graced with a name. The cathedral provides a prominent landmark in the central background and on the right can be seen the Over Causeway, a road thought originally to date back to the Romans, which is now a dual carriageway. Given the propensity of this area for flooding, it seems almost incredible to note that an electricity sub-station was built near here, on a site just to the north of the railway in the left distance. After a major flooding scare in 2007, millions of pounds then had to be spent building new flood barriers around it.

'Large Prairie' tank No. 4115 is seen approaching Over Junction with the 4.08pm from Gloucester to Hereford on 10th June 1961, in sunny contrast to the icy cold picture taken from exactly the same spot nineteen months later, which appears as the front titlepiece. Built at Swindon in late 1936, No. 4115 was withdrawn from Severn Tunnel Junction shed on 12th June 1965. The train is approaching the bridge carrying the A40 Over Causeway across the line. This road was re-routed about a hundred yards to the east circa 1975, in preparation for the construction of the Gloucester ring road; it was rebuilt as a dual carriageway but redesignated as part of the Ledbury road, the A417, the A40 becoming instead the ring road. The new bridge carries the four lanes of the A417 over the railway at a point just behind the rear coach. The left-most arm of the bracket signal in the foreground was for the Ledbury Branch. B.J. ASHWORTH

A superb study of work-stained '57XX' pannier tank No. 8745 near the top end of the Llanthony Docks Branch, wreathed in steam in the cold of a bright October morning in 1964, having just taken water at the tower here. The location was right alongside the A40 road and the fireman has climbed the low bank to lean on the fence and chat to the photographer. Beyond the water tank and the signals is the junction with the South Wales main line, whilst Thomas Telford's bridge carrying the A40 over the River Severn can be seen and, on the extreme left, Over Junction Signal Box is also just visible. Built in June 1931, No. 8745 was a Gloucester engine and was withdrawn from Horton Road shed during the week ending 21st August 1965. It was cut up by Cashmores of Newport. JOHN STRANGE/NPC

SECTION 2
The LLANTHONY DOCKS BRANCH

Gloucester had been an important trading centre for several centuries prior to the arrival of the railway, largely as a result of its position on the River Severn. Below Gloucester, the river is much more tidal, being subject to the daily bores which roll up the river, many of them reaching heights which make them an attraction to spectators and surfers. The city became a customs port in 1580 and was much used as a transshipment point, where up river vessels would transfer cargoes to and from esturial ships. The river even spawned its own wooden sailing ship design, the Severn Trow, with its flat bottom which enabled it to sit on the mud or sand at almost any small tidal inlet or port.

The restrictions to trade caused by larger sea-going vessels being unable or unwilling to risk navigating the river up to Gloucester brought the need for improvements in to sharp focus, however, and thus a plan was conceived to build a ship canal linking the port with the Severn Estuary at Berkeley. The Gloucester & Berkeley Canal gained its Act of Parliament in 1793 and the work of building it started soon after. However, the undertaking was beset by financial difficulties and work ground to a halt in 1799. The new basin at Gloucester was finally connected to the river by means of a lock in 1812, whilst the Gloucester & Cheltenham Tramroad, an early horse-drawn waggonway, had opened its line linking quarries on Leckhampton Hill with the new dock in 1811. Money was found to allow construction of the canal to recommence in 1817, under the supervision of Thomas Telford. By this time, it had been decided to shorten the canal to enter the river at Sharpness but further problems again delayed completion until 1827.

The new docks at Gloucester were, however, to prove a magnet for the various nascent railway companies a decade or so later, with Gloucester's early railways aiming for the potential goods traffic on offer, rather than passengers. Thus it was that both the Midland and Great Western railways constructed separate branches to the docks at Gloucester, with the MR serving the quays, wharves and warehouses on the east side of the canal and the GWR those on the west, alongside the 15th century remains of Llanthony Priory and from which the branch took its name. It was opened in 1854 and, after just over 130 years, the final traffic on the Llanthony Docks Branch, cement to the Blue Circle Cement terminal, ceased in 1985.

LEFT: The mile long branch from Over Junction to Llanthony Yard was built across the flood plain of the River Severn, raised on a low embankment which protected it from all but the worst floods. This DMU 'Special', which utilised a Gloucester RC&W-built Class '119' unit, is seen traversing the line on 21st November 1970 with a Railway Correspondence & Travel Society tour. On the right is the separate branch serving Castle Meads power station, with the exchange sidings for all traffic visible in the left distance. BILL POTTER/KRM

ABOVE: Extract from the 1961 WTT detailing the locomotive restrictions for the Llanthony Docks Branch.

RIGHT: A little over six years earlier, on 18th June 1964, photographer Bill Potter discovered this row of eight ex-GWR locomotives stored on the branch, whilst awaiting disposal to one of the scrapyards. At the head of the line is '43XX' Class 'Mogul' No. 6368, with some heavy damage to its buffer beam. No. 6368 had been officially withdrawn from Horton Road shed on 16th December 1963 but was not actually disposed of until 1965, suggesting that this row of engines may have continued to languish here for some months after the picture was taken. BILL POTTER/KRM

The LLANTHONY DOCKS BRANCH

Whilst many railway photographers of the 1960s went chasing the end of steam after it had ceased running on the Western Region at the end of 1965, a handful of others determined to capture what was left of their local area. Bill Potter, being resident in Gloucestershire, took a great number of colour slides locally after the demise of steam, including several superb views of BR Class '03' 0-6-0 diesel shunters at work on the Llanthony Docks Branch. Here, on 11th May 1967 No. D2136 trundles across the iron girder span carrying the railway over the eastern channel of the River Severn at Gloucester. Note the ex-GWR shunter's truck next to the engine; this series of photographs indicate that the use of these vehicles was still very much in vogue at this date. In the right background, the separate branch to Castle Meads can be seen curving away the short distance to the north to reach the power station. Shunting manoeuvres would have the Class 'D3' allocated on any one particular day shuttling back and forth across the river bridge on a regular basis, granting plenty of opportunities to any watching photographer. BILL POTTER/KRM

LEFT: At Upper Parting, 2 miles north of Gloucester, the River Severn splits in two. The Eastern Channel comes close in to the city, from which the docks are accessed by a lock still in regular operation today. It then curves round to flow under the bridge seen here and heads back west to rejoin the Western Channel at Lower Parting, about a mile distant. In 1871, a new weir was built, just out of sight to the left in this view, to ensure a minimum 6 foot depth of water in the river above Gloucester and, at the same time, Llanthony Lock was also constructed to allow craft to bypass the weir. The lock was abandoned in 1924 when its high walls started to collapse and had to be shored up. The lock was later partially infilled and can be seen, with its adjacent lock keeper's cottage, in the left background. Note the yard men hitching a ride on the shunter's truck and the footpath on the north side of the bridge.
BILL POTTER/KRM

ABOVE & RIGHT: On 23rd January 1967, Bill captured these two views of No. D2137 (later BR Class '03' No. 03137) trip working along the branch, departing Llanthony Sidings across the bridge over the Eastern Channel with a train of wagons bound for Gloucester Yard, where they would be remarshalled for onward transit. Prominent in the view above is Castle Meads power station, which ceased generating in 1973. In the second view, right, the train has just passed beneath the footbridge from which the previous photograph was taken; this remained standing for a number of years after the branch was closed. The Western Channel, which we shall see in a few pages time, flows under the bridges at Over and the land that lies in between the two channels is known as Alney Island. BOTH BILL POTTER/KRM

ABOVE: A rare colour view of the CEGB-owned 21-ton fireless locomotive used for shunting at Gloucester Castle Meads power station. Built by Andrew Barclay (Works No. 2126) in 1942, it is seen here in the power station yard, gleaming in the sunshine in 1962. The power station was opened by Gloucester Corporation Electricity Department in 1941 and the engine came here from new, painted in wartime grey livery and designated Gloucester Corporation No. 1. It was the only engine ever to work here, ceasing operation with the power station in 1969. In 1973, the locomotive was donated to the Dowty Railway Preservation Society and moved to their base at Ashchurch. In 1988, it was obtained by the National Waterways Museum, since when it has been cosmetically restored and is now back on display close to its old home. The power station was demolished in 1978, with Gloucester Round Table raffling the pressing of the detonator button to fell the chimney for charity. NPC

ABOVE: On 10th October 1970, the embryonic Dean Forest Railway Preservation Society ran a railtour by DMU which, amongst other destinations, also visited the Llanthony Docks Branch. The unit is here seen crossing over the swing bridge to run into the sidings. BILL POTTER/KRM

LEFT: Seven weeks later, the Metropolitan Cammell 3-car unit forming the RC&TS railtour of 21st November 1970 is seen crossing the swingbridge over the Eastern Channel as it departs Llanthony Docks. Castlemeads power station is seen almost in its entirety in the left background. BILL POTTER/KRM

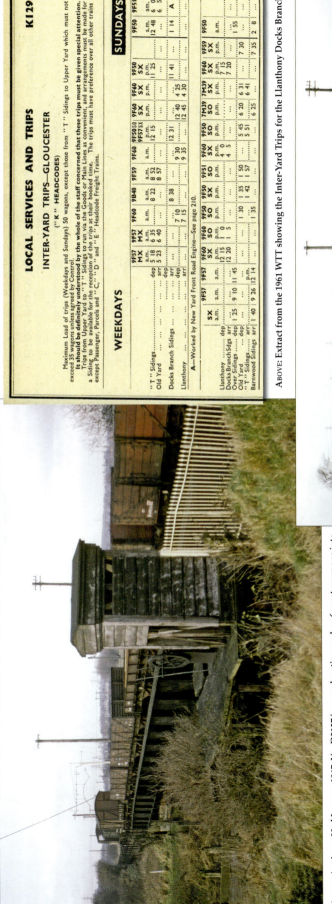

ABOVE: Extract from the 1961 WTT showing the Inter-Yard Trips for the Llanthony Docks Branch.

ABOVE: Again on 23rd January 1967, No. D2137 is seen shunting a rake of empty wagons into the docks sidings, beneath the loading gauge positioned at the far end of the bridge. It was originally a swing bridge, although it had not moved for many years when these pictures were taken. The tiny wooden cabin providing shelter for the operator and the control wheel and gear were still all in place, however. BILL POTTER/KRM

RIGHT: Later in the day, No. D2137 hauls another train away to the exchange sidings in the background; the open wagons in the centre of the consist look to be loaded with logs, which would have come up the canal from Sharpness and may be bound for the timber works at Grange Court. BILL POTTER/KRM

BELOW: Extracts from the 1961 WTT detailing particulars of work for shunting engines on the Llanthony Docks Branch, which also indicates that this had been 'dieselised' for at least six years before these photographs were taken.

The main fan of sidings comprising Llanthony Yard, seen from the top of the footbridge on 5th March 1966. Modern yellow-liveried BR trailers are in evidence, juxtaposed with a number of ancient gas lamps still painted in chocolate and cream. With its array of traffic and wagon types, along with its position alongside the Gloucester & Sharpness Canal – the buildings in the background, many of which still survive, are on the far bank – the yard and its branch would make a fascinating subject for a model. The tracks curving off on the far right served Llanthony Quay. Today, as a result of the building of the new Gloucester south-western bypass and a modern industrial development, this site has been largely obliterated. The railway bridge over the river remains and much of the course of the railway across the flood plain is now a footpath but there is little to be seen of the other branch to Castle Meads power station. Incidentally, although the GWR and Midland dock branches were always worked independently, there were connecting lines, one across Llanthony Bridge just out of sight in the left background, one running over Lock Bridge, over the canal lock out into the Severn and one to the south of Llanthony Quay, connecting to Hempsted Sidings. BILL POTTER/KRM

RIGHT: Still on 23rd January, No. D2137 is seen framed by the footbridge at the head of the yard, as it prepares to depart with another train of wagons. No. D2137's career was not a lengthy one. The 230-strong '03' Class were built at Doncaster and Swindon between 1957 and 1962, No. D2137 emerging from the latter works in 1960. After service at Gloucester, it is known to have worked at Goole docks in the mid 1970s, before being withdrawn in 1976 and cut up at BREL Doncaster the following year. Hempsted Lane level crossing lay immediately beyond the footbridge and the gates can just be made out. At this point there is now a major road junction on the Gloucester South Western Bypass, construction of which was largely completed in 2007. BILL POTTER/KRM

LEFT: On 11th May 1967, Class '03' No. D2126 was found shunting the branch, with the obligatory shunter's truck followed by a rake of cement wagons; this was the final regular traffic into Llanthony Sidings when the branch closed in 1985. The locomotive was always positioned at the Over Junction end of the train because most of the sidings at Llanthony did not have a run round facility. Note that in the few weeks since the picture at the bottom of page 41 had been taken, the chimney of the pumping engine house at the docks had been demolished. Water is still pumped from the Severn in to the docks to replenish that lost through use but no longer by steam power. BILL POTTER/KRM

BELOW: Another panorama of Llanthony Yard, from the footbridge steps on 23rd January 1967, with No. D2137 waiting to leave. The line connecting to the Midland side running via Llanthony Bridge, passed through the white gate and then ran on the far side of the brick-built, two-storey yard office in the left background. BILL POTTER/KRM

A rake of vans trundles away from Llanthony Sidings behind one of the Class '03' diesel shunters circa 1964. In the background, a line-up of eleven withdrawn ex-GWR engines, mostly tender types but with a couple of 'Prairie' 2-6-2 tanks at the nearer end and a pannier tank tucked in towards the far end, are stored awaiting their final journey to one of the South Wales scrapyards. This is clearly a different batch to those photographed by Bill Potter, seen a few pages earlier. Whilst most of them are likely to have been withdrawn from Horton Road shed, that may not have been the case for all of them and, as noted previously, they may have been stored here for some months, to give time for bids from the scrap merchants to be sought and evaluated. Barnwood shed, closed in May 1963, was also used for storage of withdrawn engines. Opposite them, a rake of steel mineral wagons can be seen at the end of the Castle Meads power station branch. NPC

A very late candidate for inclusion in these additional pages was this view of Class '57XX' No. 4698 heading on to the Llanthony Docks Branch at Over with a pick-up freight from the Forest of Dean Branch on 6th August 1965; the view also most likely dates the picture of the same engine entering Gloucester on page 23. As with that picture, No. 4698 displays another chalked 'LINER' inscription on this side but I have no idea what it means. Almost the full expanse of Over Sidings can be discerned in the background, leading down to the water tower just visible above the 0-6-0PT's cab roof. DON MANN

RIGHT: Ex-GWR 2-8-2 tank No. 7252 clanks away from Over Junction 'light engine' towards Gloucester in January 1965. The '72XX' Class were rebuilds of earlier 2-8-0 tanks, which was done following the loss of coal traffic during the late 1920s-early 1930s Depression. By extending the frames at the rear to accommodate a trailing axle, the coal and water capacity of the engines were greatly increased. They were then able to travel longer distances and were used to replace the old time-served 'Aberdare' Class 2-6-0s. The first two batches of twenty locomotives were rebuilt from '52XX' Class 2-8-0Ts between 1934 and 1936 but the final batch of twenty, of which No. 7252 was the penultimate member, were rebuilt from older '42XX' engines, between 1937 and 1939; No. 7252 was a rebuild of No. 4210, originally built in March 1912. The engine had about six months left in service when the picture was taken, being withdrawn from Severn Tunnel Junction shed on 12th June 1965. JOHN STRANGE/NPC

LEFT: On 27th April 1967, a decidedly wet and overcast day, the junction for the ex-GWR Llanthony Docks Branch is seen from the front of a DMU approaching Gloucester and just crossing the bridge over the River Severn. This was a 1958 replacement for the original bridge, on a new alignment a few yards to the south, which allowed the track across it to be on a straighter alignment and moved the junction with the Ledbury Branch. To the right, the bracket signals protecting the junction can be seen, along with another set controlling travel along the branch; note the wires controlling these signals and the rodding for the points running beside the Down line to Over Junction Signal Box. The conical top of the water tower seen earlier is also just visible on the far right. The bridge in the background carried the A40 road over the line on its way to Ross and on to south west Wales. BILL POTTER/KRM

RIGHT: A Collett '22XX' 0-6-0 heads towards Gloucester with a service from Hereford in 1964. The train is strengthed to four coaches, the leading vehicle being an ex-GWR Hawksworth Brake Composite, whilst a long wheelbase CCT parcels van with three sets of double doors either side brings up the rear. The previous alignment of the main line was to the right of the train and behind the 1958-built Over Junction Signal Box. The base of the box it replaced, which the line ran in front of, can just be seen above the roof of the parcels van. The old route of the A40 across Thomas Telford's bridge over the River Severn can be seen on the right. I have a clear memory of driving over this in a lorry with my dad around the year of this view, which also provided my only ever tantalising glimpse of Over Junction and sidings. Sadly, dad's interest in railways and industrial archaeology was yet to take root, so no effort was made at the time to explore further. COLOUR-RAIL

Work stained 'Mogul' No. 7318 drifts past Over on 22nd August 1964, with a train from Hereford which includes a Parcels coach at the rear and also some vans, probably containing perishables, picked up *en route*. The distinctive shape of Over Junction Signal Box can be seen behind, with the branch to Ledbury, closed completely three months earlier, just visible curving off beyond to the right. A demolition train hauled by a Class '08' diesel shunter can just be glimpsed waiting to come off the branch. In the left foreground, the Llanthony Docks Branch swings away east from the main line. ALAN JARVIS

Three months before the end of Western Region steam, on 22nd September 1965, '9F' 2-10-0 No. 92250, in filthy condition and with smokebox numberplate already removed, clatters past the junctions at Over with a coke train from South Wales. This locomotive made it to the very last day of WR steam, being withdrawn from Gloucester on 31st December. It held the distinction of being the last steam engine built at Crewe and was one of only two engines on BR (and the only '9F') fitted with a Giesl ejector, hence the non-standard narrow chimney. Thomas Telford's graceful arch of 1831, on the right, had sagged in the centre from the day it was built, due to an error freely admitted by its builder. The scaffolding was presumably to allow regular inspections as road traffic increased in weight and intensity. It was finally bypassed by a new road in 1975 and is now only used as a footbridge, as it is a Scheduled Ancient Monument. BILL POTTER/KRM

SECTION 3

The LEDBURY BRANCH

The 19 mile Ledbury Branch had a long and interesting history, having begun life originally as a waterway, the Hereford & Gloucester Canal. Construction of this began in 1793, from the River Severn at Over, and the canal was officially opened as far as Ledbury on 29th March 1798. Thereafter, difficulties with the terrain and shortages of capital meant that the rest of the route was not completed until 1845, when the newly built basin at Hereford was finally filled with water. For a few years the canal flourished but traffic peaked in 1860 and then went rapidly into decline as railways took over as the preferred mode of transport, with the opening in the following year of the GWR line from Worcester to Hereford, which passed through Ledbury. Soon, the residents of Newent and Dymock began the clamour for a line serving their communities.

In the event, two companies were involved in the construction of a railway from Ledbury to Gloucester: the Ross & Ledbury Railway was incorporated on 28th July 1873, with the intention of building a line between these two towns running via Dymock; the Newent Railway was incorporated a week later, on 5th August, to build a line from Newent to a junction with the GWR at Over. It was intended the two railways would make a junction with each other at Dymock but, before construction even commenced, an agreement was reached in May 1876 between the two smaller companies and the GWR for the latter to subscribe the capital; GWR nominees replaced the two boards. Progress was still slow, however, for the line's route required the takeover of the H&G Canal and it was not until 1880 that the first contract was let, for the section between Dymock and Ledbury. This was to be the only part of the Ross & Ledbury company's planned route that was ever built and was completed with double track along its near 5 mile length. Meanwhile, in June 1881, a notice was
(Continued on page 54)

The Ledbury Branch as shown on the 1961 edition one inch OS, by which date passenger services had been withdrawn, so all the stations are shown as white circles. Note: The map has been reduced by 25% to fit the page.

BELOW: Extracts from the 1955 and 1961 Working Time Tables (WTT), giving the point to point timings for goods trains between Over and Dymock, and engine restrictions over the branch – is there any record that a 'Manor' ever worked over the line?

Time Allowances for Freight Trains—continued

DOWN		Point-to-Point Times Mins.	UP		Point-to-Point Times Mins.
GLOUCESTER AND DYMOCK					
GLOUCESTER (Central)	...	...	DYMOCK	...	...
Over Junction	...	4	Newent	...	10
Barber's Bridge	...	11	Barber's Bridge	...	11
Newent	...	12	Over Junction	...	11
DYMOCK	...	10	GLOUCESTER (Central)	...	4

ENGINE RESTRICTIONS—continued   K129

GLOUCESTER, OVER JUNCTION AND LEDBURY
Route Colour – Dotted Blue.
Types of Engines Authorised—Blue, Yellow and Uncoloured Groups. Blue Group Engines are subject to a speed restriction of 25 miles per hour.

4-6-0 ENGINES, 78XX "MANOR" CLASS
May work over the Section at a speed not exceeding 25 miles per hour, subject to following prohibitions and restrictions:
Newent.—Connection in Up Main Line between platforms heading to Goods Shed. Through connection to Back Siding off Goods Shed Road. Speed not to exceed 4 miles per hour.
Dymock.—Connection in Down Line between platforms leading to Goods Shed.

ABOVE: An unusual aspect of Over Junction Signal Box, taken from the A40 road overbridge on 16th July 1964, six weeks after the line had closed, and looking towards Gloucester. Nearer to the camera is the base of the earlier Over Junction Signal Box, built by Mackenzie & Holland circa 1884 and extended in 1903. In the right background is the now closed Port Ham electricity sub-station, which was connected to Castlemeads Power Station. BRIAN MILLS

LEFT: A close-up of the Up starter for the Ledbury Branch, which had a subsidiary 'Calling-On' arm below, along with detail of the A40 overbridge, built of Forest of Dean red sandstone with a wrought iron span. The polished rails were from the demolition trains, as dismantling of the line was in process. BRIAN MILLS

BELOW: Looking north from the A40 bridge, showing the start of the single line. BRIAN MILLS

One of the finest exponents of the art of railway colour photography in the late 1950s/early 1960s was South Wales-based Alan Jarvis, who treated the medium with the same seriousness as his black and white photographs. This delightful shot of ex-GWR railcar No. W19W about to come off the Ledbury Branch at Over Junction on 4th July 1959 is one of my personal favourites and serves to demonstrate what could be achieved. The view is looking off the A40 road bridge, with red & cream liveried No. W19W about to clatter over the points leading to the main line junction. Beyond, the branch snakes off towards Newent, beneath an overgrown arch carrying a farm track over the line. The sun is high in the sky and the heat is obviously intense. Today, the A40 is a dual carriageway at this point, with the bridge on which the photographer stood long since demolished. Also gone are the farmhouse on the right, the occupation bridge and much of the trackbed, which has been 'landscaped' out of existence. ALAN JARVIS

The LEDBURY BRANCH

ABOVE: In hazy summer heat, one of the Class '45XX' 'Prairies' with straight tanks, No. 4573, skirts Lassington Woods between Over Junction and Barbers Bridge with a two-coach train on 20th June 1959. A member of a class originally designed by G.J. Churchward, No. 4573 was new into stock at the end of November 1924 but was to be withdrawn two years after the picture was taken, on 9th August 1961, by which time it had migrated down to Neyland shed, in west Wales. Locomotives in this class from No. 4575 onwards were built to a slightly modified design by Collett. B.J. ASHWORTH

RIGHT: Looking back towards Over Junction from the overbridge carrying the B4215 road over the line at Barbers Bridge, on a wintry day in early 1965, before track lifting of the closed branch had reached here. The slight depression to the right of the railway marks the route of the Hereford & Gloucester Canal at this point, whilst Barbers Bridge station was immediately behind the photographer. JOHN STRANGE/NPC

LEFT: The bare trackbed as seen from the same spot just over three years later, in April 1968. The formation and the canal bed are now bisected by the realigned B4215 but the Hereford & Gloucester Canal Trust, which is undertaking the mammoth task of slowly rebuilding the canal, are hoping to retore this section to water in the next few years. NPC

BELOW: A portion of the Newent Railway Plan No. 1, undated but circa 1873, which shows the course of the line at Barbers Bridge in relation to the already existing route of the canal. The (later B4215) road from Over to Newent can be seen crossing the canal by means of an overbridge, to the right of which the red shaded area marks the site of Barbers Bridge station. NPC

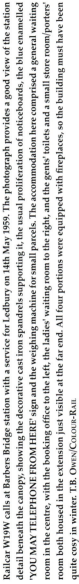

Railcar W19W calls at Barbers Bridge station with a service for Ledbury on 14th May 1959. The photograph provides a good view of the station detail beneath the canopy, showing the decorative cast iron spandrels supporting it, the usual proliferation of noticeboards, the blue enamelled 'YOU MAY TELEPHONE FROM HERE' sign and the weighing machine for small parcels. The accommodation here comprised a general waiting room in the centre, with the booking office to the left, the ladies' waiting room to the right, and the gents' toilets and a small store room/porters' room both housed in the extension just visible at the far end. All four portions were equipped with fireplaces, so the building must have been quite cosy in winter. T.B. Owen/Colour-Rail.

A view of the station looking south from the road bridge in March 1965, with the line curving off to the right towards Newent. The apparent traffic in the goods yard is deceptive; the line had closed the previous July and the crane and wagons which can just be made out belong to the demolition contractors. Clarke's distinctive station design, with its stone quoins, three tall chimneys and wide overhanging canopy, will be seen to better effect further up the branch. The original promoting Newent Railway company's initials survived until the end on the cast iron spandrels supporting the canopy. They were photographed on the same day and are seen in the lower view. BOTH JOHN STRANGE/NPC

Branch in Devon and the Bristol & North Somerset Railway. Traffic levels never justified the laying of the second track throughout and the first cutback occurred in 1898, when the loop, Down platform and signal box at Barbers Bridge were all taken out of use. Sometime during the years of the 1914-18 Great War, the double track between Dymock and Ledbury was singled, the rails presumably being taken for the war effort. In conjunction with this work, a new box, Ledbury Branch Signal Box, was opened at Ledbury on 4th January 1917. However, it appears to have been little required and was closed in 1925. Attempts to stimulate passenger traffic in the 1920s and '30s saw halts opened at Ledbury Town (1928), Greenway and Four Oaks (both 1937), and Malswick (1938). Despite this, the passenger service did not survive long enough to feature in the Beeching Report, being withdrawn on and from 13th July 1959, on which date the halts were all closed, along with the line north from Dymock to Ledbury, whilst the three original stations remained open for goods traffic worked to and from Gloucester. This service succumbed on 30th May 1964, with the complete closure of the rest of the branch. Much of the trackbed has since reverted to farmland, although in a somewhat ironic twist, it is gradually being rebuilt to its form of 150 years ago by the Herefordshire & Gloucestershire Canal Trust. Some bridges still remain, along with the station building at Barbers Bridge which was purchased and converted to a private residence shortly after closure. Dymock and Newent stations were not so lucky, the site of the latter being partially buried under a new relief road avoiding the town; a plaque beside it marks the fact that, at this point, the route has been successively, a canal, a railway and now a road.

(*Continued from page 49*) issued for the closure of the canal and the second contract for construction of the rest of the railway between Dymock and Over, to be built double track width although only a single track was to be laid, was finally let in January 1883. An unofficial first passenger train, operated by the contractor, was run between Ledbury and Newent on 5th May 1884. Board of Trade approval for the complete branch was finally received in July 1885, with the line opening throughout officially on 27th of that month. The two nominally independent companies involved in its construction were finally absorbed by the GWR in 1892.

There were originally three stations on the branch when it opened, at Barbers Bridge, Newent and Dymock, all with delightful and distinctive brick-built station buildings designed by William Clarke. Clarke designed stations on a number of other GWR lines, including the Bromyard Branch in Herefordshire (of which Rowden Mill and Fencote still survive), the Kingsbridge

On 23rd June 1962, the branch was visited by a Gloucestershire Railway Society tour, which comprised two ex-GWR auto trailers hauled by '64XX' Class 0-6-0PT No. 6424. Here, the Special is seen paused at Barbers Bridge, whilst enthusiasts have clambered down to inspect the station and small goods yard, and take photographs. The tour ran to Dymock and then returned to the main line, where it then travelled south to visit the Cinderford Branch and other lines in the Forest of Dean. Note the relatively fresh state of the ballast. BILL POTTER/KRM

On a damp and miserable spring day in May 1964, BR 'Standard' Class '2' 2-6-0 No. 78001 bundles through Barbers Bridge station with a goods train for Newent and Dymock. Any traffic to or from here will be handled on the return journey. Although the branch had always been worked by ex-GWR types, this attractively proportioned, Riddles-designed 2-6-0 worked the line regularly in the final few weeks before the goods service was withdrawn. No. 78001 was the second member of the 65-strong class to be built, emerging from British Railways' Darlington Works on the final day of 1952 and surviving to the very end of Western Region steam, being withdrawn from Gloucester Horton Road on 31st December 1965. Barbers Bridge South Ground Frame was installed when the signal box was closed in 1898, with Barbers Bridge North Ground Frame controlling the other end of the goods loop, some way behind the photographer. Also just glimpsed here on the left, behind the PW hut, is the loading platform, whilst the corrugated iron goods lock-up is situated between No. 78001 and the station building. The remains of the Down platform, also closed in 1898, are just discernable on the right, with the trackbed of the former loop occupied by a line of telegraph poles. JOHN STRANGE/NPC

LEFT: In the first of a page of views showing Barbers Bridge after closure, the station awaits its final trains on 16th July 1964, those of the demolition contractors. The platform had originally extended as far as the bridge but when it was shortened is not known. In the right foreground is part of the rear wall of the station master's house, which generally seemed to escape being captured by the camera lens. BRIAN MILLS

RIGHT: The rails recede from the platform in April 1965, as the demolition contractor starts lifting the final section back to Over Junction. Through the bridge, the demolition train can be seen at the new railhead, whilst the remains of the telegraph pole route litter the platform in the foreground, along with a velocipede which probably had previously lived in the PW hut seen on the previous page but would now most likely be heading for the scrapyard. JOHN STRANGE/NPC

LEFT: The remains of the goods yard on the same day, with what looks to be both ground frame huts joined together to form a site office on the left. The cast iron nameplate is still in situ on the nearest hut. Did the huts survive the dismantling of the line and what was the fate of the cast iron plate, worth a tidy sum on the railwayana market today? Behind, on the loading platform is the column on which the yard crane swivelled and there is just a glimpse of the station master's house beyond the station building. Note also the firebucket in the left foreground. JOHN STRANGE/NPC

RIGHT: Just over four years later, in July 1969, Clarke's station building is framed by the span of the road bridge, whilst nature has reclaimed the trackbed. Note the quality of the dressed stone used in building the bridge and the substantial cast iron girders. The road was realigned here after closure to by-pass the bridge, whilt both the station building and station master's house survive intact today, although the site has been somewhat spoilt by the construction of further housing. JOHN STRANGE/NPC

In warm summer sunshine and with newly mown hay still waiting to be collected from the field in the foreground, black-liveried Class '4575' 2-6-2T No. 5538 is seen near Newent with a two-coach train for Ledbury on 23rd August 1958. Built in 1928 and a long time resident of Horton Road shed, No. 5538 was to be transferred away from Gloucester a year or so later, ending its service at Newton Abbott on 19th October 1961. Both coaches are in the attractive but short-lived crimson & cream livery of the 1950s, with the leading vehicle an ex-GWR bow-ended 57ft corridor coach of 1920s vintage. Nearly fifty years after the line closed completely and with much of it having reverted to farm land, it is not easy to pin rural locations such as this down exactly. I am of the opinion that it is on the Gloucester side of Newent, not far from Malswick Halt, the only stopping place on the line of which I don't have a colour view. Opened on 1st February 1938 and situated on a curve in the line, Malswick was a simple wooden affair, similar to all the other halts on the line. BILL POTTER/KRM

LEFT: The year 1959 delivered one of those long, hot, balmy British summers about which we all like to reminisce – but which now come along all too infrequently. At its height, on 4th July, photographer Alan Jarvis visited the Ledbury Branch to capture the last throes of the passenger service, which was slated for withdrawal just a week later. With not a soul to be seen, Railcar W19W stands at the platform at Newent, having just arrived from Gloucester. ALAN JARVIS

ABOVE: A few minutes later, W19W departs for Ledbury, with the concrete provender store and brick-built goods shed in the left background. The figure on the left is the signalman, who has come over to the station with the single line token for the section to Dymock to hand to the driver of the railcar and to fill up his water can at the same time. ALAN JARVIS

RIGHT: As the railcar trundles away past the goods yard, the signalman walks over the boarded crossing as he makes his way back to the box. ALAN JARVIS

Only a railway enthusiast could appreciate the sheer joy of a day spent in glorious weather on the platform of a sleepy branch line station whiling away the time waiting for the next train to arrive – which could be hours. In the final view in the sequence begun on the previous page, W19W arrives back at Newent with the return working from Ledbury to Gloucester on 4th July 1959. ALAN JARVIS

No. W19W again at the Up platform on 11th July 1959, the last day of passenger services on the branch. The picture drips atmosphere and it is difficult to believe that this was the end. On the platform, the guard enjoys a joke with a passenger, whilst another couple chat to the driver through his window. Beyond the station gate on the right, one of the Red & White buses, the replacement for the rail service, waits in the forecourt. BILL POTTER/KRM

A rare colour view of trains crossing at Newent, as railcar No. W19W waits for Collett 0-6-0 No. 2207 to arrive with the branch pick-up goods on 10th July 1959. New in August 1939, the '22XX' was at Kidderminster shed from 1953, transferring to Gloucester Horton Road in March 1956, where it spent the rest of its relatively short career, withdrawal taking place in January 1961. Being a single track branch, the driver of the railcar will exchange the staff for the Dymock to Newent section with the token for the Newent to Over Junction section, about to be handed over by the fireman of No. 2207. Once the railcar has departed, the 0-6-0 will then be free to shunt the yard here, before carrying on northwards to Dymock and Ledbury. Was No. 2207 a new 'cop' for the schoolboy spotter on his bike on the left? This is another slide, bought off an internet auction site, which came with no recorded provenance, so sadly the identity of the photographer is not known to me. NPC

Collett 0-6-0 No. 2248 arrives from Ledbury with a short freight, which appears to include a horse box, on 10th March 1959. The locomotive will uncouple here and move forward, before backing over the crossover to shunt the yard and pick up any wagons for Gloucester. B.J. ASHWORTH

Manoeuvres completed and with the Up starter signal 'off', No. 2248 prepares to depart for Gloucester. Built in 1945, the locomotive spent most of its working life shedded at 85B but had been re-allocated to Reading by the time withdrawal took place during the week ending 29th August 1964. B.J. ASHWORTH

G.W.R. NEWENT

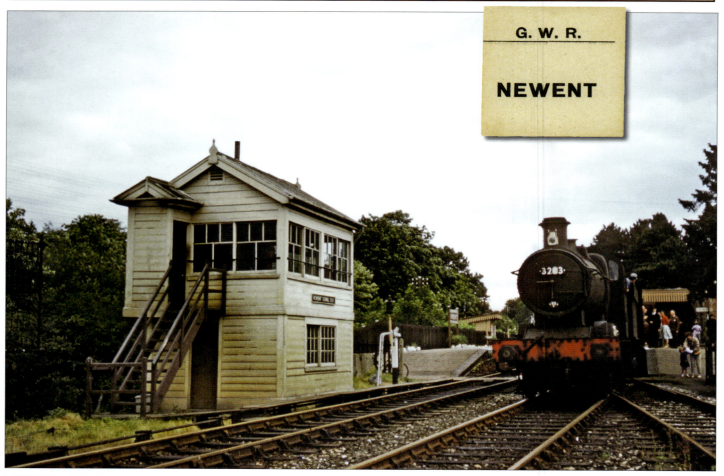

ABOVE: The passenger service on the last day, with Collett 0-6-0 No. 3203 at the head, was strengthened from the single railcar which sufficed most of the time, to an unheard of five coaches so locals could ride the branch one final time. Here, the train waits at the Down platform whilst a veritable crowd of passengers climb aboard for the trip to Ledbury. At the bottom of the platform ramp, photographer Bill Potter's wife and daughter watch as he captures the moment. Fireman Jim Kavanagh observes the throng whilst driver Jack Folley is out of sight on the footplate. BILL POTTER/KRM

LEFT: The wooden signal box is well shown in both these pictures but this view also illustrates the token apparatus, which was still in good order at this date, although probably little used, as it is likely that most exchanges were done by hand. This box was a replacement for the original cabin, provided by Mackenzie & Holland, in 1948. That was also built of wood and of a very similar design to this but was partially sunk into the Up platform. The box seen here dated from 1902 and was secondhand, having been brought here from its original site alongside Aston Magna Brickworks, on the Oxford to Worcester line near Moreton-in-Marsh, after it was made redundant following the provision in 1946 of ground frames for the sidings which it controlled. Basil Wood, the last regular signalman here at Newent, is nowhere to be seen. BILL POTTER/KRM

An interesting panoramic view of the station on 15th April 1961, looking towards Gloucester and showing the loading bay behind the Down platform, with a single mineral wagon standing in it. The cattle pens are just in view on the right; there were only two, perhaps surprising for this rural location but the movement of livestock was not a significant traffic on the branch and they appear to have fallen out of use some years before the final cessation of goods traffic. Note that with the end of the passenger service and the box now being opened as required, the Up line had ceased to be used, whilst the rusty rails indicate that shunting of the goods yard and bay was now carried out from the Dymock end of the station. The first signal box had been at this end of the Up platform, between the nameboard and the ramp. MARK B. WARBURTON

A lovely overall view of Newent circa 1961, with plenty of evidence of activity on the platform and in the yard. Beneath the canopy, platform barrows are in use for the parcels traffic which was still handled here. A carmine and cream liveried British Railways parcels van can be made out hiding behind the bushes, with the driver either loading or unloading packages for onward transit. Incoming traffic to the yard included supplies for the local coal merchant, with a BR slope-sided mineral wagon standing beside piles of recently unloaded coal in the right background, and animal feed delivered to the provender store. Outward goods included the occasional loads of timber, plus boxes of daffodils in considerable quantity when in season; indeed, the branch is sometimes referred to as 'the daffodil line'. BILL POTTER/KRM

Table of maximum speeds for the branch from the summer 1961 Freight WTT.

GLOUCESTER AND DYMOCK BRANCH

Over Junction 0 m.p. and 0m. 10c.	All Trains to and from Branch	10
Over Junction to 1 m.p.	All Up and Down Trains	30
1 m.p. to 4¼ m.p.	All Up and Down Trains	40
4¼ m.p. to 5m. 50c.	All Up and Down Trains	35
5m. 50c. to 6¼ m.p.	All Up and Down Trains	45
6¼ m.p. to 7¼ m.p.	All Up and Down Trains	35
7¼ m.p. to Newent Loop Junction	All Up and Down Trains	40
Newent Station and Loops	All Up and Down Trains	15
Newent Loop Junction to 9¼ m.p.	All Up and Down Trains	40
9¼ m.p. to Dymock Loop Junction	All Up and Down Trains	50
Dymock Station and Loops	All Up and Down Trains	15

ABOVE: The first building to go at Newent following the withdrawal of the passenger service was actually the goods shed, which was demolished circa 1960, the remaining traffic being handled at the more modern provender store. This view is undated but looking at the generally tidy condition of the rest of the station and in comparison with the June 1962 pictures left and below, it is believed to have been taken in the spring of 1961. A pair of vans stand alongside the store, there is coal visible in the yard, the platform barrows await parcels traffic and both platforms look in a reasonably well cared for state. Note also that the signal arms have been removed although the posts still remain. JOHN STRANGE/NPC

ABOVE: No. 6424 with the Gloucestershire Railway Society tour at Newent on 23rd June 1962. Railway enthusasts mill around on the Down platform for one last time, as the surrounding vegetation slowly closes in. BILL POTTER/KRM

RIGHT: No. 6424 about to leave for its final destination at Dymock with the GRS Tour. Note that the signal posts and token apparatus have all been removed since the picture top of the page was taken. JOHN STRANGE/NPC

ABOVE: No. 78001, which we last saw passing Barbers Bridge on a damp spring day, is pictured here at Newent a few weeks later on 16th May 1964, waiting to leave for Gloucester with a short goods train comprised of three vans, two coal wagons and a brake van. Withdrawal of goods traffic and final closure of the station was just two weeks away, on 1st June. JOHN STRANGE/NPC

RIGHT: Conversation piece. The driver and fireman chat as they prepare to mount the footplate for the picturesque journey back down the branch to Gloucester. JOHN STRANGE/NPC

LEFT: Another study of No. 78001 at Newent on 16th May 1964, on what would have been a very relaxed day out for the crew. They would have been aware that the end was near, so there were not many occasions left on which to enjoy rosters such as this. Although the official final closure date was given as 1st June, the last trip up the branch, by No. 78001 and a brake van to collect any remaining empty wagons, took place on Saturday 30th May. NPC

LEFT: A final brief return to better days at Newent, in this busy scene from the late 1950s. A large and varied selection of parcels and sacks can be seen on the platform, that have either just been unloaded from railcar W19W or are about to be placed on board. Is that also a goose nonchalantly wandering around? The picture gives an indication of the lifeline that the railway still provided for this small country town in north west Gloucestershire, a service, however, which would soon be taken over by road transport. COLOUR-RAIL

RIGHT: Four Oaks Halt, between Newent and Dymock, as the GRS tour passes on 23rd June 1962, the occasion saluted by a couple of passengers waving their handkerchiefs out of the windows of the auto trailer. Opened by the GWR on 16th October 1937, the halt had closed with the passenger service in 1959 but remained substantially intact three years later, apart from the nameboard being taken down from its posts and propped against a lamppost, and the removal of the wooden railings. Note the concrete sleepers on this section. The photographer was standing on the three-arch, brick-built bridge which spanned the cutting here, a pathway and steps leading down to the platform from the road above. This cutting has now been filled in but one of the brick parapets of the bridge still remains. JOHN STRANGE/NPC

LEFT: The closed single line at Four Oaks Halt on 16th July 1964, photographed from the same overbridge. The track, still in pristine condition, was bullhead rail on concrete sleepers, whilst the telegraph rig was also in excellent condition– clearly quite a recent replacement although the wires had been removed. The M50 motorway overbridge can be seen nearing completion in the distance. Note that although two years had elapsed since the previous picture was taken, the halt nameboard was still lying on the platform at the base of the lamppost. BRIAN MILLS

Two views of railcar W19W calling at Dymock station on 4th July 1959, with a trio of schoolgirls leading a group of arrivals along the Down platform, ABOVE. The unit is then seen departing in the direction of Ledbury, BELOW, beneath the attractive road overbridge. The station gardens were a delight. BOTH ALAN JARVIS

The Clark-designed building at Dymock was every bit as attractive as the others on the line and in a similarly beautiful location, the 'GWR pine trees' having matured over the years since they were planted to provide a distinctive and instantly recognisable station backdrop. On 4th July 1959, railcar W19W pauses for custom on its journey from Ledbury to Gloucester. In the distance, through the arch of the stone-built overbridge which still remains today, can just be seen the bracketed Home signal with the arm in the 'off' position giving the railcar permission to enter the station. The wide formation beyond the bridge gives a clue to the fact that, up until 1917, the line northwards from here to Ledbury had been double track. Greenway Halt was situated around a mile and a half north of the bridge. ALAN JARVIS

Looking north through the station on 15th April 1961, showing the stop blocks that were put in place following lifting of the line to Ledbury. Note the signals were still in place. MARK B. WARBURTON

The view south towards Gloucester on the same day, with plenty of vans in evidence in the yard and a glimpse too of the 5-ton yard crane that was provided here. Just beyond the goods shed is Dymock Signal Box, a wooden structure similar in appearance to that at Newent but provided by McKenzie & Holland for the opening of the line. The signalman here in the final years was actually a lady, Gladys Badham. MARK B. WARBURTON

Dymock station in all its sylvan glory circa 1962, with the platform gardens blooming and the sun shining but still with plenty of cloud in an azure blue sky. The photographer's car stands in the station forecourt whilst his wife and baby can be seen on the platform centre right and in the background beyond them the goods yard is still open for business, with a van and a couple of wooden bodied open wagons in view. The goods shed here remained in use right up until the final cessation of traffic, whilst that at Newent had already been demolished; quite why the one survived and the other did not is not known. Indeed, Dymock goods shed still stands today, although it has been converted for use as a church – the Western Way Christian Chapel – and is now almost unrecognisable from the building seen in these photographs. In the foreground, the rails lying between the tracks are from the section north to Ledbury, which was lifted between August 1960 and the end of April 1962. The rather piecemeal way in which this was carried out was in stark contrast to the rest of the branch between here and Over Junction, on which lifting commenced just two weeks after final closure. BILL POTTER/KRM

Top Left & Above: No. 6424 with the GRS tour at Dymock. Some passengers inspect the locomotive whilst others take the opportunity of a final chance to photograph a passenger train here. The platforms are stacked with sleepers from the track lifting which had taken place north from here. BOTH BILL POTTER/KRM

Top Right & Right: Extracts from the summer 1961 freight WTT: The timings of the single daily (Saturdays excepted) goods train and the maximum loads for the branch; it is highly unlikely the latter was an issue in the last years of the line's existence.

ABOVE: Greenway Halt's location, a mile and a half north of Dymock, was as rural as this rare colour shot suggests. The view is looking north, with railcar W19W heading away towards Ledbury on 21st March 1959. The halt, opened on 1st April 1937, served a handful of scattered hamlets and farms, and only ever saw light usage, whilst administration of it was undertaken by the station master at Dymock. The trackbed hereabouts today has been largely incorporated back into the surrounding fields but the brick-built overbridge on which the photographer was standing still remains. Note the PW hut in the left background which also housed a ganger's trolley, to assist with maintenance of this section of the line. COLOUR-RAIL

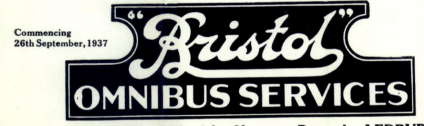

ABOVE: The writing was on the wall for the branch passenger service from the late 1920s. This is a section of the time table for the competing Bristol Omnibus service of autumn 1937; there were stops at all the places the railway called at and many more besides. NPC

RIGHT: The Down passenger service on the Ledbury Branch from the September 1955-June 1956 Working Time Table comprised just five trains daily, the journey taking 50 minutes. Note that the early morning diesel railcar service was formed by the 6.15am from Cheltenham St. James station.

Bye Street, Ledbury, looking towards Bridge Street on 18th October 1963. The road rises to cross the Gloucester-Ledbury Branch in the centre of the picture, with the brick parapets of the bridge prominent. The adverts on the grocer's shop on the right should bring back memories for some. D.J. NORTON

The remains of Ledbury Town Halt on 29th July 1961, after the track had been lifted. The short platform, barely two coaches in length, had a wooden facia with an earth and cinder infill. Note the nameboard is still in situ, along with a cast iron warning notice and a corrugated iron hut at the far end beneath the bridge. JOHN STRANGE/NPC

A second view of the halt, the first provided on the branch by the GWR on 26th November 1928. As previously mentioned, this section of the line had originally been double track and the platform was sited on the bed of the lifted set of rails. Both views show the bridge, the parapets of which are shown in the photograph of Bye Street. The road was carried across the railway on wrought iron beams, which were supported on brick abutments. Today, the road here has been lowered and widened, and the bridge no longer exists. This view also shows the passenger access from the rear of the platform and note the 4-wheeled flatbed lorry passing in the background. The corrugated iron hut seen beneath the bridge span in the previous view was used for the storage of oil and oil lamps, for lighting the platform at night. JOHN STRANGE/NPC

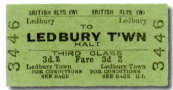

The Up passenger service on the branch, again from the 1955-56 WTT comprised a corresponding five return trains daily, with the journey taking between 47 and 53 minutes. Note the instruction to the guard of the last train to extinguish lights where necessary; the unmanned halts were all lit by oil lamps, which had to be put out at the end of services each night. The branch trains ran Monday-Saturday; there was no Sunday service.

Although the track had been lifted through the town, the section to the main line was still in place as this photograph, also taken on 29th July 1961, indicates. It was retained in use as a siding until August 1960, presumably in conjunction with track lifting at the northern end. The signal post, minus its arm which controlled the approach to the junction, stands beside the bridge carrying the line over the A438 road to Hereford. From here, the branch executed a gentle 'S' on its way through the town and its route, remarkably, is still virtually intact and easily traceable. JOHN STRANGE/NPC

Railcar No. W19W in the Down platform at Ledbury on the last day, 11th July 1959. The view is looking east towards Worcester, with the western portal of Ledbury Tunnel just visible in the left background behind the water column and signals. Behind the railcar is a glimpse of the goods shed and signal box; the latter remains in use today. The footbridge also still survives (albeit without its canopy) but whilst the station is well used, with a regular mix of local and long distance trains, passengers are served from a wooden hut alongside the Down platform, the station buildings seen here having all been demolished. The line from Worcester to Hereford was built by the Worcester & Hereford Railway and opened in stages between 1859 and 1861. By the time Ledbury station opened on 13th September 1861, the W&HR had been absorbed by the West Midland Railway (on 1st July), which in turn became a part of the GWR on 1st August 1863. BILL POTTER/KRM

LEFT: A meeting of 'Halls'. In crisp, clear winter sunshine on 24th January 1959, No. 5998 *Trevor Hall* waits for the road at Ledbury, as classmate No. 5971 *Merevale Hall* approaches with a Hereford bound train, the section through the tunnel having always been single track. It was also on a steep gradient up from the station and on a sharp curve, so was always difficult to work in steam days – hence the need for bankers – and was detested by footplate crews. Note the silhouette of the gas lamp on the coach side, whilst No. 5998 – and probably No. 5971 – is beautifully turned out in BR lined green livery. DAVID BICK/NPC

ABOVE: Locomotive servicing facilities were provided at Ledbury but although it was classed as a sub shed to 85C Hereford, there is no record of a shed building ever having existed here. There was, however, a turntable and a small coaling stage with roof and canopy, which was provided primarily for the banking engines stabled here, which were used to bank Up trains through Ledbury Tunnel. Standing alongside the stage on 11th July 1959 is '5203' Class 2-8-0T No. 5243. These tank engines always worked bunker first through the tunnel to reduce the effects of the fumes. The facilities were also used by locomotives off the branch, tender engines being turned here, whilst all could take coal and water as required. BILL POTTER/KRM

RIGHT: An unidentified 'Hymek' Bo-Bo diesel-hydraulic drifts in to the Down platform with an express for Hereford in August 1963. Although this picture is a little soft, it was worth including for the detail of the goods sidings and, in particular, the grounded coach body – probably from an old 6-wheeler – on the far side of the coal yard. JOHN THORN

LEFT: A rare and unusual aspect of Ledbury station, snapped from the window of a train approaching from Gloucester on 24th January 1959. Following rationalisation of the double track junction to a single line in September 1956, branch trains could only use the Down platform here. Note the brick wall supporting the ramped approach to the station forecourt. DAVID BICK/NPC

ABOVE: Looking north towards Hereford in June 1968, the station still exuded a distinct GWR/WR air, with its cream saw-tooth canopies, chocolate and cream stanchions, totems and signs. The footbridge, however, had lost its protective canopy but note the 'portholes' at the left-hand end; these were provided to allow the Ledbury signalmen to see the Down starter. In the distance, the line to Hereford curves round to head across the 30 arches of the brick-built Ledbury viaduct, constructed in 1859-60 and now Grade II listed. NPC

RIGHT: Ledbury Branch Junction on 29th July 1961, the rust covered rails an indication that it had been out of use for around a year; the track was finally removed in late April 1962. For most of its life, as mentioned above, this had been a double track junction, with the line becoming single track beyond the Hereford Road bridge, an attractive stone-built, skew arch structure which still stands today. JOHN STRANGE/NPC

SECTION 4

OVER JUNCTION to GRANGE COURT JUNCTION

Whilst the section of the South Wales Railway from Over Junction to Grange Court Junction is clearly part of the main line between Gloucester and Severn Tunnel Junction, in historical terms it can be treated as a separate entity, because it was built by a different company to the rest of the route. It also suits our journey, because having rejoined the main line after our lengthy sojourn up the branch to Ledbury, at Grange Court we shall deviate away once more, as this was where the cross-country route to Hereford branched off. This section of line is around 4 miles in length, virtually straight and relatively level.

The Gloucester & Dean Forest Railway was formed by an Act of 27th July 1846, with GWR support, to build 15½ miles of railway between Gloucester and Awre, where it would link up with the South Wales Railway, along with the short branch to Llanthony Docks. In the event, only the 8 miles to Grange Court were built before the Company's finances ran out, with the SWR completing the line to Awre, the whole opening on 19th September 1851. There was one intermediate station between Gloucester and Grange Court, at Oakle Street, and the route was broad gauge until 1869. The line is still in use today but nothing remains of the stations or junctions.

Gloucester to Grange Court Junction as shown on the 1961 edition one inch OS.

No. 7252 posing in front of Over Junction Signal Box in January 1965. This brick-built box, with high pitched roof, was to a design not found anywhere else on the WR system. Whilst the sidings here at Over were enlarged and extended during the Second World War, the box was a post-war rebuild, dating from 1958, when the bridge spanning the River Severn was replaced a new one being built alongside to the east, which resulted in the junction layout being altered and the old box demolished as it was in the way. Unusually, the window surrounds were in brick, whilst the roof, at a time when flat roofs were in vogue, was much higher and on a steeper pitch than any other signal box roof certainly that this author has ever seen. It had a short life, however, closing on 2nd June 1969. ALAN SAINTY COLLECTION

With its number and other numerals chalked on the bufferbeam, work-stained ex-GWR 2-8-0 No. 2890 pulls away from Over Sidings, with a long train of steel mineral wagons laden with South Wales coal, in March 1964. The locomotive was one of the later series, built between 1938 and 1942 and commencing with No. 2884, which is why they are often referred to as the '2884' Class. Construction of the earlier engines had been in several batches spread over seventeen years between 1903 and 1919. No. 2890 still had a year left in service, being withdrawn from Newport (Ebbw Junction) shed on 21st April 1965. The engine is coming off one of the loops installed here in 1904. Both Up and Down loops were doubled in length and additional siding accommodation laid in on the Up side in early 1942, to cater for the increased traffic during wartime. They acted principally as holding sidings for the Docks Branch but the loops were also used to allow faster trains to pass. With the line to Hereford and the Forest of Dean branches, along with the traffic to and from South Wales, this was an extremely busy stretch of railway. The signals seen here were all operated from Over Junction Signal Box, although the Distant arm was the Over Sidings Down Inner Distant. Exit from the two Up goods loops was possible from either box. Note the small green low-sided lorry passing along the A40 in the right background. NPC

A half a mile west of Over there is a major road junction where the A48 commences, branching off south-westwards away from the A40 towards Lydney, Chepstow and South Wales. Some 119 miles later, after following the curve of the South Wales coastline through Cardiff and Swansea, the A48 joins up with the A40 again at Carmarthen. This view of Class 9F No. 92215 heading towards South Wales with a load of iron ore was taken from the verge of the A48 near its start and close to the bridge carrying it over the line. It is undated but the engine was allocated to Banbury shed until early September 1963, so the picture is likely to be a few weeks prior to that. Upper Moorcroft Farm features in the right background. NPC

From a similar vantage point, Class '22XX' No. 2242 made for a pretty picture as it hurried by with the 12.25pm from Gloucester to Hereford on 9th May 1964. As a resident of Hereford shed since July 1957, it no doubt had come to know the route well but No. 2242 was transferred to Horton Road in November 1964 after the line was closed, where it lasted just six more months, being withdrawn in May 1965, the wholesale closure of Gloucestershire branch and secondary lines having left many of these smaller engines with little or no work. Whilst the A48 bridge has been heavily rebuilt with a massive concrete parapet which blocks all views of the railway, a photograph taken from this exact spot today will show little change apart from the loss of the telegraph pole route. NPC

Westwards from Over is a particularly attractive section of railway which, sadly, seems rarely to have attracted the attention of photographers. Passing beneath the A48 road to Chepstow, the city of Gloucester, with its distinctive cathedral tower, forms a backdrop in any view taken looking east from the bridge. Westwards, the line is straight as it heads towards Oakle Street, with the hills of the Forest of Dean in the background. On 6th June 1964, the Railway Enthusiast Club ran 'The Severn Bore', a brake van tour of the lines of the Forest of Dean, which was double-headed by two 16XX 0-6-0PTs. This was over-subscribed, so a second tour was run on 20th June, this time with just one engine, No. 1658, in charge and, on a perfect day for photography, it is this second tour which is seen first passing beneath the A48, ABOVE, and then heading towards Oakle Street, BELOW. T.B. OWEN

In a view which shows the line was not completely level, Collett 0-6-0 No. 2245 is seen coasting down a slight gradient towards Oakle Street, with a lengthy mixed freight probably bound for the Hereford line, on a gloriously hot day in the summer of 1960. This was another Gloucester Horton Road engine, withdrawn on 23rd May 1963, which met its end without leaving the county, being cut up by Cooper's Metals at Sharpness a year later. The black painted steel bridge in the left distance, carrying a farm track near Churcham, still survives, whilst on the horizon above the train is part of the sprawling Severnside village of Minsterworth, far larger than Oakle Street but which never had a station. As mentioned opposite, this attractive section of railway through Oakle Street was infrequently photographed, despite the frequency and variety of passing trains, which was rather a shame. Note the wide spacing of the tracks here, betraying the line's broad gauge origins. ALAN JARVIS

RIGHT: In obviously poor condition and leaking steam everywhere, Gloucester-based ex-GWR 'Mogul' No. 7318 starts away from Oakle Street station, with what may well be a last day Hereford to Gloucester train on 31st October 1964. The station is just beyond the bridge but little can be seen of it in this view. The large roof visible top right belonged to the Oakle Street Hotel, opened circa 1891 by Wintle's Brewery of Mitcheldean. It was renamed 'The Silent Whistle' in the 1990s but closed in 1999 and is now a private house. JOHN STRANGE/NPC

BELOW: No. 6318 gathers speed as it leaves Oakle Street for the final time. John Strange, who took his shot a few seconds earlier, will be one of the little group of photographers in the left distance. ROY DENISON

BELOW: Another grimy 'Mogul, No. 6349, pauses at Oakle Street station with a Hereford-bound train on 9th May 1964. No. 6349 was based at Hereford shed in 1948 and was withdrawn from Gloucester during the week ending 8th August 1964, so the journey between the two cities must have been a very familiar run by the time of this photograph.
ALAN CHANDLER, COURTESY ALAN SAINTY

A delightful study of the small wayside station at Oakle Street, basking in late autumn sunshine on 3rd November 1962 and showing the simple wooden buildings provided here. This sleepy halt served a small hamlet of just a few scattered cottages and farms, as well as the more distant but larger village of Minsterworth, spread out along nearly a mile of the parallel A48. Despite being on the main line, it had only a limited time table, being served by Gloucester-Hereford trains only, not those heading to and from South Wales. The station opened for passengers on 9th September 1851 but then did not appear in the timetables between 1856 and 1870. The signal box, which had been sited on the far end of the Down platform, was closed circa 1953-4, the siding and goods bay on the left then being accessed by a ground frame. The goods yard was closed on 12th August 1963, with the siding and ground frame being taken out on 13th October. Note the colour light signal opposite on the Down side. There were two minor level crossings on the short section ahead to Grange Court Junction, at Ley Road (just discernible in the distance) and Frowen's Lane, both of which are still in operation today, although the latter appears to be only a farm track and is very restricted use. ROY DENISON

A closer view of the main buildings, on the Up side and looking towards Gloucester on its last day. The nearer timber building was originally all the accommodation that was provided here. The brick building and gents urinal were later additions, probably in the 1890s but certainly by 1902, along with the brick shelter on the Down side; this originally had a small canopy but no such luxury was ever provided for the main building. Note the faded nameboard set back by the fence on the left, whilst although the ground frame and yard had been taken out a year earlier, little effort seems to have been made to remove the materials and equipment from the site. The only reminder of the station's existence today is the station master's house, the lofty red brick building visible in the centre background. ROY DENISON

RIGHT: With its 2D Coventry shedplate to the fore, Class '9F' No. 92138 catches the late evening sun as it heads south through Grange Court Junction on 23rd October 1964. New in to service on 31st July 1957, the 2-10-0 was to finish its career at Speke Junction shed, in Liverpool, exactly ten years later, on 8th July 1967. COLOUR-RAIL

BELOW: At the same location on the same day, '57XX' Class 0-6-0PT No. 4698 hurries south with a mixed train bound for the Forest of Dean, comprising empty mineral wagons for Northern United Colliery, Berry Wiggins tank wagons for Whimsey depot and some vans at the rear for Cinderford. It will probably be split in two at Bullo Junction and taken up the steeply graded branch to Bilson Junction and Cinderford in separate portions. A late GWR build, in February 1945, No. 4698 was a Gloucester-based engine and was withdrawn from 85B during the two week period ending 23rd October 1965. COLOUR-RAIL

RIGHT: Not the sharpest of shots but this view looking east towards Gloucester from the station footbridge a short while later provides a rare glimpse of the goods yard, although the track had been lifted by this date. It comprised two widely spaced sidings which were connected part way along forming a loop. One siding ran in front of the loading dock and courrugated iron lock-up, before ending behind the platform on the right alongside a couple of cattle pens. The other ran close to the fence at the back of the yard. Goods handled here comprised mostly agricultural produce and timber, and there was also a seasonal traffic in Christmas trees grown locally. An unidentified 2-10-0 storms through with a loaded iron ore train from Northamptonshire. This will have travelled via the Stratford & Midland Junction line and then south along the Honeybourne line to Cheltenham; we shall see more of these workings in a future volume. COLOUR-RAIL

LEFT: There were a number of services which ran through to Hereford which originated further out than Gloucester. In morning frost on 21st December 1963, the 8.00am train from Swindon to Hereford is seen arriving at Grange Court, with the fireman having just collected the single line token from the apparatus in the crook of his arm. The driver of BR 'Standard' Class '4' tank No. 80070 appears to be watching his colleague to make sure he had caught it safely. The goods yard was also equipped with a 5-ton capacity crane, situated on the dock next to the lock-up and seen here still in situ, although the sidings were in the process of being lifted. JOHN DAGLEY-MORRIS

Collett introduced the eighty-strong class of 'Grange' 4-6-0s to replace eighty '43XX' Class 2-6-0s, which were withdrawn in the later 1930s. Indeed, some of the new engines incorporated the wheels and motion from withdrawn 'Mogul's but their route availability was not as good, being similar to the 'Hall' Class. Their duties were also similar, being used on mixed traffic work. Here, No. 6848 *Toddington Grange* is seen in poor external condition, hauling a ballast train through Grange Court Junction on the sunny evening of 23rd October 1964. On the right is the impressive Grange Court Signal Box, opened on 17th April 1935 as a replacement for two smaller boxes situated at either end of the station, Grange Court East Box and Grange Court West Box. No. 6848 was withdrawn from Oxford shed during the week ending 18th December 1965. COLOUR RAIL

A panoramic view of Grange Court Junction station circa 1962, looking west with a train from Hereford hauled by an unidentified 'Large Prairie' just arriving under the bridge. The station was opened on 1st June 1855, although it had appeared in the October 1853 time table albeit without a train service, and was closed officially on 2nd November 1964, upon the withdrawal of the passenger service to Hereford. In fact the final trains had actually run two days before, on Saturday 31st October, there being no Sunday service on the route by this date. Early 20th century photographs of the station show that it changed little during its lifetime; the station buildings and waiting shelters were original, whilst the footbridge and the building on the left were later additions, dating from 1897 when the platforms were extended to the east. The latter, built of blue engineering bricks, housed toilets and a staff rest room, and is the only structure surviving from this view today, apart from the road bridge. Out of shot here to the left, the station master's house also still remains as a private residence. For many years there has been a goods loop on the site of the Hereford lines but this is now disconnected and out of use. It is likely that the original short posted oil lamps were replaced in the mid 1930s by the concrete lamp standards seen here, when the signalling alterations noted above were carried out. MICHAEL HALE

Whilst graced by few passengers, Grange Court Junction must have been a wonderful location to watch and photograph the plethora of passing trains. Here, on a summer's day circa 1964, an unidentified but heavily work-stained '9F' 2-10-0 rumbles through on the Down main line with a lengthy mixed freight bound for South Wales. The locomotive's smokebox numberplate is almost decipherable and it might be No. 72070, which between June 1963 and March 1965 was a Leicester Midland based engine. NPC

Whilst the number of wonderful additional colour transparencies that have turned up since this volume was first published undoubtedly justifies this enlarged second edition, my personal favourite amongst all of them is unquestionably this hugely nostalgic and rare view of the road approach to Grange Court station, surrounded by mature pine trees and beautifully lit by shafts of sunlight. Anonymous and undated, it was probably taken in 1964, a few months before closure. Coincidentally, within a short space of time I also acquired a superb black and white negative of almost the same view but taken in the mid 1950s. Nothing remains of these magnificent red sandstone buildings today, so this image serves to remind us what another architectural gem we have lost. Did the bicycle belong to the photographer? NPC

A fine overall of the station circa 1964, with a train from Hereford partially in view on the left. Vans such as the 'Fruit D' seen here, were regular additions to these services, carrying parcels and often perishable roduce. At the head of the train, which as well as the van comprises three carriages, is a Collett '22XX' 0-6-0. For the last two or three years of the station's existence, the bay window at this end of the main building was bricked up and the room presumably taken out of use. The station architecture, particularly the island platform waiting shelter, was distinctly Brunellian in style and was something of a broad gauge gem. The decorative stonework and the cast iron supports for the canopies, with their gargoyle-like outward facing ends, are all worthy of closer study. Note the Gents attached to the waiting shelter on the Hereford line side, whilst the weatherworn nameboards dated from the platform extensions in 1897. The ganger in the foreground is talking to a mate just glimpsed walking along the Up line a little way along. T.B. OWEN

An unidentified Class '9F' 2-10-0 labours through the station with a heavy train of laden coke wagons in January 1965. The line is on a curve at this point and also a slight gradient, so even a '9F' would be working quite hard at this point with a load like this. The problems for heavy Up freight trains could be compounded if they had to be looped to allow a faster Up main line passenger train to pass or if a Ross line service had priority. JOHN STRANGE/NPC

Having taken the view of the station on the previous page, photographer Trevor Owen lingered here to capture some of the varied passing trains. Here, a grimy Class '4' diesel in two-tone green livery with small yellow warning panel heads towards South Wales with a freight working (as indicated by the '7V' part of the reporting number), whilst No. 3812 rumbles through towards Gloucester with another train of coke hoppers. The decorative embellishments to the island platform waiting shelter can be studied in a little more detail and, at a time when many people did not have a telephone at home, there is another of the blue enamelled 'Telephone' notices on the end of the main building – a period piece in itself, this is not something we would ever think about today now that we all carry a phone with us. The orientation of the shelter suggests that Hereford line passengers were not considered in the original design, the door in the rear wall looking like a bit of an afterthought. T.B. OWEN

Today, 'Elf n Safety', British Transport Police, Gloucestershire Constabulary and just about anybody else with a sniff of authority would descend on you like the proverbial if you stood in this position taking photographs of passing trains but, in late autumn 1962, apart maybe for a shout from the odd officious engine driver or guard, few worried if you strayed the wrong side of the boundary to get your shot. And just as well too, for without this more relaxed attitude, a number of the photographs within these pages would not have been possible, with this one being another of my particular favourites. 'Modified Hall' No. 6993 Arthog Hall bursts out from beneath the bridge carrying the Grange Court Road – a grand sounding name for a narrow country lane – across the railway at the western end of the station, at the head of a goods train heading to South Wales. The locomotive is in far worse condition than when we last saw it, polished and gleaming in the bay at Gloucester, but it still had three years of service left. JOHN STRANGE/NPC

An unidentifed Collett 22XX 0-6-0 slows as it arrives at Grange Court with a three-coach train and van from Hereford; this is the same train as seen in the overall view of the station on page 91. The site of Grange Court West Box was between the Up main loop and the siding alongside Christie & Vesey's creosote and timber works. Originally established as the Albion Carriage Works, by the late 1920s the site housed a linoleum manufacturer and then, during the Second World War, it was used to build huts, bailey bridges and other war materials, under Christie & Vesey's ownership. After the war, the firm concentrated on the pressure creosoting of imported timber, operating here until the early 1970s. The yard had originally been rail connected from both sides, with a connection running back off the Up main loop as well. As can be seen, the company also had their own steam crane, which was also used to shunt wagons around internally. Today, the site is still in use, although no longer rail connected and, since 2000, has been under the ownership of Severn Valley Woodworks Ltd. T.B. OWEN

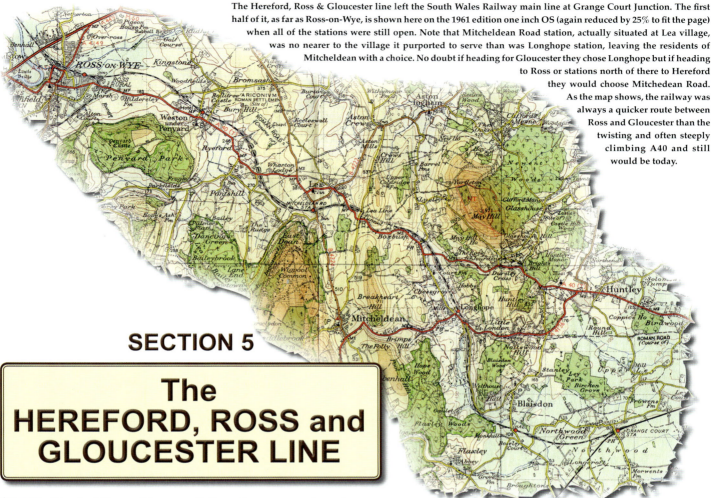

The Hereford, Ross & Gloucester line left the South Wales Railway main line at Grange Court Junction. The first half of it, as far as Ross-on-Wye, is shown here on the 1961 edition one inch OS (again reduced by 25% to fit the page) when all of the stations were still open. Note that Mitcheldean Road station, actually situated at Lea village, was no nearer to the village it purported to serve than was Longhope station, leaving the residents of Mitcheldean with a choice. No doubt if heading for Gloucester they chose Longhope but if heading to Ross or stations north of there to Hereford they would choose Mitchedean Road. As the map shows, the railway was always a quicker route between Ross and Gloucester than the twisting and often steeply climbing A40 and still would be today.

SECTION 5

The HEREFORD, ROSS and GLOUCESTER LINE

The Hereford, Ross & Gloucester Railway Company was formed in 1851, with the aim of building a line 22½ miles in length, running from Grange Court Junction to Barr's Court station in Hereford. At Grange Court, the broad gauge rails of the South Wales Railway made an end on junction with those of the Gloucester & Dean Forest Railway. At the other end of the line in Hereford, Barr's Court station was not yet open at this time; it was to be constructed by the Shrewsbury & Hereford Railway and opened to passenger traffic on 6th December 1853. In the meantime, the HR&GR began construction of their broad gauge line from the Gloucester end, with the section from Grange Court to a place called Hopesbrook opening to all traffic on 11th July 1853. Hopesbrook, or Hope Brook as it is today, is actually a part of Longhope and is a little way north of where Longhope station was sited when it opened in 1855. A temporary engine shed was built here and trains ran to and from Gloucester. This situation lasted for two years and it is presumed that the building of Lea Line Tunnel, a mile to the north, was the main reason for the hold up, although the railway company were also short of funds. The line was finally opened throughout on 2nd June 1855.

The broad gauge rails on the HR&GR line had a life of just fourteen years, conversion to standard gauge taking place in 1869. No photographs exist of the line in its broad gauge state, although an early engraving of Grange Court Junction looking west shows a broad gauge train arriving at the platforms from Hereford. Thereafter, it settled down to a largely uneventful existence as an important single line cross-country route, traversing some highly picturesque countryside – including several crossings of the River Wye, as it made its way from Gloucestershire to Herefordshire. The original stations were at Longhope, Mitcheldean Road, Ross-on-Wye, Fawley and Holme Lacy, whilst halts were later added at Blaisdon (1929), Weston-under-Penyard (1929), Backney (1933) and Ballingham (1908). Ross-on-Wye was the principal town served and had by far the largest of the intermediate stations, being also the junction for the branch to Monmouth. Traffic returns, both passenger and goods, were always greater on the eastern section of the line, the stations between Ross and Hereford generally serving much smaller and more scattered communities.

The Hereford, Ross & Gloucester line was without doubt a victim of Dr Beeching's desire to pare all duplicating secondary routes come what may. It followed a reasonably direct line between the cities of Gloucester and Hereford that, following the closure to passengers of the Ledbury Branch which had provided an alternative more circuitous route, could only otherwise be made by travelling via Worcester – a very long way round. The competing A40 road is still and will always be a poor substitute, as it winds its way up and down hill and through various villages, whilst 21st century traffic levels preclude any chance of making up time on the more level stretches. Many people now live in places like Blaisdon, Longhope and Mitcheldean but work in Gloucester, so the roads in to the city from the west are especially clogged during the rush hour. A 1970s/80s campaign led by a local man in Ross-on-Wye to reopen the line from there to Gloucester as a commuter route, along with the Wye Valley Branch to Monmouth and on to Chepstow for tourists, foundered at quite an advanced stage, when the prospects for European and other funding suddenly dried up, but also having encountered fierce oppostion from one or two local landowners who had reclaimed parts of the trackbed.

Most of the route is still easily traced today and there are important survivals at one or two stations but the chances of reopening any part of the line would now seem highly unlikely.

RIGHT: Trains on the route from Hereford could cross at numerous places, including here at Grange Court Junction, where single line working either started or finished depending on the direction of travel. No. 4161 draws its train away from the Up branch platform, having crossed a corresponding Down service in the station behind. The bare ballast in the foreground following the removal of the sidings indicate a summer 1964 date and probably on a Saturday given No. 4161's load of four coaches plus van. NPC

BELOW: The fireman on this Collett 0-6-0 heading to Hereford leans out to collect the single line token from the apparatus opposite the 60-lever signal box. The catcher can be seen on the other side of the line. These saved the signalman a walk along the platform at this busy box but to save even having to walk down the steps, they often used a pole with a hook, which they dangled out of the window to collect the token from the fireman. NPC

The service withdrawal notice in one of the waiting rooms at Grange Court. NPC

A circa 1964 close-up of the Up side branch platform waiting room at Grange Court, which was in the same style and construction as the rest of the station. It was also provided with a gents toilets, at the far end. NPC

More detail of the station buildings, showing the exposed nature of the island platform shelter, which although stylish offered little protection from the elements. In terms of passenger numbers, Grange Court was never a busy station and by the final decade this deserted scene would have been typical. It served the small village of Northwood Green just to the north-west of the line but took its name from the court and farm immediately to the south-east of the station. Apart from the sparsely populated local area, anyone travelling from stations on the Hereford line could also change trains here to head south and *vice versa* but this never amounted to any significant total either. The closure of the Hereford line was thus to sound its death knell, there being little reason to retain the station afterwards and, along with Oakle Street and Newnham, it was closed. Other intermediate stops between Gloucester and Lydney, at Westbury-on-Severn and Awre, had already gone, leaving this 22 mile section with no intermediate station, as it remains today. NPC

On 23rd October 1964, the Grange Court signalman leans out of his box holding a pole with a hook on the end to collect the single line token (a time saving trick at this busy box) for the section from Longhope from the fireman of 'Mogul' No. 7318. The locomotive has obviously had a priming problem from the state of it and note that the usual three-coach plus van formation has been strengthened by the addition of a fourth coach at the rear. A pannier tank with single mineral wagon and brake van heads the opposite way, possibly on a trip working to the timber works just beyond the bridge, or to Lydbrook Junction. The goods yard had by this date been taken out but there is a glimpse of the short goods bay on the far left. Incidentally, for anyone interested in learning more about the complexities of working this busy signal box, an interesting article entitled 'Train regulation – old style – at a Gloucestershire country junction', by J.C. Oxley, appeared in *Trains Annual* 1966. Colour Rail

Left: The list of signal boxes between Gloucester West and Hereford Barr's Court station, along with their opening hours, from the 1961 WTT. Beginning with the distances between boxes and their names, the first column then is the time the box opened on a Monday morning, the second column is for other days, the third column is closing times and columns four and five are opening and closing on Sundays.

'Large Prairie' No. 4107 pauses with a westbound train, again on the last day of services. Note that the nameboard on the Up Hereford line platform was better cared for than that on the island platform and this view also provides a closer study of the Gentlemens' convenience alongside the waiting shelter on the former. The locomotive, one of the '5101' Class of 2-6-2 tanks, was built in 1935 and withdrawn from Severn Tunnel Junction shed on 25th May 1965. John Strange/NPC

ABOVE: No. 6346 calls with a Hereford train in April 1964, in a view which also shows the rear of the island platform waiting shelter. Note the platform paving slabs only extended around the buildings; elsewhere, the surface was cinder and gravel. JOHN STRANGE/NPC

BELOW: More unusual motive power on this occasion, as BR Standard Class '4' tank No. 80100 (minus smokebox numberplate) makes a brief stop for passengers in August 1964. It may have been pressed into service by Gloucester shed, having arrived on a London Midland Region working, due to a shortage of engines. The electric flashes on the tank sides indicate the engine had also worked 'under the wires' and it was withdrawn from Shrewsbury (84G) shed on 24th July 1965. HUGH BALLANTYNE

A short while after the bottom picture on page 98 was taken, No. 4107 is seen heading off to its next stop at Blaisdon Halt, less than a mile away. A number of the enthusiasts on this final day working have their heads out of the carriage windows and consider the highly dangerous position adopted by our intrepid photographer, in between the Up loop and the Up main lines! No. 4107 and its coaches worked at least two return trips to Hereford on this day. JOHN STRANGE/NPC

No. 4107, a regular on the line in its final years, departs Grange Court on 3rd October 1964 with a Hereford train. Note the permanent way hut built against the centre pier of the bridge. M. SMITH/COLOUR-RAIL

No. 6346, heads away from the station to begin its journey across country to Hereford in April 1964. Engines in this uncared for state must have proved hard work for footplate crews, particularly on routes like this one to Hereford, with its numerous tunnels and gradients between here and Rotherwas Junction. JOHN STRANGE/NPC

A few seconds later, the train leans into the curve away from the station, the angle of the shot managing to convey an entirely unjustified impression of speed. Over the roofs of the carriages, the main line curves southwards towards Lydney, Chepstow and Severn Tunnel Junction, and the extent of the Up main loop can also be seen. In about 400 yards, the train will pass over a minor road at Church Lane crossing. JOHN STRANGE/NPC

Another of Roy Denison's superb station studies, showing the full layout at Blaisdon on 12th August 1962, over a year before the goods yard was removed, although the rust on the rails would suggest that it had not seen any traffic for some months at least prior to this view. Pre-dating the establishment of the halt, Blaisdon Siding was opened for goods traffic on 12th November 1906 and, as seen here, comprised a loop with two short stubs at either end, one of which ran alongside the dock holding the livestock pen in the left foreground. The siding was officially taken out of use on 11th October 1963 and removed the following month. Traffic to and from it would had been largely agricultural in nature, no doubt including consignments of Blaisdon plums when in season, plus consignments of house coal coming inwards. ROY DENISON

By now, readers will have got used to the idea that No. 7318 is not going to appear in these pages in anything other than filthy condition. Here, on 26th September 1964, the 'Mogul' pauses to drop off passengers at the first stop along from Grange Court, the tiny halt at Blaisdon. The three-coach train forms the 2.25pm Saturdays only working from Gloucester, so no doubt those having just got off are returning from a morning's shopping in the city. Opened by the GWR on 4th November 1929, the halt was a typically simple affair, consisting of a wooden fronted, cinder topped platform with a corrugated iron hut. Note that the attractive little brick-built weighbridge hut, here seen decorated by climbing roses, had been left in place despite the removal of the rest of the goods yard, including the fence around the livestock fence. In the right distance, the line skirts the edge of Winyard Wood, on the left, then crosses Northwood Green Lane before curving round to the junction. HUGH BALLANTYNE

Looking in the opposite direction, between them, this pair of photographs neatly document Blaisdon Halt in its final year. Another unkempt Churchward 'Mogul', Gloucester-based No. 6349, is seen arriving with a train from Hereford in summer 1964. Passenger access to the halt was either via the approach road coming in on the right, which also provided access to the goods yard, and then over the line by the boarded crossing at the end of the platform, or via steps leading down from the road just to the left of the bridge, which was a more direct route to the platform that did not involve crossing the line. The man running on to the platform is a photographer, who had used this route down from the top of the bridge. Note that, despite the time of day and the sunshine, the lamp above the hut is lit. Today, the bridge remains as a reminder of the halt's existence. ALAN JARVIS

Photographer John Ryan had just alighted from the departing Gloucester-bound train on Saturday 15th August 1964, so he could photograph Blaisdon Halt. The service comprised eleven trains each way on a Saturday, so his wait for the next Down train was probably around an hour. JOHN RYAN

Looking the opposite way from the embankment leading up to the road overbridge almost exactly a year earlier, No. 6365 drifts towards the halt with an Up train on 10th August 1963. Up on the hillside on the right is Blaisdon Hall, built in 1876 by South Wales and Forest of Dean iron master William Crawshay for his son Edwin. In 1935 it was bought by the Silesian Society and used as an agricultural school for training underpriviliged boys. It is now an upmarket wedding venue. NPC

In common with '5101' classmate No. 4161, which we have also already encountered more than once, No. 4157 was latterly another regular on the line between Gloucester and Hereford. The picture is undated but the locomotive had been transferred to Hereford from Pontypool Road in June 1964, so it must have been taken in the summer of that year. The location was also not given but I am fairly certain that is on the line just to the west of Blaisdon Halt, as it approaches Blaisdon Woods (with No. 4157 thus bound for Hereford). The road overbridge just visible in the background and the pole route being to the left (or north) of the line at this point pretty much confirm this, as, there is no other location where these two factors can be matched – Ballingham was wrong, for instance, as the pole route would have been on the other side of the line – although the distant higher ground of the Cotswold escarpment between Gloucester and Stroud, on the far side of the River Severn, seems a tad more prominent than I would have expected. CHRIS WALKER

LEFT: From the same viewpoint, this is looking the opposite way, back towards Blaisdon. Some of the scattered houses of Blaisdon village can be seen in the left background and in the days when different varieties of fruit abounded, the area became renowned for its own plum; Blaisdon Red plums, first grown here in the late 19th century are a red variety perfect for making jam. They are only grown within a 25 mile radius of the village. The bank on which the photographer was standing is heavily wooded today and it took some time and a certain amount of fieldwork to pin down the location. JOHN STRANGE/NPC

RIGHT: Looking north a few moments later, the lane in the background provided the clue to solving the location of these views. Velthouse Lane is here on its way round the hillside, dropping down from Blaisdon and now about to join with the railway and follow it all the way to Longhope. Gloucester had rostered a 'Hall' Class 4-6-0 for this turn, the identity of which was sadly unrecorded by John Strange; 'Hall's were not regular performers on the route. When visited in 2012, the lane at this point and the field corner were remarkably unchanged from this view. JOHN STRANGE/NPC

LEFT: Without the benefit of studying the previous three slides, I would never have pinned down the location of this one. No. 7815 *Fritwell Manor* rounds the curve through Blaisdon Woods with a service for Gloucester. On this warm autumn day and on a downward gradient, there is barely a wisp of steam from the 4-6-0 as it coasts towards its next stop at Blaisdon Halt, just half a mile away. It is sad to see one of this handsome class in such a poor external state but cleaning duties generally seem to have been almost totally neglected on the Western Region in the last couple of years of steam. JOHN STRANGE/NPC

RIGHT: BR 'Standard' Class '4' 4-6-0 No. 73097 on the rising gradient between Blaisdon and Longhope, with the 7.50am Swindon to Hereford service on 1st October 1964. The BR 'Standard' types only appeared on the line in the three or four years of its existence and then only intermittently, with ex-GWR engines generally holding sway. This view is slightly out of chronological order with the full page picture opposite, which was taken a short distance back down the line to the left. JOHN DAGLEY-MORRIS

After leaving Blaisdon Halt the line began a gentle climb all the way to Longhope, first heading west but then executing a long sweeping curve to the north as it skirted the lower edge of Blaisdon Wood. Photographer John Strange had positioned himself a little way up the slope on the southern side of the line, to capture this highly picturesque view of an unidentified 'Large Prairie' tank coasting downhill round the curve on its journey from Hereford to Gloucester, in the early autumn of 1964. Velthouse Lane, which also edged its way round Blaisdon Wood on its way from Longhope to Blaisdon, is just out of sight up on the right. Apart from the railway, there is no other sign of human habitation in this beautifully rural scene and the photographer's position was no doubt a surprise to the driver as he glanced out of the cab. JOHN STRANGE/NPC

RIGHT: With Hope Wood covering the steep escarpment in the right background, Collett 0-6-0 No. 2242 makes its way towards Longhope with a Hereford train on 15th August 1964. A Gloucester-based engine, built in April 1945, No. 2242 had twenty years of service, her career coming to an end on 21st May 1965. The cows, no doubt long used to the passing of steam locomotives, ignore the train. BILL POTTER/KRM

BELOW: Looking in the opposite direction from the same spot, 'Mogul' No. 7307 hurries a Gloucester-bound train, comprising three carriages and three vans, away from Longhope in April 1964. This picturesque study beautifully illustrates what we lost with the passing of the steam era; not just a railway but a way and pace of life, so different from today. JOHN STRANGE/NPC

RIGHT: A few moments after taking the picture on the previous page, the photographer turned to capture this lovely panned shot of No. 7307 coasting past, heading down the gradient from Longhope to its next stop at Blaisdon. The missing numberplate provides the clue that the 'Mogul' is near the end of its working life. Built at Swindon in November 1921, it was to be withdrawn from Gloucester shed on 1st June 1964. What a glorious run this must have been for a footplate crew on a warm spring day like this. As well as providing access to vantage points west of Blaisdon, Velthouse Lane also ran parallel to the line for much of its way to Longhope, providing vistas such as those presented on these two pages. The trackbed here is now heavily overgrown with trees for the most part (and has also been built on in several places), such that views across the valley like this are no longer possible. JOHN STRANGE/NPC

LEFT: A little while later, a dirty unidentified Class '22XX' passes the same way with a short goods train, probably from the cable works at Lydbrook Junction, off the Ross and Monmouth line, although some goods traffic was still being worked to and from Ross at this date. All the other stations between Hereford and Gloucester had been closed for goods in 1963. JOHN STRANGE/NPC

BELOW: A similar working on 1st October 1964, with No. 2287 heading an even shorter train to Gloucester. This may well be the same locomotive as in the previous shot. JOHN DAGLEY-MORRIS

This slide also came with no details on the mount and although clearly in the vicinity of Longhope, the growth of trees and bushes along the route in the years since these pictures were taken and the line was closed has again made pinning down the exact location difficult, whilst the white painted bungalow in the left background has defied attempts at finding it. However, I am fairly certain that this is a Down train heading for Hereford in 1964 and we are looking east across the valley, with Velthouse Lane running along somewhere behind the train or even behind the bungalow. The locomotive is a '41XX' Series 'Large Prairie' and the train is a typical three coach working, with a Hawksworth Brake Composite next to the engine. NPC

OPPOSITE PAGE TOP: The first of two views taken from alongside the bridge carrying the A4136 road from Huntley to Mitcheldean over the line at Longhope. On 16th June 1962, '5101' Class 2-6-2T No. 4116 is on the final approach to the station and passing some vegetable plots which were presumably the preserve of railway staff. I had not seen a picture showing these plots before, which look to have been more extensive in past times but were now clearly falling out of use and indeed, look completely overgrown by the date of the second photograph, just over two years later. MARK B. WARBURTON

Seen from the valley side a little way below the line, No. 4135 is having to work as it climbs towards Longhope with a four-coach train for Hereford (85C), its home base, on 16th June 1962. The engine was withdrawn from 85C on 8th June 1964. MARK B. WARBURTON

No. 7318 again, making a brisk getaway down the gradient from Longhope with the 2.38pm Hereford to Gloucester service on 30th July 1964. The signal in the background is the Down Distant for Longhope station. BILL POTTER/KRM

Ex-GWR 'Manor' Class 4-6-0 No. 7814 *Fringford Manor* approaches Longhope with the 2.47pm Gloucester Central to Hereford train on 15th August 1964. The overbridge was demolished after closure and the road realigned and it is quite difficult now to distinguish the course of the line at this point. Velthouse Lane runs just behind the buildings in the left background. No. 7814 was another Gloucester engine, withdrawn on 10th September 1965. BILL POTTER/KRM

Looking from the A4136 road bridge in the opposite direction opened up this vista of the approach to Longhope station, with its protecting semaphore signals. Nearest is the Home signal, positioned 'wrong side' and set lower down the post so it was visible to footplatemen through the bridge. Beyond it, the Starter is 'off' for the departing train, which here comprises three carriages, three vans and then another coach, probably a parcels GUV, at the rear, hauled by No. 7318 again. In the centre distance can just be seen the Up Home signal, which is also still 'off'. On the left, an elderly gentleman watches the train's departure over the hedge bordering Old Monmouth Road. The date is 22nd August 1964, the sun beats down and all is well in this sylvan part of rural west Gloucestershire. Over the next few pages, we shall now proceed to spend a little time at this delightful country station, of which almost nothing now remains, simply watching the trains and soaking up the atmosphere. ALAN JARVIS

LEFT: Bill Potter's visit of 15th August 1964 to Longhope produced this startling shot of BR 'Britannia' class 4-6-2 No. 70052 *Firth of Tay* departing the station with a pigeon special, which was classed as a parcels/empty stock train (3T13). No. 70052 was a Scottish Region engine, so was well off its patch here. It was eventually withdrawn from Carlisle Kingmoor shed, on 1st April 1967. Along with the 'Brit', a '9F' is known to have travelled the line and the occasional diesel put in an appearance, including at least one 'Hymek' and a 'Warship'. BILL POTTER/KRM

BELOW: From the same vantage point and on the same day, ex-GWR '61XX' Class 'Large Prairie' No. 6128 provided more usual motive power for this Hereford to Gloucester service as it worked back to its home base. The engine was withdrawn from Gloucester shed on 26th March 1965. BILL POTTER/KRM

RIGHT: '5101' Class No. 4107 leaves Longhope for Gloucester with a train from Hereford in 1964. The '5101's were Collett's modification of Churchward's successful '51XX' Class 'Large Prairie' tanks. Although a little grainy due to the lack of light down at track level at this location, the view does provide a glimpse of the stone-built A4136 road bridge in the background, which was demolished, it is believed, in the late 1970s. Note the token catching apparatus in the foreground. JOHN STRANGE/NPC

Steam shrouds 4-6-0 No. 7801 *Anthony Manor* as the Starting signal gives the 'off' and the driver opens the regulator on a misty autumnal day. Taken on 30th October 1964, one of the local population leans over the fence on the right, by the path leading up to the road from the station, to take in a scene that would be no more within a few days. T.B. OWEN

The '61XX' Class were another Collett enlargement of the '51XX's, designed for London suburban services but they eventually found their way out across much of the GWR system. No. 6137, which ended its career at Stourbridge Junction during the week ending 21st November 1964, waits at Longhope in August 1962. DEREK CHAPLIN

Another '5101' Class 'Large Prairie', No. 4135 draws in to the Up platform with a Gloucester-bound train on 16th June 1962. The leading vehicle, a parcels GUV, is clearly identified in the picture below. MARK B. WARBURTON

Having been given the 'off', No. 4135, beautifully turned out in British Railways smart lined green passenger livery, starts away towards Gloucester. MARK B. WARBURTON

Although the main building at Longhope could justifiably be described as unprepossessing at best, the station nevertheless managed to maintain an air of attractive charm which certainly drew in the photographers. There is little to enable us to guess at a date here and the 'Mogul' is not unidentifiable but some time during the last months of operation in 1964 would again seem a fair bet. A solitary passenger almost hidden behind the porter on the right would appear to be the only custom for the Gloucester-bound train on this occasion, along with perhaps the photographer. The bicycle propped against the seat on the Down platform probably belonged to the signalman – one of Trevor Owen's views shows a moped parked at the same spot. NPC

LEFT: A closer view of the stone-built waiting shelter on the Up side, which, like that at Grange Court, had a gents toilets attached at the nearer end; in the Victorian age, ladies were often not provided for in the same way! The station site is now a private garden and this building survives converted for use as a summer house. NPC

BELOW: Collett Class '22XX' 0-6-0 No. 3242 can just be seen in the background, drawing in with the 12.38pm train to Hereford, as the Longhope signalman ambles along the platform with the single line token for the section to Mitcheldean Road. The exchange could have been effected in front of the box but he then would not have had the chance to pass the time of day briefly with the footplate crew, before the train went on its way again. JOHN RYAN

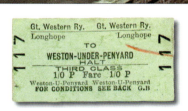

BELOW: Longhope was photographed on the same day as Oakle Street and Blaisdon by Roy Denison, 3rd November 1962, the bright sunshine seemingly coming in between bouts of showery rain. The intention was clearly to record the stations themselves, with no interference from passing trains, and the viewpoint and the lighting clearly helped to show off Longhope's idyllic location to its very best. ROY DENISON

Longhope station on 30th October 1964, the final day of services, looking north from the opposing platforms. After climbing most of the way from Grange Court, the line levelled out through the station, before commencing a further gradual climb from here to Lea Line Tunnel. For the signalmen at this two-shift box, there were numerous periods of quiet like this. The loop was a provision from opening of the line but the Up side platform and shelter were only added in 1897. In the top picture, the 5-ton goods crane can just be seen beyond the level crossing in the background but the track in the yard had been lifted. BOTH T.B. OWEN

On 30th July 1964, No. 7815 *Fritwell Manor* calls with the 2.25pm from Gloucester, which is made up of the usual three-coaches. No. 7815 spent most of its life based at Gloucester and withdrawal was just three months away, on 23rd October. The station building and Down side platform dated from the opening of the line throughout on 1st June 1855. The goods lock-up on the right, with its twin elliptical roofs, was constructed of corrugated iron sheet and was another later addition. It was used mostly for parcels and small goods, and was worked from the station platform, no siding ever being laid alongside it. This low viewpoint shows the down gradient which began just at the far end of the platforms. BILL POTTER/KRM

A couple of minutes later, *Fritwell Manor* pulls away from the platform as it begins the 2.75 mile journey to its next stop at Mitcheldean Road. Since closure of the line, a large house has been built across this end of the station site. Considering some of the work the 'Manor' Class undertook on routes such as the Cambrian main line, with its steep gradients and much higher loadings, the run between Gloucester and Hereford must have been something of a breeze. BILL POTTER, KRM

Hereford-based Collett 0-6-0 No. 2241 straddles Station Lane level crossing whilst shunting its train at Longhope in August 1962. This Hereford-based engine was withdrawn on 14th February 1964. DEREK CHAPLIN

Photographer Derek Chaplin took three views of No. 2241 shunting at Longhope and there are no apologies for reproducing a second one – because what a delightful scene it shows. With a service of only eight passenger trains a day, each way, there was plenty of time for the pick-up goods to attach and detach wagons at the various stations *en route*, which was just as well because it invariably involved blocking the running line. The point beneath the engine's tender was a single slip, giving entry to the passing loop and the yard. The short loading platform beyond the two open wagons rather oddly curves away from the siding and the hut is likely to have housed a weighing machine. Beyond it, the end of the second siding here can just be seen, with a couple of vans parked close to the buffer stops. Station Lane, passing over the crossing, fortunately led only to a couple of farms, so was not busy. Remarkably, one of the crossing gates still survives here today. DEREK CHAPLIN

LEFT: Longhope Signal Box, a standard GWR design in red and blue brick, with a hipped slate roof, dated from 1st November 1897, when a new layout at the station was brought into use. NPC

ABOVE: Bill Potter's visit of 30th July 1964 resulted in views of a couple more trains. Here, No. 4161, a regular performer on the line in its last months, calls with the 12.15pm Gloucester Central to Hereford train. BILL POTTER/KRM

INSET TOP RIGHT: The point to point time allowances for Up and Down freight trains on the Hereford, Ross & Gloucester line, from the 1961 WTT.

RIGHT: Ex-GWR '51XX' Class 2-6-2T No. 4157 with the 1.40pm from Hereford to Gloucester Central at Longhope on the same day, with a parcels/GUV in addition to the three carriages. Although the station was a crossing place, it only happened once a day, when the 7.33am Down train crossed with the 7.41am Up (see the time table extracts on pages 152-53), hence the dearth of pictures showing this happening. The Down train proceeded on its way at 7.43, after a 10 minute wait. BILL POTTER/KRM

LEFT: The 85B shed plate can be clearly seen on the smokebox door of No. 6330 as it makes its brief stop at the station in the crisp spring sunshine of April 1960. The fireman leans nonchalantly on the cab side as he awaits the guard's signal for the 'off'. The whitewash on the platform edges looks to have been reapplied fairly recently. No. 6330 spent its final years at Gloucester, being withdrawn from there on 7th September 1962, although Cashmores of Newport did not cut it up for another two years. ALAN JARVIS

ABOVE: Another of the '5101' Class 2-6-2Ts, No. 4171, ambles away past the small goods yard with a train for Hereford on 2nd October 1964. The end was nigh for line and locomotive, with both having succumbed by the end of the month, No. 4171 having migrated to Leamington shed, from where it was withdrawn during the week ending 24th October. The yard had closed by this date, the sidings having been lifted in the July, a row of chairs in the foreground marking the line of the loop siding running beneath the loading gauge. This shot also provides a good view of the permanent way sheds on the left, which housed the trolleys used by the local platelaying gang for inspecting their stretch of line. ALAN JARVIS

RIGHT: BR Standard Class '2' 2-6-0 No. 78006 makes a photographic stop at Longhope with the last goods from Kerne Bridge on 29th October 1965, which was also the final train between Ross-on-Wye and Grange Court Junction. DAVID BICK/NPC

RIGHT: One of the services from Hereford which ran through Gloucester rather than terminating there was the 4.30pm to Cheltenham St. James, seen here on 9th August 1963 with 0-6-0 No. 3205 in charge. The signalman is strolling back to the box, having just exchanged the single line token with the footplate crew. The smoke just visible in the far distance is unlikely to have been from a Down train as I originally thought, as the Up Home signal is still showing clear for the train at the platform; it is probably therefore smoke from a bonfire. The attractively proportioned Collett '22XX' Class engines were a direct replacement for the ageing 'Dean Goods' 0-6-0s and were built between 1930 and 1948. They were popular with footplatemen, being relatively fast and versatile, and it is perhaps a surprise that only one example survived into preservation. Coincidentally, it was No. 3205, which first found its way to the Severn Valley Railway after withdrawal in 1965, hauling the inaugural train on that line in 1970, but can now be found on the South Devon Railway at Buckfastleigh. JOHN DAGLEY-MORRIS

LEFT: No. 4123 was another member of the '5101' Class of 'Large Prairie' tanks, of which 140 were built, the last few emanating from Swindon Works in 1949, under British Railways. With its copper capped chimney not completely obscured by soot, this Gloucester-based engine waits patiently for the right away from Longhope on 1st August 1959, its train including a 'Fruit D' van at the front. New into stock at the end of January 1938, No. 4123's career was a relatively short one. It left Gloucester Horton Road on 17th November 1961, after a working life of just twenty-three years, and was cut up at Swindon in June the following year. T.B. OWEN

RIGHT: Although trains only infrequently crossed here, Gloucester-bound trains always used the Up platform. This meant passengers had to cross the tracks by means of the boarded foot crossings at each end of the station, as a footbridge was never provided. In the last month of passenger services on the route, an unidentified 'Large Prairie' 2-6-2T arrives with a Gloucester train. The third carriage straddles the slip point giving access to the loop but it can be seen that the connection into the goods yard has been lifted. In the distance, the line is dead straight for around half a mile until it crosses the A40 road and starts to curve round to Lea Line Tunnel and Mitcheldean Road. JOHN STRANGE NPC

LEFT: The goods workings on the line were much less frequently photographed. However, on his visit of 3rd November 1962 Roy Denison captured Collett No. 2242 as it made its way through with a Hereford to Gloucester pick-up goods. A branch regular, we have seen it several times already and it features at most of the locations we shall visit on our way to Hereford.
ROY DENISON

RIGHT: A view of the station from the second carriage behind 'Large Prairie" No. 4115 as it threads a service to Gloucester over the level crossing and into the Up platform on 7th June 1962. NPC

BELOW: A circa 1962 view of No. 6304 arriving over the level crossing with a train for Gloucester, past a line of vans in the double-ended goods siding. Unlike regulars such as No. 2242 above, this is the only time within these pages that we shall encounter Gloucester Horton Road-based No. 6304, which was to spend its last five years in service working from 85B, up to its withdrawal in January 1964. New in December 1920, the outside steam pipes were fitted by BR at Swindon in January 1952. NPC

Above: Few photographers seem to have ventured to the eastern end of Lea Line Tunnel, although it was only a couple of hundred yards away from the A40 road but, fortunately, John Dagley-Morris and his late brother Richard did. Here, on 1st October 1964, John photographed No. 7318 as it burst back out in to warm autumn sunshine, heading down gradient to Longhope with the 10.25am Hereford to Gloucester service. Note the mile post on the right, showing 126¾ miles from Paddington. Both portals of the tunnel are accessible today, albeit with a little difficulty, this end being still completely open. JOHN DAGLEY-MORRIS

RIGHT: A view from just above the western portal of Lea Line Tunnel, taken in August 1963 and looking towards Ross, as Class '43XX' No. 7335 drifts towards it with a train for Gloucester. This was the highest point of the line and from here there was a falling gradient of 1 in 144 through the 771 yards bore of the tunnel, which is completely straight. It had no ventilation shafts but was provided with refuges inside for the benefit of permanent way men. A PW hut can be seen level with the rear of the train and there was another structure to the left of the locomotive, almost hidden by the bushes but better seen in the view below, which presumably was also for use by track workers. No. 7335 had begun life in 1932 as No. 9313, the twenty engines of the '93XX' series forming a sub-class of these popular 'Moguls'. However, in the later 1950s, all were given modifications which altered them to '73XX' series and they were renumbered onwards from 7322 to 7341 as a result. No. 7335 was withdrawn from Gloucester during the week ending 7th September 1963 and cut up at Sharpness the following year. Incidentally, Alan Keef's renowned narrow gauge railway engineering works can today be found in premises just beyond the trees on the left. DAVID BICK/NPC

Ubiquitous No. 2242 strolls away from the smokey confines of Lea Line Tunnel with the 12.25pm from Gloucester to Hereford on 9th May 1964. The footplate crew were clearly aware of the photographer, the fireman also taking the chance for a breather on the coast downhill towards the next stop at Mitcheldean Road, half a mile away. NPC

The HEREFORD, ROSS and GLOUCESTER LINE

ABOVE: 'Mogul' No. 6330 with a six-coach train between Lea Line Tunnel and the A40 road bridge on 23rd June 1962. The single lamp mounted at the top of the smokebox indicates that this is an ordinary stopping passenger train, so the reason for the heavy loading is not known. The appearance of chocolate & cream stock on Gloucester-Hereford train services was also not common by this date, as the pictures in this section indicate. In the foreground is the Mitcheldean Road Distant signal, which was permanently fixed at caution. MARK B. WARBURTON

LEFT: A rare view from the top of the hill, from a poor colour print but worth including as a 'snapshot'. An unidentified 'Mogul' heads towards the tunnel and Lea village can be seen in the background. IAN POPE COLLECTION

Another unidentified 2-6-2T steams hard towards the confined bore of the tunnel on 10th March 1959, the driver no doubt intending to shut off steam and coast through once he has passed the entrance. This end is npw bricked up, apart from a small gap at the top to allow bats inside to roost. B.J. ASHWORTH

Having passed through the tunnel and then under the A40, No. 4107 is seen on the down gradient to Mitcheldean Road station with the 4.00pm service from Gloucester on 17th October 1964. The road bridge is just out of sight, obscured by the hedge on the right. The bridge was demolished some years ago and the trackbed here has been landscaped. JOHN DAGLEY-MORRIS

A change from the usual ex-GWR motive power is provided by BR 'Standard' Class '5' 4-6-0 No. 73031 of Gloucester Horton Road shed, which is seen arriving at Mitcheldean Road station on 30th October 1964 with a four-coach train for Hereford. Note that the platform edges had been cut back to those short sections of the platform which were still in use. Although closure was imminent, the rest of the station was still well maintained, with a full compliment of fire buckets and a colourful selection of posters on display. As the station's name indicates, it was some distance from the Forest of Dean village of Mitcheldean it purported to serve, being situated in the Herefordshire village of Lea. Indeed, it was a moot point as to which station was nearer for the inhabitants of Mitcheldean – Mitcheldean Road or Longhope. The station opened with the line in 1855 but the building seen here, to a standard GWR design, was a later addition, dating from the opening of a new layout including a second platform in 1898. No. 73031 was built at British Railway's Derby Works in July 1953 and was withdrawn from Oxford shed in August 1965, after just twelve year's service, surely a poor return for such a fine design of engine. T.B. OWEN

In another of Derek Chaplin's delicious views from August 1962, '5101' Class 2-6-2T No. 4135 is seen framed by a flowering rhododendron bush and abundant green leaves as it draws in to Mitcheldean Road station with a Hereford-bound train. The edging on the Up platform extended right to the end, where the ramp ran down to the boarded foot crossing but that on the Down side had been removed; would today's Health & Safety executive permit this arrangement? Almost certainly not and probably quite rightly so, because of the chances of slipping down on to the track, but back then, personal responsibility was much more the way things were. This is our third encounter with No. 4135, which was to be withdrawn from Hereford shed on 8th June 1964. The locomotive is crossing the bridge over the B4224 road leading to Mitcheldean. DEREK CHAPLIN

BELOW: The first of a pair of summer 1964 views, showing Collett 0-6-0 No. 2287 setting off from Mitcheldean Road having slowed to exchange the single line staff with the signalman, walking back to his box on the left. Note the new BR vans at the front of the train, which is likely to be the Lydbrook goods, serving the cable works at Lydbrook Junction on the Ross-Monmouth Branch. In filthy condition, No. 2287 is sporting a Severn Tunnel Junction 86E shedplate on its smokebox door but had been transferred to Gloucester Horton Road 85B by the time of its withdrawal in May 1965. NPC

LEFT: Looking east through the station, as No. 2287 heads away towards Gloucester. NPC

LEFT: Winter sunlight brightens this view to The Lea from beneath the canopy of the main building on 7th March 1964 To save passengers using the Up side from having to walk any further than necessary, a carriage length of edging stones were left in place at the east end, so all anyone had to do was cross the line and climb the ramp but such practice all looks very unsafe now. TIM STEPHENS

ABOVE: Taken on the same day, the light dusting of snow would undoubtedly have made conditions on the platforms even more treacherous, albeit whilst serving to enhance this Christmas card-like panorama of the station for a 21st century audience. The leaden sky above The Lea carries a promise of more snow to come. TIM STEPHENS

RIGHT: A sprinkling of passengers gather on the short section of the Up platform that still retained its edging stones, ready to board the 11.03am from Hereford to Gloucester, hauled by No. 6128, on 15th August 1964. The crew had already exchanged the staff with the signalman, who can be seen heading back to his box in the left background. JOHN RYAN

I love views with human interest and this shot of Mitcheldean Road station, with ex-GWR 'Mogul' No. 6364 disappearing off towards Weston-under-Penyard with the 9.48am train from Gloucester to Hereford is particularly delightful. Grandad may have just got off the train to be met by the children or he may have brought them here to watch a few trains passing through as closure – and the end of an era – loomed. Meanwhile, the station master and signalman have a chat before the latter heads back in to his box. No photograph of the original Mitcheldean Road station building has ever been seen but it is likely that it was in the same style as those that survived until the end at Longhope and Holme Lacy; the signal box dated from the addition of the Up platform in 1898. This view shows well the paraphernalia that went to make up a steam age railway station scene – the various signs and posters, including an enamelled GWR notice, the loaded parcels trolley and the token apparatus. The floral display on the Down platform was also a sight to behold. JOHN RYAN

ABOVE: Whilst motive power on the line was very varied, particularly on the 7.50am Swindon to Hereford service, which Richard Dagley-Morris tells me often had a Shrewsbury engine on the front, this slide is without doubt the most remarkable discovery to date – I never expected to find that a 'Jubilee' had featured on the line and it has rather surprised everyone else I've spoken to! From October 1961 to its withdrawal in November 1964, No. 45699 *Galatea* was a Shrewsbury based engine, so it was clearly conforming to the rule above but the very fact that the crew are posing for the sadly unknown photographer indicates that all concerned were very aware of the unusual nature of this particular working. No. 45699 is happily still with us, having been rescued from Barry scrapyard in 1980 and is now based at Carnforth. NPC

RIGHT: Gloucester Horton Road's ex-GWR 'Mogul' No. 6349 was clearly sporting a home-made smokebox door numberplate and other depot staff 'embellishments' to its front end steelwork when it was photographed heading light engine past the signal box in the summer of 1964. Transferred from Llanelly in September 1963, it was to be withdrawn in early August 1964. CHRIS WALKER

BELOW: A closer study of the Up side waiting shelter from a Down train. NPC

Taken on 30th October 1964, this view is part of Trevor Owen's attempt to document the stations on this half of the line at closure. In the steam age and, latterly, against all the odds, staff mostly did their utmost to look after their own personal bit of the system, as the neatly trimmed hedges and general air of tidiness here demonstrates. Standard 'GWR evergreens' line the station approach road behind the hedge on the left, whilst the goods yard was also on this side but behind and to the left of the station building. Note the Wickham permanent way trolley at right angles to the Down line just beyond the end of the platform. The scattered and sparse population served by the station ensured that passenger ticket sales were never substantial but the goods yard provided reasonable quantities of traffic for most of its existence, mainly agricultural produce in later years. Previously, like Longhope, timber traffic had also been important. T.B. OWEN

Although the camera did not manage to 'freeze' the front end of No. 7318 in this October 1964 view, it does provide us with a glimpse of the Up side waiting shelter, with the outside Gentlemen's convenience at the western end, facilities which dated from the station's 1898 rebuilding. Note that the fireman is in position to make the token exchange with the signalman. JOHN STRANGE/NPC

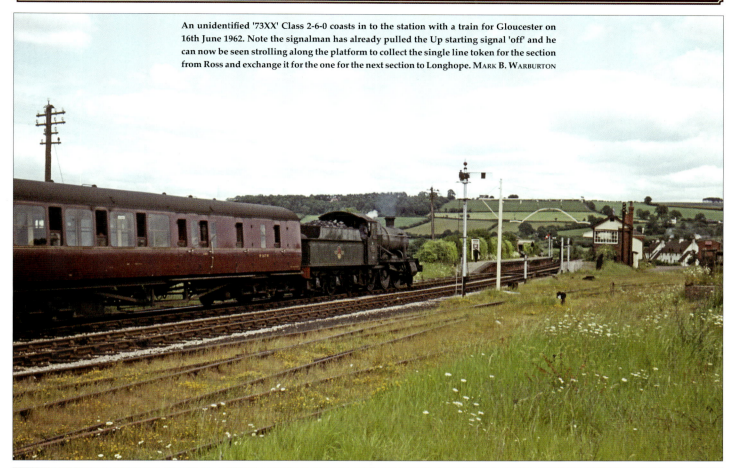

An unidentified '73XX' Class 2-6-0 coasts in to the station with a train for Gloucester on 16th June 1962. Note the signalman has already pulled the Up starting signal 'off' and he can now be seen strolling along the platform to collect the single line token for the section from Ross and exchange it for the one for the next section to Longhope. MARK B. WARBURTON

A couple of minutes later and the train can be seen heading away, whilst the signalman ambles back to his box. MARK B. WARBURTON

No. 4135 starts its train away from the station, heading for the next stop at Weston-under-Penyard. On the right is the goods yard which, like Longhope, never had a goods shed. Although the sidings are well overgrown with grass, there are still a number of wagons in the yard, although the livestock pen looks not to have seen any use for a while. Only a small yard crane was provided here, of $1^1/_2$ tons capacity and just visible to the right of the van. DEREK CHAPLIN

No. 6330 ambles away from Mitcheldean Road on 23rd June 1962; this is the train also shown on page 130 and Bill Potter photographed it here too, which suggests there was something unusual about it. The station was the destination of the Mitcheldean Road & Forest of Dean Junction Railway, a company incorporated by an Act of 1871 to build a line just over $4^1/_2$ miles long from Whimsey, near Cinderford, to Mitcheldean Road. After numerous difficulties, the project was taken over by the GWR and the line was completed, the first section – around a mile – opening in 1885. In 1907, the GWR opened a further section to Drybrook but the line through Euroclydon Tunnel to Mitcheldean Road, some 2 miles of fully laid and maintained railway, was never opened and the rails were finally taken up in 1917. The MR&FDJR did not make a direct junction with the main line but ran into the yard here; its route was just to the right of the grass bank in the foreground and then in front of the livestock pen (which was provided in 1898). Most of the trackbed can still easily be traced today. JOHN STRANGE/NPC

The debris in the right foreground gives a clue that we are near the end here, as the fireman of No. 7318 waits to receive the single line token for the section to Ross from the Mitcheldean Road signalman in October 1964. The weeds have gone from the Up loop though! JOHN STRANGE/NPC

With the token safely exchanged, No. 7318 blows off steam and slowly pulls away from the platform. The track in the goods yard was lifted sometime in 1963 – exactly when is not clear – but a pile of coal still remained, whilst recovered sleepers and rolls of signal wire await collection in the foreground. JOHN STRANGE/NPC

RIGHT: A final shot of No. 7318 departing the station, which also shows the end of the loop and the onward continuation of the line here to the west. The headshunt seen in previous views had split where the loop ended into two sidings, to which there was also a facing connection from the loop. These had all been lifted and the relevant arm on the bracket, presumably a shunt signal, was also removed. JOHN STRANGE/NPC

LEFT: 'Mogul' No. 7317 arriving with a Gloucester-bound service in the summer of 1964. Note the connection to the goods yard in the left background had already gone, so the sidings must have been taken out early in the year. The loss of goods services must have made life very quiet for the signalmen at this rural outpost, with only the passenger trains left to administer. No. 7317 had only a few months of service left, gravitating to Taunton shed by the end of the year, from where it was withdrawn on 28th December. COLOUR-RAIL

RIGHT: Withdrawal of the passenger service in 1964 did not quite spell the end for the Ross-on-Wye to Grange Court section. Goods traffic was still maintained to both Ross and to the cable works at Lydbrook Junction, on the Ross to Monmouth Branch. The final official closure of the line occurred on 1st November 1965 and this view of the station building was taken from the last Lydbrook goods as it rattled through on 29th October. A couple of locals had come out to pay homage as it passed by – the next train here would belong to the demolition contractors. The signal box closed when the passenger service was withdrawn and the Down loop was disconnected at the same time. DAVID BICK/NPC

LEFT: Like many closed stations, once the track had been removed the structures were left to rot. This view looking west through the derelict Mitcheldean Road station was taken on 13th September 1970 and shows the Up side waiting shelter being absorbed by the undergrowth, whilst grass has also colonised the platforms. Today, a small housing development occupies the site of the station and nothing physical remains to mark its existence. However, the small estate is named Noden Drive, after Reginald 'Dick' Noden, who was station master at Mitcheldean Road from the mid-1940s up until the line's closure. NPC

The line ran through a curved length of cutting (marked by the line of trees just to the left of the top of the telegraph pole) crossing then from Gloucestershire into Herefordshire, as it continued to traverse some highly attractive countryside. With the wooded slopes of Lea Bailey in the background and Mitcheldean Road station off in the left distance, this three-coach train is about to pass under Wharton Lodge, on its way to Weston-under-Penyard, again in the final month of operation. The Mitcheldean Road Distant signal can just be glimpsed above the end of the rear coach. The route of the abortive MR&FDR runs from left to right, along the lower slopes of Lea Bailey, on its forlorn and unused way up into the Forest of Dean. Apart from being an all round delightful view, this slide was a fortunate find for another reason; whilst much of the route of the railway is still visible today, from the end of the treeline on the centre right, this section of trackbed has been ploughed back into the fields. Road improvements have seen the bridge under which the train is about to pass swept away, whilst the cutting on the other side, behind the photographer, has been filled and is now also a field, so the existence of the railway hereabouts is no longer apparent to the casual observer. Incidentally, this view shows one of the 'Large Prairie' tanks travelling bunker first towards Hereford; bunker first working in the Gloucester direction seems to have been much more common. JOHN STRANGE/NPC

LEFT: Immediately after leaving Mitcheldean Road the line ran through a short but rather dramatic cutting, lined with stone buttress walls at the base. This 7th March 1964 view is looking towards Ross. TIM STEPHENS

ABOVE: A field level view of the same section of line shown on the previous page, heading round from Mitcheldean Road and Lea Bailey Hill, in the right background, with No. 2242 coasting gently past towards the A40 overbridge with the 12.25pm train from Gloucester to Hereford on 9th May 1964. The low viewpoint clearly shows the downward gradient here, which extended all the way through Weston-under-Penyard and almost to Ross. NPC

RIGHT: One of the sections of line that I was unable to illustrate in the first edition of this volume was that on the other side of the A40 at Wharton Lodge – a gap that we can now fill. Taken on the same day as the previous picture, No. 4161 was working bunker first back to Gloucester with the 1.40pm from Hereford, through another length of cutting lined with stone buttress walls. The pine trees on the right formed a protective barrier on the western boundary of Wharton Lodge House and are still there today. The cutting, however, has gone, filled in to the level of the land either side. The stone-built overbridge in the background, which carried a farm access track, has also gone, although whether it was demolished or still lies buried beneath the infill I have been unable to ascertain. NPC

A number of John Strange's slides which I acquired were simply marked 'Gloucester-Hereford', although sometimes with an engine number too. This one defied my attempts to locate it exactly, although I knew it was near Weston-under-Penyard but in the first edition I plumped for just to the west of the village. I now know the location to be just to the east and the photographer was standing with his back to the A40. On a low embankment, surrounded by park land, a Collett '22XX' Class 0-6-0 trundles past with a combined Lydbrook goods/track removals train, with lifting underway on the section of line between Monmouth May Hill and Lydbrook Junction, in April 1964. It was the underbridge on the right which threw me, as it is no longer there, whilst the lane that ran beneath it has been raised. JOHN STRANGE/NPC

The photographer noted that this picture of No. 4100 with the 10.25am Hereford to Gloucester service, on a crisp December morning four days before Christmas Day 1963, was *'after Weston u P'*. Weston-under-Penyard Halt was situated just over a quarter of a mile behind the train, whilst the local parish church, St. Lawrence, can just be made out in the left distance. This was another rarely photographed section of the line. JOHN DAGLEY-MORRIS

No. 4107 again, coasting to a halt at Weston-under-Penyard on 12th September 1964, with the 12.15pm train from Gloucester to Hereford. JOHN DAGLEY-MORRIS

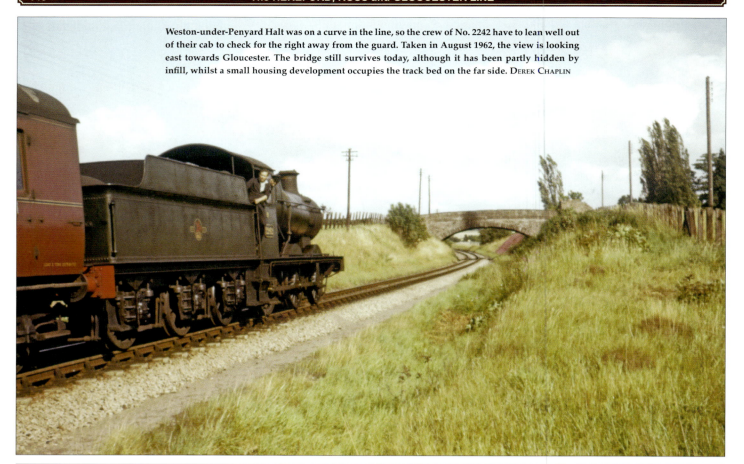

Weston-under-Penyard Halt was on a curve in the line, so the crew of No. 2242 have to lean well out of their cab to check for the right away from the guard. Taken in August 1962, the view is looking east towards Gloucester. The bridge still survives today, although it has been partly hidden by infill, whilst a small housing development occupies the track bed on the far side. DEREK CHAPLIN

Weston-under-Penyard Halt in 1961, as seen from the road overbridge in the picture above. The platform was lit at night by oil lamps, which were extinguished by the guard of the last train of the day. Today, the cutting has been filled in and a new estate has obliterated the site of the halt. T.B. OWEN

This view of Weston-under-Penyard Halt from the base of the embankment provides us with a rather more dramatic indication of its situation. On 3rd November 1962, Class '2XX' No. 2286 pauses with a train for Ross and Hereford. The locomotive had transferred from Machynlleth to Hereford about a month before this picture was taken. ROY DENISON

LEFT: A rare survivor, this poster timetable for Weston-under-Penyard Halt dates from the final year of services. Note that the 10.21pm to Gloucester and the 8.04pm train to Hereford were Saturdays only workings. It is in reality approximately 2ft in width and would have been pinned to a noticeboard on the platform. NPC

BELOW: Summer sunshine colours this picturesque view of the halt, as 2-6-2T No. 4107 departs bunker first with the 1.25pm Sundays only train to Gloucester Central on 22nd August 1964. BILL POTTER/KRM

Having received the 'right away' green flag from the guard on the platform, the driver has opened the regulator of No. 2242 and smoke and steam blast forth from the chimney as it prepares to move off bound for Gloucester. Taken during the final few days of passenger services on the line, the engine is in typically grimy condition. As can be seen from these pictures, the halt was situated on an embankment, with the hut mounted on a timber framework at the back of the platform and a wooden staircase leading up to it from the path below. JOHN STRANGE/NPC

Also photographed in the last few days of passenger working and in an even more filthy state, No. 7815 *Fritwell Manor* pauses with a Gloucester-bound train. Although perhaps more usually associated – certainly in later years – with the Cambrian main line between Shrewsbury and Aberystwyth, engines of the 'Manor' Class, the GWR's final design of 4-6-0, were also regularly seen on the Gloucester to Hereford route and 85B maintained an allocation of them right to the end of services. At the far end of the halt, the line crossed over a minor lane but there is nothing left of the bridge today, the stone from the abutments having been re-used in the building of a new house. JOHN STRANGE/NPC

The 13.25pm from Hereford to Gloucester heads away from Weston-under-Penyard behind No. 4157 on 15th August 1964. This is the best detail colour view seen to date of the basic facilities provided here and shows the non-standard colour in which the hut and nameboard support posts were painted. Note the temporary speed restriction signal on the left; presumably work was being carried out on the line a short distance further on. JOHN RYAN

A classic shot of No. 7822 *Foxcote Manor* in April 1964, coasting on a slight downgrade the exact whereabouts of which is again unknown but on the same stretch of embankment as the previous view; it could be along the gently graded 2 miles between Weston-under-Penyard and Ross-on-Wye. The engine is most likely not doing any more than 40mph but a piece of expert panning on the part of the photographer has given an impression of greater speed, with engine name and numberplate still just sharp enough to read. Silhoutted against the skyline, No. 7822 here shows off the graceful lines of the 'Manor' Class to good effect. JOHN STRANGE/NPC

The approach to Ross-on-Wye station from the west, as seen in April 1964, with more unusual motive power in evidence on this occasion, in the form of No. 6872 *Crawley Grange*, which is seen here in a sequence of views whilst working a Gloucester to Hereford and return service. After climbing over and through the hills around Longhope and skirting the slopes of Lea Bailey, the last couple of miles into Ross were over relatively flat terrain. Looking east from the end of the platform here at Ross, the line curves first to the left but just beyond the tree line in the middle distance, it began a long sweeping curve to the right, to head towards Weston-under-Penyard. Meanwhile, on the right, the branch from Monmouth is also on a sharp curve as it enters the station, with the engine shed positioned in the fork between thr two lines. Note the old yard lamps and the slight downwards slope on the line running in to the engine shed. JOHN STRANGE/NPC

LEFT: Moments later, No. 6872 *Crawley Grange* slows as it passes the engine shed and arrives at the station. Even on this route, three coaches would have barely taxed the capabilities of a 'Grange'. JOHN STRANGE/NPC

RIGHT: The stop at Ross was a fairly leisurely one, with most trains allowed between 3 and 5 minutes, so there was plenty of time for photographer John Strange to get to the other end of the station for another shot of No. 6872 waiting to leave for Hereford. Note the rake of mineral wagons on the left; they appear to be examples of those built by Metro-Cammell for the Ministry of Supply, 7,000 of which were shipped out to France in 1946. Many of them later found there way back for use over here. JOHN STRANGE/TOWY COLLECTION

BELOW: The photographer spent the day taking pictures at Ross in the company of a friend, so was able to catch No. 6872 again, when making the return journey from Hereford to Gloucester. Behind the engine, there is just a glimpse of the standard GWR concrete provender store provided here. JOHN STRANGE/NPC

LEFT: With a cheerful grin from the driver, No. 6872 *Crawley Grange* departs Ross-on-Wye on the return journey. The scenic route from Gloucester to Hereford and back on a sunny spring day – all in all, a very pleasant day's work for the footplate crew. No. 6872 was withdrawn from Oxford shed on 31st December 1965, the very last day of Western Region steam, and was cut up by Cashmores of Newport the following year. JOHN STRANGE/NPC

BELOW: By contrast, the driver of 'Mogul' No. 6346 is more interested in the progress of the approaching train in this view on the same day. Once the crew of the unidentified 'Large Prairie' have handed the single line token to the Ross signalman, No. 6346 will be able to proceed on its way. JOHN STRANGE/TOWY COLLECTION

ABOVE: Collett 0-6-0 No. 2242 at Ross with a three-coach train for Hereford on 30th October 1964. Note the wind shelter protecting passengers from the elements beneath the Up platform awning and also the wooden bicycle shed on the Down platform. T.B. OWEN

LEFT: No. 6349 calls at Ross on a damp day in July 1964. The picture is out of focus slightly but the view was worth including for the oil tank wagons, seen in the yard in the left background, in the process of being emptied. JOHN STRANGE/NPC

BELOW AND OPPOSITE PAGE BOTTOM: Extracts from the *Working Passenger Time Table* for 19th September 1955 to 10th June 1956, detailing the Up and Down passenger services on the line. There were several long stops at Ross, for Up and Down trains, of between 6 and 12 minutes, no doubt a result of the need to wait for crossing trains on this long, single track, cross country route. The eight trains each way per day service was maintained till the end.

Ross was a very attractive station, as this overall view taken looking west in the summer of 1962 shows. The main station building was on the Down side, largely hidden from view here, and the Down platform at the east end was covered by a handsome canopy that was supported by some beautifully ornate ironwork, which also protected passengers using the Monmouth bay platform, on the far left. The wooden footbridge was completely enclosed and a supplementary station building, which included a waiting room (originally for the benefit of Third Class passengers), was also provided on the Up platform. The goods yard on the right comprised three long loop sidings, which could be accessed from either end. The crew of No. 6137 replenish the tanks of their engine from the water column on the platform, although it seems unlikely that they are waiting to cross a Down train as the signalman has already cleared the starting signal for their departure onwards to Gloucester. DEREK CHAPLIN

In the early 1960s, few mastered the art of colour photography, with its slow film speeds, as well as this. With not a soul in sight, bar the feint blur of the signalman inside his cabin, nor a piece of rolling stock to be seen, this is Trevor Owen's magical study of the east end of Ross station at dusk on the evening of 30th October 1964. The luminescence from the signal box interior, coupled with the light beneath the platform canopy shining on the rails in the foreground and the signal lamps glowing red, all combine in a picture of enchanting quality. Ross Signal Box was brought into use on 12th November 1938 and replaced two earlier boxes, Ross South, which was situated just beyond the headshunt hidden behind the bracket signal, and Ross North, at the other end of the station. The new box was built into the Monmouth bay platform, which had been extended in 1896. The Monmouth line branches off right from the main line and we shall return to travel along this a little later on. T.B. OWEN

ABOVE: The fireman of No. 7815 *Fritwell Manor* leans out ready for the token exchange with the Ross signalman as they pass the box, to save him a walk down to the other end of the platform to effect the handover once the train had come to a halt. No. 7815 was withdrawn days before the line closed. NPC

BELOW: Roy Denison's visit to the line of 3rd November 1962 ended at Ross, where he took three pictures, one of which was this fine panorama of the eastern approaches and the engine shed, with an unidentified Collett 0-6-0 standing outside. In the foreground is the bay platform Starter signal for the Monmouth Branch, which was clearly still well maintained although had not been in use for nearly three years. ROY DENISON

RIGHT: 'Large Prairie No. 4135 throws up a plume of white steam as it heads smartly away with a service for Gloucester on 3rd November 1962. Note the centre coach of its train is still in the 1950s carmine and cream livery, a fairly unusual sight by this date. On the left, the weeds growing between the sleepers and the rust on the rails of the Monmouth bay mark the fact that nearly three years had passed since branch services had been withdrawn. ROY DENISON

LEFT: No. 7814 *Fringford Manor* arrives with the 14.38pm train from Hereford on 14th August 1964. The view provides useful detail of the underside of the canopy and the cast iron support columns. The station looks quiet for a Saturday, perhaps a sign that the withdrawal of passenger services was just ten weeks away. JOHN RYAN

RIGHT: More under canopy detail in this view of another 'Manor Class', No. 7815 *Fritwell Manor*, arriving with the 14.47pm train to Hereford, which photographer John Ryan will board to travel further on up the line. Ross was the only intermediate station on the route to be provided with a footbridge, a handsome affair with a covered roof, glazed windows and quite substantial for a station of this size. JOHN RYAN

There is much to study here in Roy Denison's third and final view of Ross-on-Wye, another panoramic shot which shows this delightful, rural market town station in all its glory. The 1st edition 25 inch Ordnance Survey of 1889 appears to show the the original station at Ross, opened on 1st June 1855, had an overall roof or train shed, which would have been typical of a broad gauge station of that period. However, no photographs of it or indeed of the railway here pre-1900 have ever been seen. The buildings seen here all dated from the station's reconstruction in 1892. The Up side shelter had a brick building behind it, the chimney of which can be seen jutting up above the roof, which housed waiting rooms and toilets, whilst the extensive facilities on the Down platform included a refreshments room. The station's name was simply Ross from opening up to 1933, when it became Ross-on-Wye, no doubt to better reflect its location as the local tourist industry became an ever more important part of the area's economy. ROY DENISON

ABOVE: No. 4161 draws in to the Up platform with the 9.40am service from Hereford on 9th May 1964. The weekday service in the final year comprised eight trains each way, with a journey time between Ross and Hereford of 25-30 minutes, which would still compare favourably with the road journey today, particularly when taking in to account that the train made four stops on the way. NPC

RIGHT: A nice detail study of the GWR conical water tower, locomotive watering facilities and short parcels bay on the Down side at the west end of the station, with No. 4157 waiting to cross with the arriving train before proceeding on its way to Hereford. CHRIS WALKER

BELOW: No. 6993 *Arthog Hall* (which we saw earlier bursting through the bridge at Grange Court Junction) coasts in to Ross with a four coach train for Gloucester on a warm summer's day circa 1963. The picture provides us with another partial view of the goods shed and of the livestock pens in the right background but colour photographs of the goods facilities in any detail have still yet to be found. NPC

ABOVE: Dusk also colours this view of the station, showing trains crossing in October 1964, with the headlamp of the Gloucester-bound train hanging from the rear bunker of the unidentified 'Large Prairie' tank. In the Down platform, the tail lamp of the Hereford train also stands out. The provender store is seen almost in its entirety on the right but the yard appears deserted. The station site is today a modern industrial and retail park, and this building, along with the station, has gone. However, the engine shed and goods shed still survive, having found alternative uses, the former currently as the hub of a garden centre and the latter in use by a plant hire company. Regrettably, the nearby attractive red and yellow brick weighbridge hut which had also survived was demolished in 2011. The column on the platform was fed from a large GWR water tank out of sight here on the far right of the yard. T.B. OWEN

LEFT: A cosy glow from the grate of No. 2242, whilst the longer exposure required for this evening shot has caused the driver to 'ghost' as he acknowledges the photographer. The GWR parachute-style water tank was also fed from the main tank and there is a partial view of the east end of the goods shed beyond. This was a fairly substantial building, with two roads running through it either side of a central loading platform. Like the engine shed, it dated from the line's broad gauge period. T.B. OWEN

No. 6330 in the typically work-stained and run down condition of this late period, arriving with a train from Hereford in April 1964. The leading parcels GUV is also covered in a thick layer of grime. Until 1959, the running in boards had stated 'CHANGE FOR MONMOUTH' beneath the station name. Note the complicated pointwork serving the goods shed and short goods bay platform, partly a result of the GWR's abhorrence of facing points on running lines. JOHN STRANGE/TOWY COLLECTION

No. 2242 again but looking in far better cared for condition in this 1962 view, its Brunswick green paintwork having been given a clean before setting out from Gloucester. In hot, dry weather, coal dust was a problem in steam days and the fireman is here seen damping down the coal in the tender by spraying it with water from an armoured hose, referred to as a 'pet pipe'. Departure is imminent with the starting signal having been pulled 'off' and there is a glimpse through one of the goods shed roads in the left background. In the distance, the line curves away to the right as it heads towards Hereford. ALAN JARVIS

With several of the carriage doors hanging open, No. 4161 waits for prospective passengers on 25th May 1963. There was no rush for station staff, as the arrival of a crossing Up service was awaited. This view also affords us a glimpse of the large water tower at the rear of the goods yard. MARK B. WARBURTON

A couple of minutes later and Collett 0-6-0 No. 2249 trundles in with the Down train. In BR goods black livery with 'cycling lion' emblem, this is our only encounter with this engine, which was withdrawn from Reading shed during the week ending 29th August 1964 and cut up by Cashmores at their Great Bridge yard in the West Midlands. MARK B. WARBURTON

Moving to the Gloucester end of the platform, the photographer then captured No. 2249 as it departed, in a view which also shows a little more of the southern approach to the station. MARK B. WARBURTON

Whilst waiting for the arrival of the Up train and with No. 4161 waiting patiently at the Down platform, Mark wandered out of the station and a little way along the approach road to record this view of the exterior, just managing to fit in the little Massey Ferguson tractor on the left. MARK B. WARBURTON

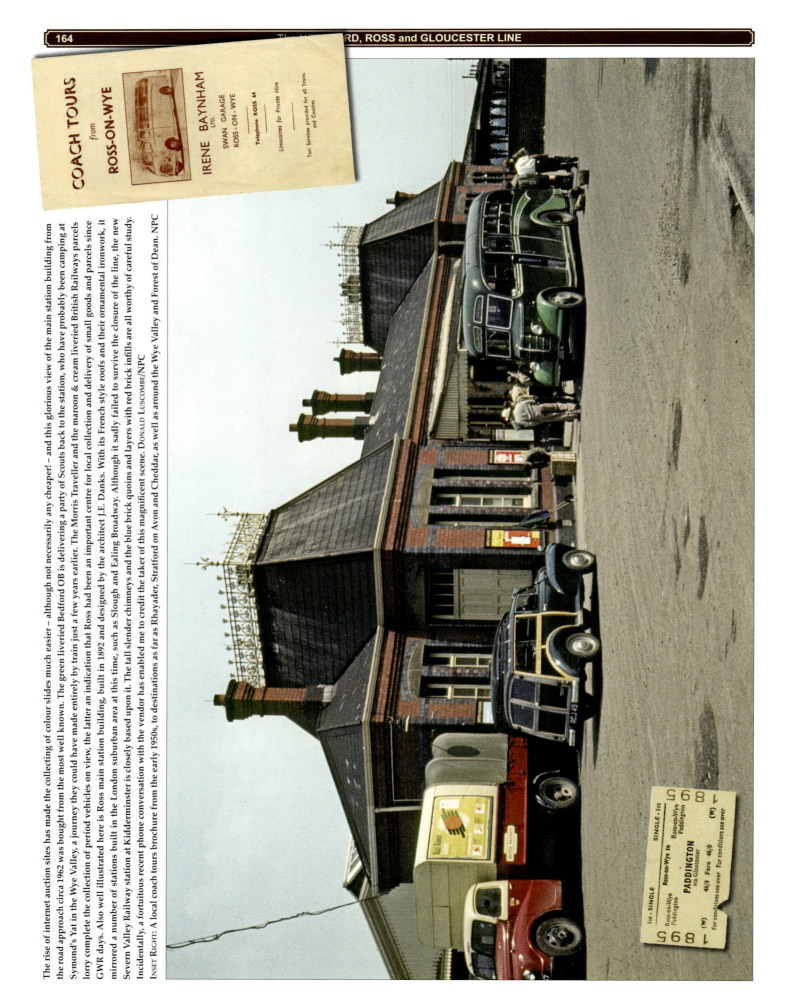

The rise of internet auction sites has made the collecting of colour slides much easier – although not necessarily any cheaper! – and this glorious view of the main station building from the road approach circa 1962 was bought from the most well known. The green liveried Bedford OB is delivering a party of Scouts back to the station, who have probably been camping at Symond's Yat in the Wye Valley, a journey they could have made entirely by train just a few years earlier. The Morris Traveller and the maroon & cream liveried British Railways parcels lorry complete the collection of period vehicles on view, the latter an indication that Ross had been an important centre for local collection and delivery of small goods and parcels since GWR days. Also well illustrated here is Ross main station building, built in 1892 and designed by the architect J.E. Danks. With its French style roofs and their ornamental ironwork, it mirrored a number of stations built in the London suburban area at this time, such as Slough and Ealing Broadway. Although it sadly failed to survive the closure of the line, the new Severn Valley Railway station at Kidderminster is closely based upon it. The tall slender chimneys and the blue brick quoins and layers with red brick infills are all worthy of careful study. Incidentally, a fortuitous recent phone conversation with the vendor has enabled me to credit the taker of this magnificent scene. DONALD LUSCOMBE/NPC

INSET RIGHT: A local coach tours brochure from the early 1950s, to destinations as far as Rhayader, Stratford on Avon and Cheddar, as well as around the Wye Valley and Forest of Dean. NPC

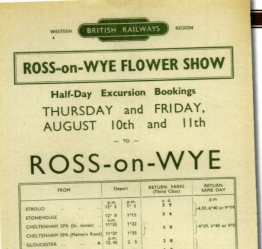
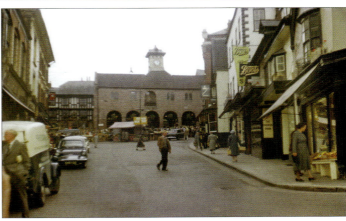

Having 'detrained' at Ross, we will take a few moments to explore the centre of this attractive market town, as it appeared in the early 1960s. The first view, ABOVE, was taken in July 1960. Ross's 17th century market hall still stands and still houses a regular market beneath its arches but you can no longer park in front of it, the cars would all now feature at a classic motors event and RAC signposts have been confined to history. The picture, RIGHT, is looking up Broad Street in 1962. The name on the blue and cream local delivery van on the left is unfortunately not quite readable but the vehicle is likely to be familiar to older 'Rossonians'. The market is in full swing around the market hall but note the road sign on the lamp post is now yellow, Ross having been resigned in late 1960 following the opening of the M50 'Ross Spur' motorway. The final view, BELOW, also taken in July 1960, mirrors what was the standard postcard view of Ross for several decades, complete with policeman on point duty. This area has now been partly pedestrianised, with one way traffic down Broad Street and along Wilton Road. As well as another fine array of period motor cars, note also the two delivery vehicles parked at the end of Wilton Road, a bright yellow Corona lemonade lorry and a chocolate and cream Fry's cocoa van, the front of which can also be seen on the right in the top picture. All NPC

RIGHT: Bennett's garage at Wilton, on the western outskirts of Ross, in 1962, which at that time was selling Regent petrol. It was situated at the major road junction between the A40, which here turns south west towards Monmouth, and the commencement of the A49, heading initially to Hereford but ultimately to Bamber Bridge near Preston. The A40 is today a dual carriageway, part of a route connecting the M50 at Ross with the M4 at Newport and there is still a petrol station on the roundabout here but it is a modern facility and all of the buildings in this view have gone. NPC

LEFT: The classic view of Ross-on-Wye from the west, again taken in 1962, with St. Mary's church dominating the skyline as it has done for around 700 years. Beneath the church, the houses border Wye Street, which was previously known as Dock Street, from the time when wooden sailing trows used to call here with cargoes of Forest of Dean coal or other commodities and coracle fishermen used to take to the river in their distinctive basket shaped craft to fish for salmon. The railway to Hereford is hidden in the trees on the extreme left of the picture. Incidentally, anyone wishing to model this line and looking for an authentic backdrop might be interested to know that one of the Gaugemaster backscenes is actually a photograph of Ross-on-Wye taken from a similar position as this. NPC

Back to the station again, to recommence our journey to Hereford. On 21st July 1962, '61XX' Class 2-6-2T No. 6137 waits for the road west, which it will shortly gain following the arrival of 2-6-0 No. 7314 with a Gloucester train. The 'Mogul' was withdrawn from Shrewsbury shed during the week ending 23rd February 1963. The goods shed unfortunately tends only to feature in the background of these views of Ross station. A. PAFRY/COLOUR-RAIL

BRITISH RAILWAY HISTORY IN COLOUR: 1. WEST GLOUCESTER & WYE VALLEY LINES

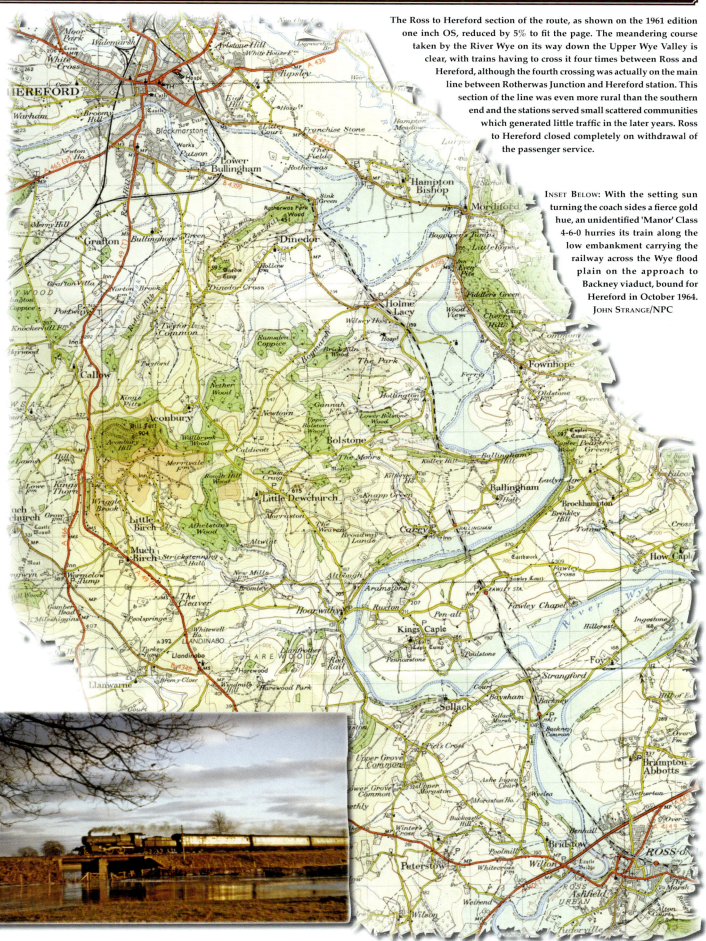

The Ross to Hereford section of the route, as shown on the 1961 edition one inch OS, reduced by 5% to fit the page. The meandering course taken by the River Wye on its way down the Upper Wye Valley is clear, with trains having to cross it four times between Ross and Hereford, although the fourth crossing was actually on the main line between Rotherwas Junction and Hereford station. This section of the line was even more rural than the southern end and the stations served small scattered communities which generated little traffic in the later years. Ross to Hereford closed completely on withdrawal of the passenger service.

INSET BELOW: With the setting sun turning the coach sides a fierce gold hue, an unidentified 'Manor' Class 4-6-0 hurries its train along the low embankment carrying the railway across the Wye flood plain on the approach to Backney viaduct, bound for Hereford in October 1964.
JOHN STRANGE/NPC

LEFT: A Hereford-bound train on the embankment approach to Backney Viaduct in October 1964, hauled by an unidentifed ex-GWR Class '61XX' 2-6-2T. JOHN STRANGE/NPC

RIGHT: Through goods trains between Hereford and Gloucester continued right up until the closure of the northern half of the route in 1964 but were rarely photographed in comparison to the passenger services. Consequently, although lacking a little in quality, this view of a grimy unidentified 'Manor' rumbling across the viaduct with a mixed goods in August 1964 is well worth including. The consist is a motley assortment of open wagons and box vans but with a couple of BR 'Conflat' container wagons as well. There were three workings each way a day, as the 1961 *WTT of Freight Trains* extract, BELOW, shows and this Up train is likely to be the 7.35pm ex-Hereford Barr's Court, which was due past Backney at around 8.20. JOHN STRANGE/NPC

In the golden glow of an autumn evening in 1964, a work stained Collett Class '22XX' 0-6-0 trundles across Backney Viaduct with a Hereford to Gloucester train. When the railway opened in 1855, the four viaducts which spanned the River Wye between Ross and Hereford were, essentially, identical in size and construction. Each comprised five stone piers, with stone abutments either end, supporting six wooden truss spans 44 feet in length; such uniformity of construction across four viaducts, even though they were only a few miles apart, is quite remarkable. However, time was to treat them all quite differently, with the Eign viaduct at Hereford being replaced in 1866 when the double track line between Hereford Barton and Rotherwas Junction was completed. The others had their timber trusses replaced with wrought iron plate girder spans at the end of the 19th century, Backney being rebuilt in 1899 to the form seen here. A capping of blue engineering bricks was laid on top of each pier to support the new spans. Following closure of the line north of Ross in 1964, the viaduct spans were removed the following year. Happily, the piers were left standing and remain today, as silent sentinels in the river, although the embankment and abutment on the north side has been largely cleared to make way for a car park for a picnic site beside the river. At least one '9F' and a 'Britannia' are known to have crossed this graceful structure. JOHN STRANGE/NPC

A few moments after capturing the view at the top of page 168, photographer John Strange fired off another frame as Class '61XX' 2-6-2T made its way onto the viaduct. Looking at the selection of pictures taken here, it is not difficult to understand the attraction of this location or the ease with which a day in glorious autumn weather could be wiled away beside the banks of the River Wye. With the nearest main road some miles away, the occasional passing train was the only intrusion in these otherwise tranquil surroundings. The stone piers of the viaduct were remarkably slender, a fact which led to problems with the two other viaducts on the route, at Strangford and Ballingham, as we shall find out in due course. Strangford was just a mile further north but the water running beneath the viaduct at Backney had flowed nearly 6 miles from there, following a large meander in the River Wye. The view is looking north east and the area of land enclosed by this meander, part of which can be seen in the background and which extends up to the higher ground seen in the distance, is known as the Foy Peninsula, after the tiny village which constitutes the only community within it. Reached only by a minor lane, it remains largely unspoilt. JOHN STRANGE/TOWY COLLECTION

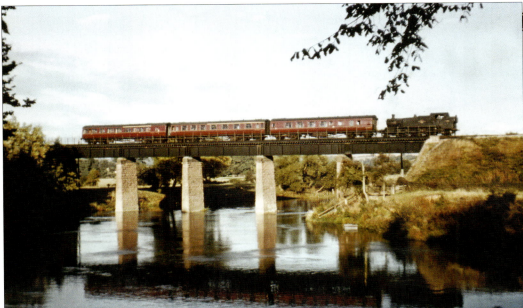

Working bunker first, an unidentifed '51XX' Class 2-6-2T makes its way over the viaduct with a return working to Gloucester in October 1964. BILL POTTER/KRM

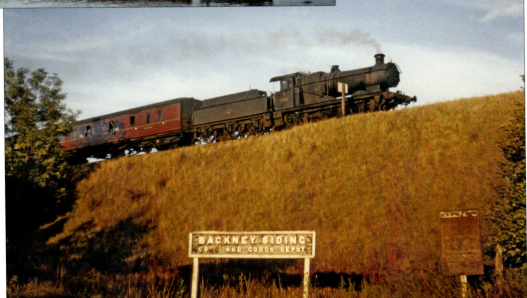

No. 2242 passing Backney Halt in October 1964, with the GWR nameboard at road level proclaiming 'BACKNEY SIDING COAL AND GOODS DEPOT' having survived the closure of the facilities here. Opened on 23rd March 1933, the halt comprised a short wooden platform and pagoda style shelter; passenger services were withdrawn on 12th February 1962, after the wooden platform collapsed. The goods yard consisted of a loop with short stub sidings at each end, the points controlled from two ground frames, North and South, and livestock pens were also provided. The yard was removed in July 1964 but had closed some time previously. JOHN STRANGE/NPC

A lovely and unusual view of the line at Backney on 17th October 1964, sadly not quite showing the halt – fractionally out of sight round the curve – but looking across Backney Common and the vale towards Ross-on-Wye, with the church spire just discernible in the centre distance. The picture was taken from a stone access bridge at Strangford, one of two which spanned this deep cutting. Today, the cutting has been completely filled in along its entire length, with only the stone parapets of both bridges remaining above ground. TIM STEPHENS

A mile north of Backney Halt, the line crossed the River Wye again, by means of Strangford Viaduct but I have not located a colour view of this. This might in part be because it was a less photogenic structure than the other two, having been rebuilt after being partly washed away by heavy floods in 1947. On the night of 1st March 1947, floods caused by melting snows from the great winter of that year washed away the central pier and the two spans either side collapsed into the river. Fortunately no trains were involved. The destroyed pier was not replaced and the bridge was rebuilt with a single plate girder span in the centre, with the two piers on which it rested being encased in reinforced concrete to carry the extra weight of the heavier span. These piers were also given streamlined cutwaters to lessen the effects of the water flow on them. The line reopened in 1947, the passenger service having been replaced with buses in the interim, whilst goods trains were routed over the Gloucester to Ledbury branch. Today, the four piers still stand, the spans having been dismantled in 1965.

ABOVE: Fawley station from the west in autumn 1964, with a train for Gloucester at the Up platform and the signalman chatting with the footplate crew after exchanging the single line token. He will have collected the one for the section just completed from Rotherwas Junction and changed it for the Fawley to Ross token instead. The starting signal is off and the train is about to depart but despite that, hands in pockets, one of the station staff is about to stroll over the boarded crossing. Note the pair of railwayman's cottages on the right and the detached station master's house alongside, all of which remain today. JOHN STRANGE/NPC

LEFT: No. 6330 with a Hereford-bound train at the Down platform in 1962. Whilst the communities served north of Ross were somewhat scattered and sparse, the trains were quite well used between the individual stations because the railway provided the most direct route across the meanders of the River Wye. ALAN JARVIS

A lovely overall view of the passenger facilities at Fawley in August 1962. The entire station was rebuilt in 1897, during a period in which a great deal of modernisation was carried out along the line. What form the original building took is not known (similar to that at Holme Lacy is likely) but the new station was almost identical to that provided at Mitcheldean Road and followed a design used extensively by the GWR at this time. The unidentified 'Prairie' tank just arriving is hauling a 'Fruit D' van and three coaches. Note the signalman waiting at the end of the platform on the right with the Fawley to Ross token, with its hooped end to enable it to be caught easily from a moving train, whilst beneath the far end of the canopy, the porter stands ready to deal with any passengers or parcels. A more peaceful location it would be difficult to imagine. DEREK CHAPLIN

RIGHT: In a warm summer haze, turned blue by the drifting smoke, No. 7325 waits at Fawley with the 7.58am service from Swindon to Hereford on 9th August 1963. One of only two ex-GWR 'Moguls' to survive into preservation, No. 7325 can now be found in the Engine House at Highley on the Severn Valley Railway. The train had arrived here at 10.35 and is waiting to cross with the 10.25 from Hereford, which was due in at 10.37 – 12 minutes after departure with intermediate stops at Holme Lacy and Ballingham; smart working indeed. However, whilst we wait for the 10.25 to arrive … JOHN DAGLEY-MORRIS

LEFT: The first in a sequence of three photographs of Fawley on 25th May 1963, showing No. 4161, which we saw at Ross a few pages ago, on the return run to Gloucester. It was a warm sunny day and the signalman is chatting to a lone lady passenger as they await the arrival of the train, which can be seen through the bridge arch just exiting Fawley Tunnel. The station looks beautifully kept, with a rockery along the base of the approach road embankment at the back of the platform and everything neat and tidy in proper railway fashion.

BELOW: As the train draws in and with token at the ready, the signalman has moved in to position to make the exchange and gets a final goodbye from the lady passenger as she prepares to climb aboard. No doubt she used the trains regularly and the two knew each other well, part of what made working in rural outposts such as this so acceptable.
BOTH MARK B. WARBURTON

Our photographer then moved to the end of the loop to capture No. 4161 departing. In so doing, he also managed to give us another view of the station master's house in the right background. As we saw at Mitcheldean Road, the Down starter would have been pulled off before the train arrived and would not be returned to danger until the signalman had made his way back to the box on the Up platform following its departure. MARK B. WARBURTON

Completing the short story started on the opposite page top, No. 7335 bustles in with the 10.25am from Hereford on 9th August 1963, to cross with No. 7325. The train includes a cattle wagon at the front and possibly a van at the rear, and was photographed from the goods loading dock. JOHN DAGLEY-MORRIS

Looking from the road bridge at Fawley, as No. 7326 calls with a Down train in 1962, whilst an Up train heads off to Ross behind. The driver waits by the box for the signalman to return with the token for the Fawley-Rotherwas Junction section, which he has just collected from the Up train. He will have to place it in the token machine first, however, before handing it back out. This is likely to have been a Saturday, because both trains are loaded to four coaches. No. 7326 was another of the '93XX' series, originally No. 9304, which were all renumbered in the later 1950s after modifications to reduce weight. It was withdrawn from Taunton shed during the week ending 9th September 1963. T.B. OWEN

Hauled by an unidentified 'Mogul', the morning mixed goods to Gloucester draws to a halt at the Up platform in September 1964. JOHN STRANGE/NPC

A short while later, No. 4161 has arrived with the 10.35am service to Hereford (9.40am ex-Gloucester), from which several passengers have detrained. They will have to wait to cross the line until the goods has cleared the loop. We can see more of the consist in this view and what a typically mixed bag it is, with numerous sheeted opens, several vans, a single wagon of coal, and a large crate of perhaps machine parts or engineering equipment and an agricultural implement loaded in the two nearest open wagons. The signal box dated from 1897, having been built to replace an earlier box which is believed to have been sited a little further down the platform, the track layout being substantially altered at the same time. Note that since Trevor Owen's 1962 photograph, opposite, the 'L' in Fawley has come loose and been reaffixed at a different height, suggesting the nameboard timber was rotting, whilst as at Mitcheldean Road, the platform edging has been partially removed. Within a couple of months of this picture being taken, such a scene as this would be consigned to history and all would be quite in this unspoilt part of Herefordshire, the silence no longer to be punctuated by the passage of steam trains. Fawley is today the only reasonably complete station remaining on the route. However, the station building has in recent years been converted in to a private residence, with an L-shaped extension built across the trackbed. The shelter on the Down platform remains as a separate building. JOHN STRANGE/NPC

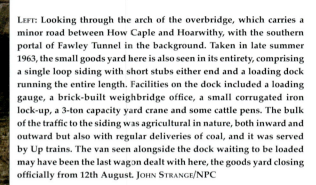

RIGHT: On a blisteringly hot day in the August of 1963 and proving that 'Granges' were no strangers to the line, this is the second member of the eighty strong class to feature. No. 6821 *Leaton Grange* enters the station having just cleared the smoky depths of Fawley Tunnel. The engine was withdrawn from Llanelly shed on the last day of October 1964, so presumably was being utilised by Gloucester to cover this diagram before being returned home. It was cut up by Birds of Bridgend the following year. JOHN CHAMPION/COLOUR-RAIL

LEFT: Looking through the arch of the overbridge, which carries a minor road between How Caple and Hoarwithy, with the southern portal of Fawley Tunnel in the background. Taken in late summer 1963, the small goods yard here is also seen in its entirety, comprising a single loop siding with short stubs either end and a loading dock running the entire length. Facilities on the dock included a loading gauge, a brick-built weighbridge office, a small corrugated iron lock-up, a 3-ton capacity yard crane and some cattle pens. The bulk of the traffic to the siding was agricultural in nature, both inward and outward but also with regular deliveries of coal, and it was served by Up trains. The van seen alongside the dock waiting to be loaded may have been the last wagon dealt with here, the goods yard closing officially from 12th August. JOHN STRANGE/NPC

BELOW: Fawley circa 1962, during a quiet time between trains and illustrating everything that was attractive about a British country railway station and a way of life now gone forever. JOHN TARRANT/KRM

LEFT: A close-up of the Down side waiting shelter circa 1963, with a lone lady passenger about to board a Hereford bound train. NPC

RIGHT: The Fawley signalman waits to greet and exchange tokens with the 16.48pm from Hereford, with No. 2286 at the head, on 14th August 1964 but there are no passengers waiting, apart from the photographer who was about to climb aboard. JOHN RYAN

LEFT: This service for Hereford in summer 1964 has just been given the 'off' and will shortly head in to the narrow confines of Fawley Tunnel in the middle distance; note how the line breasted a summit beneath the bridge and then drops on a shallow gradient towards the tunnel mouth. A Wickham maintenance trolley belonging to the local permanent way gang can be seen parked on the goods yard siding and note that the letter 'L' on the nameboard had finally lost its battle with gravity. CHRIS WALKER

ABOVE: Time for a smoke for the crew of Collett '22XX' No. 2286, as they await the arrival of a southbound working which will cross with them here, after which the section will be clear for them to proceed on their way to Hereford. Note the signal by the tunnel mouth is 'off' for the expected train. This August 1963 view also shows the facilities on the loading dock, with a ballast wagon alongside. JOHN CHAMPION/COLOUR-RAIL

LEFT: Moments later, the awaited service arrives, hauled by a 'Large Prairie' tank travelling bunker first. JOHN CHAMPION/COLOUR-RAIL

RIGHT: No. 7318 exits Fawley Tunnel in late October 1964, still working hard as it bursts out into the daylight and with its headlamps glowing red in the gloom. As a prelude to complete closure on 2nd November 1964, the redundant goods yard was taken out on 20th October, the rails having been mostly cut into short lengths, whilst the cast iron chairs are stacked on the wall of the dock. A brick-built PW hut is just visible alongside the engine and note, too, the GWR notice on the right, near the bottom of the vehicle access running down from the lane. The Down starter was on a short post so as to be visible through the bridge arch. JOHN STRANGE/NPC

A stunning view of the railway from above the western portal of Fawley Tunnel on 16th May 1964, with the line heading over Ballingham Bridge towards the station in the centre distance. The signal in the foreground is the Fawley Distant, which was permanently fixed at caution. Tim Stephens

The third viaduct was crossed shortly after leaving Fawley Tunnel. It was named Carey Viaduct by the GWR in their early official documents, after an adjacent small hamlet but is more commonly referred to today as Ballingham Viaduct, after the nearby station opened in 1908. Identical in size and appearance to the other two viaducts, it was rebuilt from its original form in 1897, two years prior to those. It is not known when or why the upper sections of the piers were encased in concrete. It would seem logical that it was done at the same time as the collapsed Strangford Viaduct was rebuilt, in 1947 but in that case why encase the upper part of the piers and not the lower half in the river, where water erosion was likely to cause damage? The only conclusion seems to be that the upper sections, which had been extended when the old wooden spans were replaced with those seen here, had suffered weather damage of some sort and needed reinforcing. As with its two sisters, the piers stand today as a reminder of its existance. Incidentally, the pronounced right to left downward slope is not an illusion or a result of the photograph being poorly orientated. As one of the other photographs will shortly show, the line dropped quite markedly down from the northern portal of the tunnel. Photographer Bill Potter was not close enough to record the number of the heavily stained 'Mogul' heading across with its three-coach train for Hereford in October 1964 but it may be our old friend No. 7318 again. BILL POTTER/KRM

One of the beauties of the steam age for both photographers and spotters was the variety of motive power, the not knowing what would turn up next. Here, one of the 'Modified Hall' Class 4-6-0s, No. 6991 *Acton Burnell Hall*, makes light work of its three-coach load as it rumbles across the viaduct in August 1964. Built by British Railways at Swindon in November 1948, this engine finished its career at Oxford, being withdrawn on the very last day of Western Region steam, 31st December 1965. M. SMITH/COLOUR-RAIL

A north easterly view, probably with the same work stained 'Mogul' as on the previous page but here seen heading back to Gloucester. The photograph is believed to have been taken on the same day, so is probably no more than a couple of hours later. A little extra water would been taken on board somewhere on route but a 'Mogul' could easily make it to Hereford and back on a tender full of coal. The bovine inhabitants of the river bank are unconcerned with the passage of the train. JOHN STRANGE/NPC

A fine detailed study of the viaduct in 1962, showing how the upper sections of each pier had been completely encased in concrete. The northern portal of Fawley Tunnel was less than 100 yards from the end of the viaduct, the southern end of which was supported on a substantial stone abutment, with a slightly smaller one at the northern end. Both abutments also still survive today, as does the isolated cottage seen through the centre span. NPC

The view towards Ballingham, looking across the bridge (the railings and the far side stone abutment can just be made out through the leaves) from close to the western portal of Fawley Tunnel on 9th August 1963. No. 6365 is near the top of the climb from Ballingham station, with the 2.43pm from Hereford which was loaded to three coaches on this occasion. JOHN DAGLEY-MORRIS

A little later on the same day but standing on the road overbridge which divided Ballingham station from its small goods yard and looking back to where he had been a short time before, 'Mogul' No. 7335 was photographed arriving with the 2.30pm train from Gloucester. JOHN DAGLEY-MORRIS

Another filthy 'Mogul' is seen heading away from Ballingham past the small goods yard on 25th May 1963. The yard was still open at this date – it was not officially closed for another eleven weeks – but it is quite clear from the covering of rust on the rails that it had been some time since the siding had seen any traffic. There was a brick-built weighbridge hut at the entrance to the yard and various small storage sheds but the yard crane which had been provided here appears to have been removed by this date. Note the corrugated iron lock-up on the loading platform and the loading gauge look freshly painted; was this an example of BR's notorious accounting practices of this period, whereby unnecessary work was carried out on certain lines, in order to bump up the costs and further increase any supposed losses, thereby justifying their closure? Black humour of the day had it that if you saw your local station being painted, you knew it was for the chop! MARK B. WARBURTON

RIGHT: Although technically not the best of slides (a result of the low winter sun and the proximity of the dark mass of the overbridge), this February 1959 view is invaluable because it shows the goods yard at Ballingham when it was still in use. The photographer unfortunately neglected to record the number of the green-liveried 'Mogul'. The siding, a loop with short stubs either end similar to the arrangement at Fawley, was brought in to use on 9th February 1908 and was also provided with cattle pens (visible on the right), as well as the other facilities shown in the picture on the previous page, apart from the 6-ton capacity yard crane. As that cannot be discerned here either, it is likely it had been removed prior to 1959. Ballingham North Ground Frame can be seen in silhouette under the bridge, with the South GF just visible in the centre distance. DAVID BICK/NPC

ABOVE: One of the '73XX' series 'Mogul's (the second two digits are not clear but the number series only ran up to 7321) drifts in to Ballingham, with a four-coach train for Hereford in the summer of 1964. The pronounced gradient down from Fawley Tunnel and across the viaduct is clearly visible in the distance, with the railings on the left-hand side of the structure just visible in front of the Distant signal, near the entrance to the tunnel. The goods yard was closed on the same day as Fawley and the rails and the ground frames were taken out on 20th July 1964, which must have been only a week or so after this photograph was taken. MICHAEL HALE

LEFT: A Gloucester train pulls away hard from its stop at Ballingham, the crew taking the opportunity to get a run at the short bank up to the tunnel, in October 1964. Loose rails and chairs from the dismantled siding lie in the foreground. JOHN STRANGE/NPC

To match his view of the line from above Fawley Tunnel, Tim Stephens also took this superb study of the small goods yard at Ballingham, looking from the stone bridge carrying the lane from Carey to Ballingham over the railway. Trees now occupy much of the site today, obscuring the view east. TIM STEPHENS

A delightful view of the small single platform station at Ballingham, taken from beneath the road overbridge in 1962 but showing it little changed from GWR days. JOHN TARRANT/KRM

A couple of passengers get ready to clamber aboard this three-coach train for Gloucester, in the charge of No. 7801 *Anthony Manor* in September 1964. This was a Shrewsbury-based engine, so may have been pressed into service by Hereford shed. It was withdrawn during the week ending 10th July 1965. HUGH BALLANTYNE

A young girl and her mother leave a Down train at Ballingham. The bridge survives today, with the trackbed beyond for around 100 yards in the direction of Fawley now seemingly part of the garden for the private house that the station building has been converted to. NPC

Photographer John Ryan, having just alighted from the departing train, took this view of No. 7815 *Fringford Manor* as it made its way off round the curve towards Ballingham Tunnel on 14th August 1964. Having to make use of the time table to visit and photograph as many of the stations and halts as possible, it made for an interesting exercise planning where and when to get off and then be able to get back on again within a reasonable time. Ballingham village, which was and still is little more than a scattered collection of a few houses and farms, lay half a mile off to the north-east, with the equally small hamlet of Lower Pen-alt a little closer to the south-west but road transport was always going to erode the station's meagre ration of passengers and so it proved. JOHN RYAN

No. 4107 calls at Ballingham in early October 1964. During the last few weeks of the line's existence, it seemed to enjoy plenty of fine weather, aiding those who wanted to photograph it before it passed into history. Ballingham was a late arrival, the GWR opening the station here on 1st September 1908. Situated in a shallow cutting, just beyond the southern portal of the 1,206 yard long Ballingham Tunnel, it comprised a single platform, with a brick-built station building, in a similar style to the late 19th century buildings provided at Fawley and Mitcheldean Road; no passing loop was ever provided and there was never a signal box. Station and goods yard were divided by an overbridge carrying a lane between the hamlets of Carey and Ballingham, and there is some suggestion that the GWR originally intended to name the station Carey Road Bridge. After closure, the building stood abandoned for many years but more recently it too has been converted to a private residence. However, this involved removing the roof to build a second storey, so it is practically unrecognisable now as the building seen in these pictures. JOHN STRANGE/NPC

LEFT: Whilst again being of lesser quality, this view is useful for being the only colour shot I've discovered looking back along the platform towards Gloucester. Taken in October 1964, No. 7318 is again the 'star' of the show and, as can be seen, nature was rapidly reclaiming the Hereford end of the platform. JOHN STRANGE/NPC

In autumn sunlight just a few weeks prior to closure, the Ballingham station master is pictured chatting with a couple of enthusiasts, in the shadow of the canopy. The typical GWR pine trees also throw their shadows across the platform, whilst beyond the far end of the platform, the line curves to Ballingham Tunnel, the southern portal being hidden by the cutting. JOHN STRANGE/NPC

Two views at the western end of the 1,208 yards long Ballingham Tunnel, both taken on a beautiful autumnal day, on 19th September 1964. In the top picture, a 'Mogul' 2-6-0 hurries towards the tunnel with a train for Ross and Gloucester whilst, below, an unidentified 'Manor' in typically sadly neglected condition for this period, coasts downhill towards its next stop at Fawley. The three-coach set seen above comprises a First/Third Class Corridor Composite coach of 1940s vintage, flanked by two Hawksworth Third Class Corridor Brakes. The 'Manor' is hauling a similar but slightly earlier set, consisting of a Corridor Third sandwiched between two Third Class Corridor Brakes all dating from the 1930s, with the addition of a Full Brake at the end for parcels traffic. BOTH DAVID SOGGEE

ABOVE: The same train a few moments later, coasting downhill towards its next stop at Holme Lacy. When I first saw this view reproduced elsewhere, I knew it was one that had to grace these pages. The top end of the line was not so well photographed as the section south of Ross and David Soggee's photograph is a wonderful portrait of the rural beauty encountered in this part of south Herefordshire. The view is looking almost due north and the line can be seen curving north west towards the village in the far left distance, with Hereford also lying some distance off in this direction. With river and railway having almost collided as the latter exited the tunnel, the Wye then takes a sharp meander to the north east and in this view is now beyond the line of trees in the centre distance. The lane also runs from Ballingham to Holme Lacy but was on a much less direct route than the railway. The photographer informed me that he was also keeping a wary eye on a bull in an adjacent field whilst taking these three lovely pictures. DAVID SOGGEE

RIGHT: We move back down to track level again now, for this picture of No. 4107 approaching Ballingham Tunnel with the 1.40pm service from Hereford on 17th October 1964. It is clear from many of these pictures that there was an 'Indian Summer' that year, which those wishing to capture the last few weeks of the line's existence were able to make the most of. The sleeper boarding in the foreground denotes the presence of a PW hut out of sight on the left, which was obviously equipped with a small hand trolley. The sleepers were positioned to aid the track gang in getting it on and off the rails. JOHN DAGLEY-MORRIS

Holme Lacy station was also in a picturesque location but, by the 1960s, its situation had been somewhat blighted by the overgrown passing loop and the establishment of a scrap merchant's yard on the old goods loading dock. The signal box, which dated from 1902 and replaced an earlier box sited nearer to the overbridge on which the photographer is standing, was reduced to ground frame status in early BR days and the loop taken out of use for crossing trains; it would never, in any case, have been used for crossing two passenger trains. Thereafter, the section became Rotherwas Junction to Fawley. The station building was original, dating from the construction of the line and it would seem likely that Fawley had an identical building prior to its replacement in 1897; Longhope station was also quite similar, although without the tall chimneys. The goods office on the right is also almost certainly original and merits closer study. This 8th August 1962 view is interesting, too, for the elderly Gresley Brake Third in BR maroon livery immediately behind the engine. T.B. OWEN

As mentioned earlier, bunker first working by the 'Large Prairie' tanks seems to have been mainly from the Hereford direction but was by no means the norm on the route. The line was generally worked by locomotives from Gloucester shed but there are numerous photographs showing the large 2-6-2 tanks working smokebox leading back to Gloucester, so were they turned at Hereford? No. 4135, seen here with a four-coach train in 1964, was actually fresh off Hereford shed, with a bunker full of coal, to which it would later in the day be returning. MICHAEL HALE

A view looking towards Ross, with a lone mineral wagon in the siding, circa 1962. The line had been on a gentle climb from Ballingham, the summit of which was passed just beyond the overbridge. All of the overbridges north of Lea Tunnel seem to have been built with this graceful shallow arch design; south of the tunnel, the overbridges at Longhope and Blaisdon had the more usual inverted U shaped arch. The station building was constructed of stone blocks but over the years had gained an add-on at this end, a wooden waiting shelter which was tacked on to the front of the Gents. A fine array of BR(WR) posters adorn the boards along the front of the building and the end of the shelter, whilst the nameboard is also a BR metal replacement for an earlier GWR wooden board with cast iron letters. JOHN TARRANT/KRM

A view of the west end of Holme Lacy station building, from a Down train on its way to Hereford circa 1963. Although serving a slightly larger – and growing – community than Ballingham, Holme Lacy remained as built for its entire existence, surprising perhaps given that the isolated Mitcheldean Road station was rebuilt. The overbridge survives today but nothing of the station remains, its site remaining undeveloped but heavily overgrown. NPC

A detailed view of Holme Lacy station building's east elevation, as No. 4152 arrives with the 13.26pm from Hereford on 14th August 1964. I had originally thought that the bag prominent in the foreground here, which matched one also seen a little earlier on the platform at Fawley, was a mail sack – until John Ryan told me that it was actually his rucksack, which held a day's provisions, notebooks and pencils, time tables, his camera and anything else required to facilitate a day out riding and photographing the line! Now you know this, it can also be spotted in his views at Longhope and just creeping in to the bottom of the picture at Blaisdon. Note the corrugated iron goods lock-up shed behind the station building on the right. JOHN RYAN

ABOVE: The sidings and ground frames were officially taken out of use on 12th February 1964 but as this view from the late summer of that year shows, the rails were not lifted. The signal box, which had acted as the North ground frame, was demolished, however, as the patch of rubble indicates. No. 7319 is just departing southwards, past a couple of old buses which will end their days in the scrapyard here; the nearer vehicle, possibly a Leyland, has a Harrington body, distinguished by its dorsal fin at the rear, which was designed to act as an air extractor, as well as for streamlined good looks. The livestock lorry is worth a second look as well. There was a corrugated iron lock-up behind the station building for the storage of small goods and a loading gauge on the dock but Holme Lacy was never provided with a yard crane; presumably, in times past, a rail mounted crane was brought in for the times when lifting power was required. COLOUR-RAIL

No. 7335 pauses at Holme Lacy with a three-coach train for Hereford on 25th May 1963. Few photographers ventured to this end of the station to take their pictures, so this is an unusual aspect, one which clearly shows the 'hump' in the line just beneath the bridge and the pronounced drop down through the platform. MARK B. WARBURTON

ABOVE: Moments later, the 'Mogul' starts away to its destination at Hereford. It was almost impossible not to take a good shot on this line and this was yet another pleasing vista, with the river having curved back round towards the railway once again but hiding just out of sight behind the trees in the right background. MARK B. WARBURTON

RIGHT: BR promotional handbill of 1950, with day excursion tickets available from Newent, Dymock and all stations between Gloucester and Hereford, to the Shrewsbury Musical & Floral Fete. NPC

BELOW: Looking back though the cutting, 'Large Prairie' No. 4161 drifts away from the station with the 12.25pm Gloucester to Hereford train on 9th August 1963. JOHN DAGLEY-MORRIS

LEFT: Plumbing new depths of neglect, No. 7320 is seen in desparate condition on 17th October 1964, near Holme Lacy with the 2.38pm service from Hereford. The locomotive had come up to Gloucester Horton Road from Taunton shed earlier on that year and, unsurprisingly, had only a few days left in service when seen here. Gloucester shed lost quite a chunk of its steam allocation following closure of the line to Hereford.

BELOW: The 2.25pm train from Gloucester, with 4-6-0 No. 7815 *Fritwell Manor* in charge of the usual three-coach set plus van, is seen north of Holme Lacy also on 17th October.
BOTH JOHN DAGLEY-MORRIS

BELOW: A little further along but earlier in the day, No. 4157 heads towards Hereford with the 12.15pm train from Gloucester. To the left of the line, the river can be made out curving in towards it again, whilst on the right are some of the outbuildings of the late 17th century Dinedor Court Farm. Hereford Bull Cider is produced here today and part of the farm has also become the site of a select housing development. The train is approaching Rotherwas Tunnel, the entrance to which was a couple of hundred yards behind where the photographer was standing.
JOHN DAGLEY-MORRIS

A rare view of Rotherwas Tunnel, as BR 'Standard Class '2' No. 78004, of Gloucester Horton Road shed, bursts out on 24th March 1962, with the 1.40pm service from Hereford to Gloucester. This was before the rot set in and the engine cleaners had got No. 78004 looking very spruce. JOHN DAGLEY-MORRIS

ROTHERWAS JUNCTION

About three quarters of a mile north of Holme Lacy, the line burrowed beneath Rotherwas Park Wood by means of Dinedor Tunnel, the shortest on the line at just 110 yards in length. Beyond the tunnel, the line curved north west through Rotherwas Park to join the Newport to Hereford main line at Rotherwas Junction. This is the southern half of the 'North & West Route', from Newport to Shrewsbury. However, despite its junior status at the junction, the Gloucester to Hereford line predated the main line by some eleven years, as the Newport, Abergavenny & Hereford Railway was only extended to join with it after the former was converted from broad to standard gauge. The fourth crossing of the River Wye, Eign Bridge on the outskirts of Hereford, was originally very similar in appearance to the other three viaducts except that it was lower and had flood arches one end. However, with the arrival of the NA&HR, it was rebuilt with iron spans in 1866 to carry two lines. It was subsequently rebuilt again in 1931, as a two span plate girder bridge, in which form it still survives today. Unfortunately, the railways of Hereford, generally, seem to have attracted the attention of photographers far less than Gloucester and views of the section north of Holme Lacy are scarce. I have not seen a photograph of Rotherwas Junction in black & white, let alone in colour, nor do we have a steam age colour view of the Eign Bridge.

Details of engine restrictions on the Hereford-Ross-Gloucester line from the autumn 1955-summer 1956 *Working Time Table*. Whilst engines of various classes were prevented from accessing certain sidings because of weight and the larger locomotives were restricted to 20mph, the only prohibitions from the route were 'King' ('60XX') Class 4-6-0s and the heavy '47XX' Class 2-8-0s. NPC

The early railway history of Hereford is complicated, involving five companies, all attempting to build competing lines to different stations. As a result, the railway map of the city did not evolve either logically or sensibly. Hereford Barrs Court station was opened on 1st June 1855, as a result of a rare burst of local co-operation between the GWR, the Hereford, Ross & Gloucester Railway and the Shrewsbury & Hereford Joint Railway. Initially a temporary station building was provided, designed by William Eassie, timber-built in Gloucester and delivered to the site by barges on the Hereford & Gloucester Canal. The permanent station, built largely of red brick and which still stands today, was completed the following year. The Barrs Court part of the name seems to have been used intermittently over the years and, as the nameboard indicates, had been dropped by the date of this July 1963 photograph. No. 2286 stands at the Down Main line platform with a train which will shortly depart for Gloucester. New in to service at the end of January 1936, this engine spent much of the 1950s working around the mid Wales and Cambrian lines, moving to Hereford in October 1962, from where it was withdrawn on 28th September 1964. JOHN CHAMPION/COLOUR-RAIL.

No. 2285 simmers gently alongside the Down main platform at Hereford in the summer of 1959, as it awaits departure time for Gloucester. No. 2285, seen here in lined green passenger livery but with the paintwork around the boiler, footplate and smokebox looking very tired, was to be an early withdrawal later that year, from Machynlleth shed on 2nd November. Incidentally, whilst the motive power attractions of the Gloucester to Hereford line included such possible delights as various types of GWR 4-6-0s, occasional BR 'Standard classes, '22XX' 0-6-0s on passenger duties and the odd real surprise, the one class that you almost never see any photographs of are the '45XX' 2-6-2Ts. Quite why they were so rarely rostered for duties on this line I would love to know. MICHAEL HALE

Covered in limescale, only the cab and tender sides show evidence of No. 7335's lined green passenger livery, as the crew wait for departure time with a Gloucester-bound train in 1963. COLOUR-RAIL

ABOVE: Sporting a makeshift smokebox door numberplate, No. 7319 is also seen waiting at Hereford with a train for Gloucester, in 1964. The station boasted two goods sheds, serving Up and Down yards opposite each other on the main line; the Down yard goods shed can be seen in the background here. COLOUR-RAIL

BELOW: A lovely view of the handsome station frontage and the forecourt circa 1962, with a fine array of period motor cars on view. With assistance from Malcolm Bobbit, we can identify them as (left to right from the lamppost): A Ford Zodiac, a Hillman Minx and a Ford Prefect (with a Morris Traveller in front). In the right foreground is a Morris Eight Series II which, from the registration number, dates from circa 1936. Note the odd headlamps – that on the near side of the car looks the original, the off-side being chromed and more modern, whilst the bumper is missing, so perhaps the car had been in an accident. NPC

RIGHT: A short goods departs from the Up side yard via the through goods line running behind the Up platform, heading for the Ross and Gloucester line behind Collett 0-6-0 No. 2286 in August 1964. The locomotive is partially obscuring the signal box nameplate, Aylestone Hill, the lack of the words 'Signal Box' on the plate giving a clue as to its joint GWR/L&NWR origins. It was one of only nine built to the Joint Type 2 design, by the Railway Signal Company, fitted with a 62 lever Saxby & Farmer rocker frame and opened in July 1884. A replacement 69 lever GWR vertical tappet 5-bar frame was installed in June 1938. The box was renamed Hereford on 9th June 1973 and the frame reduced to 60 levers around the same time. A Kearns-Barker one control switch signalling panel was commissioned on 11th November 1984 to control Shelwick Junction, allowing the box there to be closed. Hereford box is still in operation today but was fitted with uPVC windows in the mid-2000s. CHRIS WALKER

LEFT: Photographed on the same day, No. 4157 runs round its three coach train in preparation for making the return journey to Gloucester. CHRIS WALKER

BELOW: Photographer Chris Walker photographed No. 4157 departing the station (page right) before returning to catch the next eastbound service, behind classmate No. 4161. Aylestone Hill signal box can be seen again in the background, with the bridge behind carrying the road from which the box took its name. The semaphore signals have gone, as have the carriage sidings running behind the box but the scene is otherwise still recognisable today. CHRIS WALKER

Arguably, this is the classic view at Hereford station, from the A465 Aylestone Hill overbridge, with No. 4157 departing bunker first for Gloucester. The station footbridge, partially seen in the left background, has been rebuilt to conform to modern disability requirements, so now has new lift towers either end and a new span, albeit to a similar design to that seen here. The Hawksworth coach in the carriage sidings on the right may well be part of another Ross/Gloucester line set, whilst the houses behind front on to Barrs Court Road, from which the station at first (and periodically afterwards) took its full name. The houses still remain but the pre-fab buildings of the school in the centre background have been rebuilt and now house Barrs Court Special School. CHRIS WALKER

Hereford engine shed was numbered 85C by BR(WR). Here, 'Large Prairie' No. 4107 stands alongside the brick-built repair shed circa 1964. The engine is facing roads No's 5 and 6 (left) of the 8-road stone built main shed. As we have seen, this engine was a regular performer on Hereford-Gloucester line trains. DAVID BICK/NPC

The depot steam crane at Hereford no doubt had various uses but prime amongst them would have been for loading the ashes from locomotives in to wagons for removal. The crane, about which nothing else is known, is seen here on 26th June 1964 loading a steel mineral wagon with ash. H.W. ROBINSON/NPC

ABOVE: An array of ex-GWR locos outside Hereford shed circa 1960. They are, from left to right, '74XX' Class 0-6-0PT No. 7437, 'Hall' Class 4-6-0 No. 5947 *Saint Benet's Hall* and '57XX' Class 0-6-0PT No. 9665. The latter was a local engine, which ended its service here on 16th February 1963, whilst No. 5947 was withdrawn from Banbury shed during the week ending 7th July 1962. No. 7437 lasted until the week ending 13th March 1965, its last home shed being Llanelly. Hereford supplied the engines for Ross-on-Wye shed up until the end of 1960, so either of these pannier tanks may have spent time there. Built by the NA&HR, Hereford shed opened in 1853 and was closed in December 1964. The main shed, 135ft long by 120ft in width, built of stone, with three transverse pitch roofs originally of slate (replaced with corrugated iron sheet by this date) is behind No. 5947, whilst part of the west wall of the repair shop features on the right. Note the turntable pit on the left; the turntable was resited here by the GWR circa 1923. The 'Hall' is standing on shed road 10 whilst the two pannier tanks are on road 11. JOHN TARRANT/KRM

ABOVE: A glimpse of the front of the main shed, with ex-GWR '28XX' Class No. 3863 standing alongside on road 9. Whilst engines working the line to Gloucester were regularly serviced here, it is unlikely that this 2-8-0 appeared on the route, although it was only the heavier '47XX' Class which were actually precluded. Built in 1942, No. 3863 lasted nearly to the end of WR steam, being withdrawn from Bristol Barrow Road during the two week period ending 23rd October 1965. JOHN TARRANT/KRM

LEFT: WD 'Austerity' 2-8-0 No. 90672 was some way from base, being a Woodford Halse engine. Built as No. 79204 in November 1944, it was shipped to Rouen the following month and did not return to home shores until 1947. Loaned to the L&NER from October that year, renumbered 90672 and initially based at Annesley, the engine remained in ex-GCR/L&NER territory for the rest of its career, being withdrawn in from Woodford Halse shed during the week ending 25th April 1964. 'Dub-dees' could work over the Ross line but it is unlikely that this one did. JOHN TARRANT/KRM

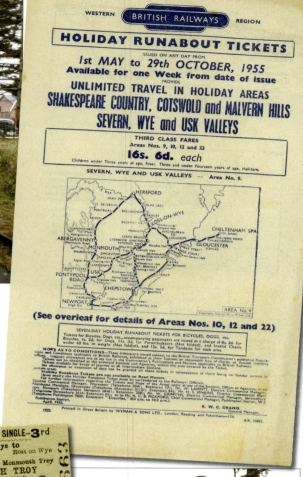

ABOVE: The Monmouth bay at Ross-on-Wye, photographed on 3rd April 1966, after the complete closure of the station. The canopy at this end of the platform made for an attractive feature and, in earlier times, when passengers were changing trains, this area would have been the scene of much hustle and bustle. Tourists with their luggage, scouts going to and from camp, and market day shoppers leaving Ross laden with their weekly shop would all have used this platform to reach the stations nestled along the River Wye between here and Monmouth. NPC

BELOW: An earlier view of the bay in 1962, after closure of the line from Monmouth (although the nameboard still reads 'CHANGE FOR GLOUCESTER AND HEREFORD') and showing the rear of the signal box in detail; note that there was also a nameplate on this side of the building as well. The point and signal rodding running out of the rear of the floor, beneath the platform and through the large aperture in the platform wall, operated the points and signals controlling access to the bay and the main running lines for the Monmouth Branch as it curved in to Ross station. T.B. OWEN

SECTION 6

The ROSS and MONMOUTH RAILWAY

The highly picturesque branch line running from Ross-on-Wye along the Wye Valley to Monmouth was opened on 4th August 1873, under the auspices of the Ross & Monmouth Railway, although it was operated from the outset by the GWR. Intermediate stations were provided at Kerne Bridge, Lydbrook Junction (where a junction was made with the Severn & Wye line coming from Lydney), Symonds Yat and Monmouth (May Hill). It was not an easy or cheap line to build, requiring the construction of two lengthy tunnels, at Welsh Bicknor and Symonds Yat, and three viaducts spanning the River Wye, at Kerne Bridge, Lydbrook and Monmouth. At Monmouth Troy station, the branch met with the Wye Valley Railway from Chepstow and the Coleford, Monmouth, Usk & Pontypool Railway from Pontypool Road, both of which we shall examine in more detail further on in these pages.

The line was never busy and produced little in the way of goods traffic, with the exception of the Edison Swan cable factory at Lydbrook Junction. Kerne Bridge had a small goods yard, at Lydbrook Junction there were exchange sidings with the S&WR line and there were sidings serving a saw mills and small gas works at Monmouth May Hill. Symonds Yat, however, had no goods yard at all, although several private sidings in the vicinity, mostly for loading timber, came under the control of the Symonds Yat station master. Local passenger services were provided by auto trains or by railcars. In GWR days, prior to the First

The Ross to Monmouth Branch, as shown on the 1961 edition one inch OS (reduced by 25% to fit the page), by which date passenger services had been withdrawn. BR had agreed, however, to leave the track in situ for a minimum of three years in case of a possible reopening using diesel railcars. In the mid 1950s, BR had taken the ex-GWR railcars off Wye Valley services and reintroduced steam push-pull workings, a move that did little to improve the economics of operating these lines.

World War, passenger trains ran between Ross and Pontypool Road, with services from Chepstow connecting at Monmouth (Troy). However, from around 1920, all three lines meeting at Monmouth were operated separately and this situation carried on into the BR era.

In recognition of the spectacular terrain through which it passed, the GWR made great efforts to develop the tourist traffic on the Ross to Monmouth Branch, including the positioning of Camp Coaches at Kerne Bridge and Symond's Yat, and the opening of a new halt at Walford. BR continued this, promoting the line as part of a Wye Valley Tour through various hand bills and even opening another new halt, at Hadnock in 1951. All was to little avail, however, and passenger receipts proved too low to keep the line in operation. Services were withdrawn as from 5th January 1959, with the section between Monmouth (May Hill) and Lydbrook Junction closing completely. May Hill stayed open for goods until November 1963, whilst Lydbrook Junction to Ross continued for goods traffic for a further two years.

ABOVE: With the Wye Valley branches from Ross to Monmouth and Monmouth to Chepstow scheduled for closure on and from 5th January 1959, the Stephenson Locomotive Society organised a farewell tour of both lines. With the 5th being a Monday, as was often the case the last regular passenger services thus actually ran on the Saturday, this being 3rd January and the SLS Tour was set for the following day, Sunday 4th. Whilst the weather was kind in as much as there was bright sunshine, a heavy snowfall the previous day hampered photography because of the glare from the snow. Consequently, almost none of the many colour shots taken that day are of the highest quality but a selection nevertheless merit inclusion. Here, the train waits at the west end of Ross station, providing a view of the approach from the Hereford direction. Note the auto trailers on the right, from the previous day's final passenger workings. COLOUR-RAIL

ABOVE: The train was top and tailed by two '64XX' Class auto-fitted pannier tanks, No's 6439 and 6412, which were both resplendent in what looks to have been fairly recently applied British Railways lined green passenger livery. The tour commenced from Chepstow, running via Monmouth and then to Ross, so these first two views show it running round at what was the northern-most extent of the trip. No. 6439, seen here, was a Newport Ebbw Junction based engine and lasted in service only until 10th May 1960. COLOUR-RAIL

RIGHT: A lovely study of No. 6412 waiting to start out on the return run. Allocated to Gloucester, from where it was withdrawn during the week ending 21st October 1964, No. 6412 was fortunate to be bought for preservation by the embryonic Dart Valley Railway. Later transferred to the Paignton line, the engine was sold to the West Somerset Railway in 1976. However, in 2008, it was sold back to the South Devon Railway, where it still resides today. BILL POTTER/KRM

Looking east from the end of the platform on 30th October 1964, showing the sweep of the lines curving in from Monmouth, as they split to serve the bay platform and loop, and the Up and Down lines between Gloucester and Hereford. On the left, a Gloucester-bound train heads off towards Weston-under-Penyard, with its tail lamp forming a comet-like blur, whilst in the right background, a pannier tank can just be glimpsed with a goods train from Lydbrook, which by this date was the terminus of the branch; with the Gloucester service on its way, the Up Branch Home to Down Main signal arm, visible in front of the engine, has just been pulled off for the train to proceed. Note the corrugated iron lamp hut on the right, situated well clear of the platforms. In front of it runs the rodding for the points and the wires to the signals controlling the Monmouth lines. T.B. OWEN

As dusk falls, '57XX' Class 0-6-0PT No. 4623 stands at Ross with the daily goods train from Lydbrook Junction; this is the train glimpsed in the right background of the previous picture. As the 1961 WTT extract, LEFT, shows, this had been a twice daily out and back service previously, with the engine based at Ross shed but changed over by Hereford every Saturday. From January 1961 the locomotive was provided by Gloucester, with the Lydbrook goods then being worked out and back from there after the closure of Ross shed. No. 4623 was later transferred to Cardiff East Dock shed, from where it was withdrawn during the week ending 12th June 1965. T.B. OWEN

LEFT: A grimy Collett '22XX' Class 0-6-0 on Ross-on-Wye shed in 1960, coupled to the local GWR 'Toad' brakevan and with a loco coal wagon alongside. Engines allocated here were provided by Hereford up until January 1961, when Gloucester took over reponsibilities instead, and in later years were usually '57XX' Class pannier tanks. The '22XX' seen here was certainly not allocated and was most likely resting between Lydbrook goods duties; note the 'Toad' is lettered for local use only. Ross-on-Wye shed opened in 1855 and originally catered for broad gauge engines, hence the partially bricked-up entrance aperture. It closed in October 1963. MICHAEL HALE

ABOVE: No. 2287 arriving at Ross with a goods bound for Lydbrook Junction in April 1964. As well as serving the cable works there, the lifting of redundant track from the branch was also underway, hence the bogie bolster wagons. Gloucester-based No. 2287 lasted in service until 21st May 1965. JOHN STRANGE/NPC

RIGHT: Later in the day, the Collett 0-6-0 arrives back from Lydbrook with an empty coal wagon, several opens loaded with cable drums and the bolsters laden with lifted track panels; these would have come from the Lydbrook Junction to Symond's Yat section of the branch, which was being lifted at this time having stood derelict since the withdrawal of services in January 1959. I wonder, where had No. 2287 ventured to receive the overhead line warning flashes on its tender? JOHN STRANGE/NPC

RIGHT: A lengthy stop was made at Ross by the special run on the last day of passenger services on the Wye Valley lines on, which allowed enthusiasts the chance to inspect the engine shed. Whilst the train itself was hauled by two immaculately turned out pannier tanks, both in fully lined green passenger livery, resident on shed was No. 7437, in the sort of condition more associated with these engines. No. 7437 had another six years left in service, however, being withdrawn from Llanelly shed during the week ending 13th March 1965. BILL POTTER/KRM

LEFT: Although a little blurred, due no doubt to the movement of the carriage, this view is included because it shows the sharply curved departure of the Monmouth Branch from Ross. Just to the right of the telegraph pole, there is also a glimpse of the bridge carrying the A40 over the line and into the town. Like much of the railway infrastructure around Ross, this too has long since disappeared. BILL POTTER/KRM

BELOW: Ross-on-Wye station with the final Lydbrook goods, having used the water column one last time, waiting to depart on its journey back to Gloucester on 29th October 1965; the line was closed officially from 1st November. BR Standard Class '2' 2-6-0 No. 78006 of Gloucester Horton Road shed was in charge, its condition indicating that it, too, had only a short time left in service. The engine was withdrawn two months later, during the week ending 12th December, at which time it was just $12\frac{1}{2}$ years old. Goods services from Ross finished at the same time but what is not clear is if this train also cleared the yard here; there are still wagons visible in the goods shed in the background. NPC

Having curved through more than 90 degrees as it left Ross and headed out into the countryside, the branch to Monmouth then turned in a more southerly direction as it made its way across largely flat terrain, past the village of Walford. A station was not provided here when the line opened, residents instead having to make their way to and from Kerne Bridge. Very belatedly, a halt was finally opened by the GWR to serve the village, on 23rd February 1931. The facilities comprised a standard GWR timber platform, with a corrugated iron pagoda hut serving as a waiting shelter. This view, looking towards Ross and dating from the summer of 1964, was taken five and a half years after passenger services had ceased; the nameboards and oil lamps had been removed shortly after, although the metal frame of the one above the door still just survived. The GWR motor train timetable board from Walford Halt is a rare piece of surviving railwayana from the branch, which today can be found on display at the Kidderminster Railway Museum. This view, incidentally, has been changed from that appearing in the first edition, simply because the photographer stood slightly further back and angled his camera a little to the left, thus showing the line curving away across the short span over the lane to Hom Green. NPC

Two views of No. 2287, with the train we saw arriving at Ross a few pages ago, departing Kerne Bridge along the banks of the River Wye. This is a lovely location, with the railway squeezed in between the road and the river, and it was from high up in one of the trees behind the line that Ben Ashworth took his classic black & white view of the Lydbrook goods in the early 1960s. JOHN STRANGE/NPC

The same train a few moments earlier, about to depart Kerne Bridge station, the road frontage to which can be seen between the trees on the left. In a region which abounds with beautiful locations and vistas, this is undoubtedly one of the best, although one that is perhaps not quite so appreciated by railway enthusiasts these days with the loss of the line. The river at this point takes a large meander through this wider section of the Wye Valley. Having passed beneath the arches of the five-arch Kerne Bridge just out of view to the left (a toll bridge built in 1828; the toll house at the east end was demolished many years ago) and then in front of the photographer, the river will shortly arc sharply to the left (east) to flow along the lower slopes of Coppett Hill in the background and finally under the railway as the line crosses over on its way in to Lydbrook Tunnel. The large house behind the station was 'Castle View', so called because it looked across the river to Goodrich Castle, high up on the north west side of the valley and built in the 13th century to guard the river crossing. JOHN STRANGE/NPC

This delightful view of Kerne Bridge station, taken in the summer of 1958, shows the BR Camping Coach in its final year of operation. The points at the north end of the loop were removed in 1901 and the Down platform taken out of use, the line alongside it becoming a siding which for many years was used as a horse loading dock. From 1935 to 1939, the GWR installed a Camp Coach (as they termed them) here, which could be hired by the week for family holidays. The scheme was very popular and the GWR had sites at many locations. It was revived after the war and continued by British Railways (see map opposite), and the Kerne Bridge coach, with its proximity to the river and Goodrich Castle, was very popular. Such was the draw of the castle for visitors that the station nameboard also carried the announcement 'FOR GOODRICH CASTLE', as can just be made out. The station building, constructed of red sandstone, was designed by the R&MR's engineer, Edward Richards, who was also responsible for building the Northampton & Banbury Junction and East Gloucestershire railways, and it bears a close resemblance to stations on both of those lines. The wooden waiting shelter had originally been sited on the Down platform, although it was many years after closure of the loop before it was moved across. Note the coal wagon positioned next to the Camping Coach (as BR termed them) and another of the ubiquitous blue enamelled 'Telephone' signs above the station door. The colourful display from the flowering tubs and the gardens was clearly the pride and joy of the two remaining station staff. The diamond shaped cast iron sign visible above the coach roof advised road vehicles of the weight restriction on the bridge and survived in situ here up until the 1980s at least. The freshly laid ballast on the running line would have contributed to the imbalance between receipts and expenditure which lead to the branch's closure. DEREK CHAPLIN

COACH SITE NUMBERS

HISTORY IN COLOUR: 1. WEST GLOUCESTER & WYE VALLEY LINES

ABOVE: A rare colour shot of the Monmouth to Ross railmotor train at Kerne Bridge in autumn 1958. Ex-GWR '14XX' Class 0-4-2T No. 1424, built in 1933, spent much of its life working from Gloucester and was also regularly to be seen on the Stroud Valleys auto trains as well. Shedded at Gloucester at Nationalisation, it was withdrawn from there during the week ending 13th November 1963. The Kerne Bridge station master, watching proceedings from the platform, also had responsibility for Walford Halt. DAVID BICK/NPC

LEFT: The map of Camping Coach sites from the 1958 BR Camping Coaches leaflet; Kerne Bridge is 99, Symond's Yat 98 and Tintern 102. NPC

In stark contrast to the picture opposite, this 16th August 1965 view shows the semi derelict station awaiting final closure of the line which was just a few weeks away. The station was named after the bridge alongside which it was built, there being no community of that name here at that time, and served the local villages of Bishopswood, behind the photographer, and Goodrich, which lies on top of the hill to the left. Part of Goodrich Court Farm can be seen in the left background and the ruins of Goodrich Castle can just be discerned on the skyline above. The building in engineers blue brick is believed to have been a lock-up for small goods and parcels, there being no shed in the yard here, whilst in the foreground is a standard GWR corrugated iron lamp hut. The signal box had closed in 1901 upon removal of the loop, the sidings here thereafter being worked from two ground frames, North and South. BILL POTTER/KRM

The purpose of Bill Potter's visit to Kerne Bridge on 16th August 1965 was to photograph the Lydbrook goods on its way back to Ross. On this occasion, it was in the hands of '57XX' Class No. 3775 of Gloucester Horton Road shed; the engine had just three months of service left, being withdrawn during the week ending 11th December. The gate on the left had provided access when the old Down platform was used as a horse dock and had also been the entry point for Camping Coach residents. After closure, the station building was used as the base for an outward bound centre from the 1970s to the 1990s and the accommodation here was supplemented by the provision of an old BR Mk 1 BSO coach. Following closure of the activity centre, the building was sold for use as a private residence. It has since been much extended, losing most of its original charm and character in the process, whilst landscaping of the surrounds has largely now hidden it from view from the road. Coppett Hill, with its scattered housing, again dominates the background. BILL POTTER/KRM

ABOVE: A photographic charter was organised to record the running of the last Lydbrook goods service on 29th October 1965 and three 'Toad' brake vans were added to the train to carry the passengers. This view is taken looking back from the footplate of No. 78006, as the train rattles through Kerne Bridge on its way to Lydbrook, a view which emphasises the sharp curve through the station. In the right foreground is the sleeper remains of the point at the northern end of the goods loop siding. The track had all been removed in June 1964. As a matter of record, note that the Mk 1 BSO appears to have been delivered here by this date and can just be seen on the platform in the background. DAVID BICK/NPC

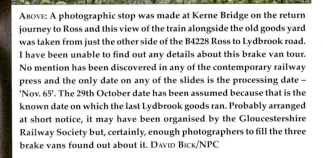

ABOVE: A photographic stop was made at Kerne Bridge on the return journey to Ross and this view of the train alongside the old goods yard was taken from just the other side of the B4228 Ross to Lydbrook road. I have been unable to find out any details about this brake van tour. No mention has been discovered in any of the contemporary railway press and the only date on any of the slides is the processing date – 'Nov. 65'. The 29th October date has been assumed because that is the known date on which the last Lydbrook goods ran. Probably arranged at short notice, it may have been organised by the Gloucestershire Railway Society but, certainly, enough photographers to fill the three brake vans found out about it. DAVID BICK/NPC

LEFT: A most unusual shot, taken from the footplate of No. 2286 on 3rd June 1964, of the Monmouth end of Kerne Bridge goods yard; the South Ground Frame point lever can just be made out above the corner of the handrail. The nearer wooden hut was for PW stores, whilst the other one housed the PW maintenance trolley for this section of the line. In the background, the line can be seen snaking across the bridge over the Wye and then curving to the left as it heads towards Lydbrook Tunnel. Regrettably, this bridge was demolished after closure of the line. A canoe hire centre now plies its trade from a base just on the left of this view. ALAN MAUND, COURTESY MICHAEL CLEMENS

LEFT: After crossing the river at Kerne Bridge, the line turned south east to run alongside it for just under half a mile, before turning southwards again as it plunged into the 630 yard Lydbrook Tunnel, which burrowed beneath the promontory of Coppett Hill. The rarely photographed north portal is seen here from the footplate of No. 2286. The retaining wall on the right is about 20 yards in length. The tunnel was on a southwards curve until nearly half way through, straightening then to head towards Lydbrook Junction. ALAN MAUND, COURTESY MICHAEL CLEMENS

ABOVE: Shortly after leaving Lydbrook Junction, the last Lydbrook goods rattles across the River Wye and into the tunnel on its way back to Ross. The next train across here would be that of the demolition contractors. DAVID BICK/NPC

A final view from the footplate of No. 2286, heading tender first back to Ross and about to plunge into the south portal of Lydbrook Tunnel. The foreshortening effect again disguises the retaining walls, which extended around 30 yards on either side. Note the banked stone retaining walls above the tunnel mouth as well, along with the PW hut on the left, whilst on the right is the Lydbrook Junction Distant signal. ALAN MAUND, COURTESY MICHAEL CLEMENS

One of the joys of compiling this volume has been the unearthing of numerous photographs which simply made the heart leap – and this is yet another one. Taken in early 1964, with the trees just starting to bud, work stained Collett '22XX' 0-6-0 No. 2287 appears to have stopped on the viaduct over the River Wye on the approach to Lydbrook Junction with its short mixed goods train just for the benefit of the photographer. Miles from officialdom and with a very generous time table to work to, you could do things like that back then. The tunnel mouth seen in the previous picture is just off to the left, whilst just out of view on the right on the far bank beyond the bridge is a Youth Hostel, still in operation today, which the author recalls staying at in 1967, when the rails were still in situ; at the tender age of 12 and not knowing that the line had shut, I sat for hours in the garden waiting to see a train! This distinctive and attractive viaduct still stands, having been used as a footbridge carrying the Wye Valley Walk regional trail. However, it was closed in February 2016 due to structural problems. The Wye Valley AONB has applied for heritage lottery funding to repair it but, even if successful, the bridge will not be re-opened until late 2019 at the earliest. JOHN STRANGE/NPC

ABOVE: The SLS tour of the Wye Valley lines on 4th January arriving at Lydbrook Junction station. Haing commenced its journey from Chepstow at 11.20am, the outward arrival at Lydbrook was booked for 13.10pm with a 10 minute stop. The junction here was with the former Severn & Wye Railway line from Lydney, which made its way northwards through the Forest of Dean via Parkend, Serridge Junction and Lydbrook, a line which we shall study in detail in the next volume in the series. It is seen here coming in on the right of the picture but had been closed for a number of years by this date. The passenger service had ceased in 1929 and the last goods traffic ran in 1951. Lydbrook Junction station building was of similar design and construction to Kerne Bridge. The signal box, a standard GWR red brick design, dated from 1908, being a replacement for an earlier box. B.J. ASHWORTH

ABOVE: There was a 10 minute stop at Lydbrook Junction, so that passengers could detrain to inspect and photograph the station. This view is taken from what were the exchange sidings with the Severn & Wye line. BILL POTTER/KRM

RIGHT: After the passengers had clambered back aboard, the tour is seen departing the platforms at Lydbrook bound for Ross, where it was due at 13.36pm. B.J. ASHWORTH

A short while after posing on the viaduct, No. 2287 has its portrait taken standing in the old station platforms. JOHN STRANGE/NPC

Photographed a few moments earlier, No. 2287 draws past the cable works factory siding. Lydbrook Cable Works factory was built in 1912 and was then enlarged during the First World War, during which there were 650 employees here, mainly producing cable for field telephones. The company got into serious financial difficulties in the slump of the early 1920s but around 1925 the works was acquired by the Edison Swan Electric Company, a member of the AEI Group, who traded as Ediswan. A great expansion then took place and a large amount of equipment was subsequently supplied to the Admiralty and the mining industry. The company also bought the adjacent Stowfield Farm, 160 acres of woodland and grazing, with a long stretch of riverside meadows and fishing rights. The company shipped all of their products out by rail and were by far the most important goods provider on the branch, with materials and coal also coming inwards. Special excursion trains were run from time to time for the workforce, many of whom also travelled to work here by train from Ross and Monmouth. During the Second World War, camouflage experts disguised the works as a village, as viewed from the air, with the lacquer plant tower becoming a church. Evacuees were housed within one of the buildings, Standard Telephones moved in with their equipment and London office staff were set up in temporary offices. Over 1,200 people worked here at the height of the war but afterwards, the isolated nature of the site began to become a factor and the works closed in 1965, with the loss of 840 jobs; this also proved the final nail in the coffin of the railway. In 1966, the site was taken over by Reed Corrugated Cases, who produced a million square metres of corrugated fibreboard every week. In 1990, they merged with Svenska Cellulosa Aktiebolaget, becoming part of the SCA Group, Europe's leading forest and paper products company. However, as part of a restructuring process, the factory was closed in 2002, with the loss of 150 jobs, and the site is now derelict. JOHN STRANGE/NPC

The sidings on the old Severn & Wye line platform side at Lydbrook on 3rd June 1964 contained a contractor's train, engaged on lifting the rails from the section between here and Monmouth May Hill. The lifting of the lines featured in these pages was rarely photographed so this is a very interesting picture. The contractor is believed to have been Pittrail Ltd, of Middlemore Lane, Aldridge, near Walsall. This firm tended to operate on something of a shoestring, as evidenced by the Broom Wade compressor behind the diesel locomotive, which was on hire from Eddison Plant; larger firms such as T.W. Ward's had own their plant, rather than hiring it in as required. Pittrail also carried out a number of track lifting contracts in this area in the mid 1960s, including in the Forest of Dean. The locomotive is a 150hp centre cab John Fowler 0-4-0DM and is almost certainly Works No. 22892 of 1940, new to ROF Glascoed in March 1940 but transferred later to ROF Risley in Lancashire and purchased by Pittrail at an unknown date. The wagons were supplied by BR as was standard practice on these jobs, whilst no doubt the lifting contract specified what reuseable material was to be returned to BR and what material the contractor was free to sell for scrap or industrial siding reuse or whatever. The driver would have been a Pittrail man but the rest of the workforce on the contract were most likely hired locally on a casual basis. ALAN MAUND, COURTESY MICHAEL CLEMENS

ABOVE: A general view of Lydbrook Junction looking north, as it appeared in its final years following the withdrawal of passenger services between Ross and Monmouth. The station building had been rather overshadowed by the cable factory since WW1 and by this date had been further hidden by a stack of pallets. The early withdrawal of the Severn & Wye Railway passenger service had also left that side of the station looking rather neglected for years. Note the water tank mounted on a red sandstone plinth on the right; this was built by the S&WR to provide water for their locomotives and was similar in design to other water towers on their system, such as at Serridge Junction. The left side of the picture is all GWR, however, with the handsome brick-built signal box, corrugated iron lamp hut and pine trees behind the platform. BILL POTTER/KRM

ABOVE: No. 78006 shunts the cable works siding for the final time on 29th October 1964. DAVID BICK/NPC

LEFT: The last rites at Lydbrook Junction, with No. 78006, having completed shunting of the yard, getting ready to depart. The remains of the partially lifted exchange sidings between the GWR and the S&WR can be seen on the left. DAVID BICK/NPC

RIGHT: An unusual shot, from the verandah of one of the GWR 'Toad' brake vans, looking back along the train and through the platforms as the small group of photographers gather ready for departure. The station building had become almost impossible to photograph clearly by the end, surrounded as it was by detritus from the cable works. With the works also closing, the metal cable drums in the wagons were most likely going for scrap. On the left of the group, facing the camera with his hand on the fence, is Bill Potter, many of whose pictures grace these pages. DAVID BICK/NPC

ABOVE: Another study of No. 78006 standing at the Down platform, which more clearly shows the triangular layout here with the S&WR line on the right. This also boasted two platforms originally but the one on the far right behind the wagons seems to have fallen out of use quite early on and was thereafter used for goods until the withdrawal of the S&W line passenger service in 1929. The wooden Nissen hut just visible beyond the pallets is believed to have been a war time addition but whether provided for railway company or cable works use is not clear. Behind it can be seen a part of the Lydbrook Junction station master's house. DAVID BICK/NPC

LEFT: Not the best quality of photograph by any means, this view is included because it gives another glimpse of the station building, whilst the low sun lights up the red sandstone nicely. In the distance, the disused track bed continues on towards Symond's Yat and Monmouth. The cable drums on the track give a clue as to the date; the picture was taken in spring 1966, after closure, with the station now awaiting the demolition contractor, presumably Pittrail again. The site of the station was swallowed up in the factory grounds after closure and nothing is left of it today. JOHN STRANGE/NPC

RIGHT: Heading southwards from Lydbrook Junction, for the next mile the line stayed close to the eastern bank of the River Wye as it meandered through the valley. This view, taken on 17th August 1958 from Riddings Wood, near the famous Log Cabin, shows the course it took as it approached this towering outcrop. There was no way round the obstruction, so the railway builders had to tunnel through. The eastern portal was to the right of and almost directly below where the photographer was standing. Probably due to his slightly precarious position, whilst the image looks correctly orientated from the trees in the foreground, looking at the railway shows that it is actually quite severely skewed. However, because it was about 10 degrees out, to straighten it would have also meant cropping it too hard, so I left it as it was. BILL POTTER/KRM

LEFT: I was fortunate indeed to acquire, via the internet, a small collection of late 1930s Dufaycolor slides, which were taken by a family on a trip up to North Wales from Hampshire. Travelling in two cars and with a caravan also in tow, they apparently stopped in the Wye Valley for a couple of days, visiting Tintern and Symond's Yat. I have included the Symond's Yat views here simply out of interest, because neither actually show the railway. This first slide is taken from a spot close to where Bill Potter took his picture, above, but looking in the opposite direction, down river. The Wye curves left round the end of the hill, to meet up with the railway again on the other side. It would seem that possibly the camera and film were new to the person who took the pictures, as a number suffered from slight light incursion and have had to be 'Photoshopped' as a result. NPC

RIGHT: This view is looking down onto Symond's Yat, with the railway and station unfortunately being just off picture to the left. The red roofed, mock half-timbered house in the foreground, which still exists today, stands almost above the southern portal of the tunnel, whilst the flat roofed property just visible in the trees to the left (now the Forest View guest house) looked out on to the railway. This point on the river was (and still is) where the ferry operated, from the Old Ferrie Inn, just below the red roofed house, across to the cottages on the river bank opposite. The large Wye Rapids Hotel, upper left, which advertised itself with white stones placed in the gardens below, is no more, the site now being occupied by cottages. Centre left is the Bungalow Pavilion, which is believed to have been used for local gatherings and river events; this is also still in existence. In stark contrast to today, just one motor car can be seen. The pictures were taken in circa 1937. NPC

On 5th October 1957, Bill Potter photographed the Ross-Monmouth auto train on the short curve between Symond's Yat Tunnel and the station, watched by his wife and young daughter on the far platfrom. The tunnel mouth is hidden by the evergreens in the garden on the right but just above the train, the red roofed house seen in the previous picture can be discerned through the trees, with the Forest View guest house on the left. Propelling the coach was '14XX' Class 0-4-2T No. 1426, which was allocated to Hereford at this date but sub-shedded at Ross for working the auto trains. It was withdrawn from Gloucester on 3rd April 1962. The northern end of the loop was taken out on 1st March 1953, reducing it to a siding which terminated just behind the photographer. Sadly, Bill appears not to have taken any other colour shots of the line on this occasion. W. POTTER/KRM

ABOVE: In the age of steam, there was very little of the Wye Valley, from Hereford all the way down to Chepstow, that could not be seen and enjoyed from the train. That this opportunity has been completely lost is, frankly, heartbreaking, as scenes like this cannot be appreciated from a car, either because you are too busy keeping your eyes on the road or because, as here, the road did not reach past where the photographer was standing in any case. This is the classic three counties view, with the left bank of the river here in Gloucestershire, the right bank in Herefordshire and with Monmouthshire straight ahead. Photographed on 4th August 1958, Class '14XX' 0-4-2T No. 1445 approaches with the usual single auto trailer strengthened by the addition of two extra coaches in crimson & cream livery; perhaps this was a Saturday or market day service. On the left, a rare glimpse of the Symond's Yat Camp Coach, which was in its last year of operation. The loop here had been converted into a siding specially for the coach, one of three Camp Coaches in the Wye Valley, the others being that already seen at Kerne Bridge, whilst the third we shall see a little later on when we reach Tintern. Note the board fixed to the old gas lamp standard on the Down platform advising: 'PLEASE NOTE. THIS PLATFORM FOR USE OF CAMP COACH VISITORS ONLY'. A lone fisherman stands in the river.
COLIN HOGG/COLOUR-RAIL

RIGHT: The cover of the 1958 British Railways Camping Coaches leaflet, the last edition in which the coaches at Symond's Yat and Kerne Bridge featured. They were 8-berth, in common with all other WR coaches and part of the page giving the weekly hire rates is also shown. NPC

RIGHT: A Monmouth to Ross railmotor working at Symonds Yat in autumn 1958, with No. 1424 in charge. This is an earlier view of the same train we saw at Kerne Bridge a few pages back and is again of indifferent quality but worth including for its rarity. DAVID BICK/NPC

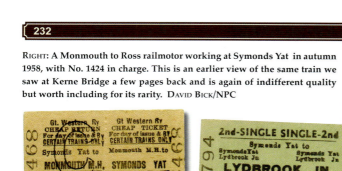

ABOVE: In poor light, No. 6412 is seen at the 'pushing' end of the SLS Tour on 4th January 1959, on the return journey from Ross to Monmouth. Note the intrepid 'photter' apparently on top of the carriage roof; quite how he would have got up there is not clear but surely, even back then in those less health & safety conscious times, it would have been frowned upon. Following the cessation of passenger services and the complete closure of this section of the line, trippers wishing to visit Symond's Yat had to get here by different means, as the excursion ticket, top, indicates. Travelling by bus from Evesham might at first glance seem a little odd but this was a trip organised jointly by British Railways and Midland Red, with the Worcestershire town being the southern limit of the latter's normal operations. W. POTTER/KRM

RIGHT: With the sun shining on the far end of the station, this view of the SLS Tour, the cover of the souvenir brochure for which is shown above right, is included because it shows the southern end of the loop with its catch point and also just how close the Up platform was to the river, with the wooden waiting shelter supported on stilts and jutting out over the riverside pathway. COLOUR-RAIL

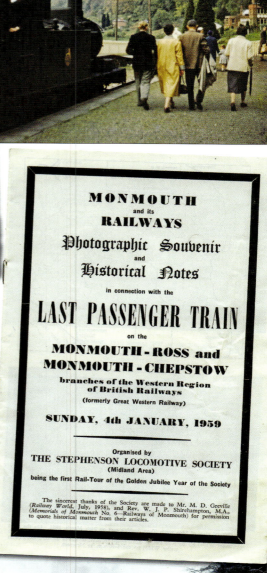

With nature taking over, the station is seen awaiting its final fate in the summer of 1961. The buildings were eventually demolished and the site is now a car park for visitors who all arrive by road but the platform edges can still be made out in its surface. There may have been a handful of stations which were in equally beautiful situations but there were none that bettered Symond's Yat. Many years ago, a signalman who began his career here told me that they nearly always won the station garden competitions, because the judges were always bowled over by the location. PETER BARNFIELD

The station as viewed from across the River Wye in 1961. It was perfectly situated for the area it served but unfortunately seasonal tourist traffic was not enough to sustain the line's finances. It would have made for a stunning preserved railway though. MICHAEL HALE

Although a county town, Monmouth is relatively small even today, so it did well to boast two stations during the decades it was served by the railway. May Hill, on the line from Ross, was the slightly better situated station for the town, being just across the Wye Bridge, which was adjacent to the road bridge which the railway passed under just off picture to the left. However, it was also much the smaller station, with a single platform for trains and no goods yard, although there were sidings serving the Monmouth Steam Saw Mills and Monmouth Gas Works, both just off to the right of this view; the latter had closed just before the Second World War but a military storage depot was then opened a little further up the line during the war. The line skirted the eastern bank of the Wye for some distance on its journey from here towards Symond's Yat and a mile and a half from here – at the base of the hill above the nearest trailer and to the right of the trees – was the short lived Hadnock Halt. This opened as late as 7th May 1951 and closed with the line, representing something of a half-hearted attempt to serve the tourist market – those who wanted to walk by the river mainly, as there was no community nearby to serve. May Hill station was quite well used as a result of its situation and is seen here in 1958 with a Ross to Monmouth auto at the platform, strengthened to two trailers, so perhaps a Saturday service. Note the local staff's vegetable patch in the foreground. DEREK CHAPLIN

The line from Ross to Monmouth May Hill opened on 4th August 1873 with, for the first nine months or so of its life, the station acting as a terminus. In May 1874, the bowstring girder bridge across the River Wye was completed and the branch was then able to run in to Monmouth Troy station. The station at May Hill was originally built as a temporary facility but, after a trial period when it continued to be well patronised, it was decided to keep it open permanently after a petition by local townsfolk. The original wooden buildings, seen here on 17th April 1960, were therefore still in remarkably well kept condition despite being nearly eighty-six years old and having been out of use for over fifteen months. The signal box, however, was slightly younger, dating from 1905 when it was erected to replace an earlier cabin sited on the platform. There had been a goods loop here, on the right, which was purely for shunting; trains were never crossed here and this end of the loop was removed in 1953, leaving only a connection at the north end into the saw mills. Although there were no public goods facilities here as such, it is thought that the wooden building at the far end of the platform was used for small goods and parcels, again being more handily sited for the town than the goods yard at Troy. MICHAEL HALE

LEFT: In the summer of 1961, the Birmingham Locomotive Club organised a brake van trip with the Wye Valley goods. Only a small party of photographers travelled with it, which required just one extra 'Toad' brake van to be attached to the train. By great good fortune, through a friend at university in Birmingham, Peter Barnfield also managed to get on board for the trip, the party joining the train at May Hill station. Peter could not find his notes for this trip, which is why the date is a little hazy, whilst the '57XX' pannier tank, here seen at the northern limit of operations, is also sadly unidentified. He does recall W. 'Cam' Camwell being on the trip, however. PETER BARNFIELD

ABOVE: Some twenty months after closure to passengers, the station buildings at May Hill were still in good condition. The attractive twin arch stone bridge seen in the background, which carried the A4136 road over the line, still stands and is all that remains here of the railway today, the rest of the site having been redeveloped. The saw mills has also gone but the industrial buildings on the right in the top photograph are still in use. PETER BARNFIELD

G.W.R.
Monmouth
MAY HILL

RIGHT: The pannier tank shunts the saw mills siding, via the connection which was retained at the north end of the loop. PETER BARNFIELD

BELOW: This glorious view of the bowstring girder bridge carrying the Ross to Monmouth Branch over the River Wye between May Hill and Troy stations was taken from the SLS Special on 4th January 1959. The structure, sometimes referred to as the Duke of Beaufort Bridge, is 99 yards long in total, with a main span of 50 yards and was built by Edward Finch & Co. of Chepstow. Finch had been responsible for building Brunel's tubular bridge spanning the Wye at Chepstow between 1849 and 1851, and the yard he established there for ironworks fabrication was rented from the Duke of Beaufort. BILL POTTER/KRM

RIGHT: The bridge in 1976; it still stands today, now in use as a footbridge. In the background is the remains of the Wye Valley Railway viaduct. Although the stone arches were built to carry a double line of rails, the metalwork span was only ever wide enough for a single line and trains first traversed it in 1861 when the CMU&PR's line was extended to Wyesham. With twenty arches on the Monmouth side, plus a further two on the Chepstow side, all constructed of local red sandstone, the bridge, sometimes referred to as Chippenham Meadow Viaduct, was 200 yards in length. It was built by the line's contractor, Joseph Firbank, with the ironwork being supplied by Kennards of Crumlin, responsible for Crumlin Viaduct and, more locally, Lydbrook Viaduct. The girder span which gave about 50 foot of clearance over the river level, was scrapped circa 1967, leaving the stone arches. However, more recently, these have deteriorated to the extent that there are real fears they may be demolished, which would be a huge shame. DENNIS PARKHOUSE

LEFT: On an overcast day in late 1958, No. 1456 waits with its single auto coach to make the return run to Ross. The 0-4-2T spent much of its career working from Gloucester Horton Road shed, where it was allocated at the time of Nationalisation in 1948, and it was to be withdrawn from there just a few weeks after this photograph was taken, on 16th February 1959. BILL POTTER/KRM

RIGHT: The running in board at Monmouth Troy was so long it had been made originally in two parts and was mounted above some attractive but non-standard wooden fencing, believed to have been supplied by the contractor who built the CMU&PR. The stone-built Down platfrom waiting shelter was rather outshone by its canopy, which protected passengers right to the edge of the platform. On 28th May 1958, a two-coach Wye Valley train stands alongside a single coach service from Ross. Prior to the summer of 1955, when the passenger service to South Wales was withdrawn, Monmouth Troy enjoyed occasional intense periods of activity when the three trains from Ross, Chepstow and Pontypool Road all met. After this, Ross and Chepstow trains still connected here, so that passengers could generally make the journey between Ross and Chepstow without having to wait too long. T.B. OWEN

LEFT: Despite careful study of the picture, the reason for this manouvre is not clear. Taken a little later on the same day, the Ross auto is seen crossing over from the Up to the Down platform, which will involve shunting almost right back into the tunnel, although it will eventually, as we shall see, depart from the Up platform. Ross trains generally arrived in the Down platform and departed from the Up. The driver is operating the controls at the front of the trailer, whilst the fireman carries out his duties on the footplate and the guard can be seen through one of the windows of No. W237W sat down taking a break. The route down the Wye Valley, which we shall embark on in a few pages time, can be made out in the right distance. T.B. OWEN

Following on from the two pictures on the previous page, a short while later '14XX' No. 1455 and auto trailer depart once again for Ross-on-Wye, via the Up line. Although not as handily placed for the town as May Hill, Troy station was in a glorious setting as this view well illustrates. What this view also shows is that the two viaducts spanning the Wye were at different heights, with the line to Ross dropping away to the left as it heads for the Duke of Beaufort Bridge, whilst the line to Chepstow, having branched right, is on a climb as it approaches the stone arches leading to the spans over the river. Note also the rather unusual arrangement of the goods yard sidings, which all fan out from the one access road off the Ross line. The yard could not therefore be directly accessed by Wye Valley goods trains and it may have been because of this that, by the 1950s, branch freights from Chepstow often worked only as far as Redbrook. The engine of a goods working arriving from Chepstow had to run round its train in the platforms using the crossover and the connection seen in the distance here by the PW hut and then draw it clear of the loop towards Ross, so as to access the yard connection. Shorter trains could also be run round in the tunnel, where there was a second crossover. T.B. OWEN

An undated overall view of the station but seemingly when the passenger service was still in operation, so prior to early January 1959. The handsome stone buildings seen here were not original, dating from the later Victorian era when the station was substantially improved, which included the provision of refreshment rooms which were housed in the building towards the far end of the Up platform. The station also boasted a covered footbridge but this seems to have been removed after the cessation of the Pontypool Road passenger service in 1955. The yard looks busy, with plenty of wagons on view and in the background, the line to Ross can be seen curving away across the Duke of Beaufort Bridge. In the left distance are the playing fields of Monmouth Grammar School. After complete closure of the station in 1965, it lay derelict for many years, although the goods yard remained in industrial use. In the late 1980s, the station building was bought and dismantled stone by stone by the Gloucestershire Warwickshire Railway, who subsequently re-erected it at Winchcombe, where it now serves once again as a station, mid way on the line between Broadway and Cheltenham Racecourse. JOHN TARRANT/KRM

LEFT: No. 1455 at Monmouth Troy with a two-coach train for Ross on 3rd January 1959. This was another of the '14XX' Class which seems to have spent much of its life in the area. Built at Swindon in the summer of 1935, it was allocated to Hereford at the time of Nationalisation in 1948 and was withdrawn from Gloucester on 6th May 1964. The refreshment rooms to the right of the engine, whilst constructed in the same style as the station building, was never provided with a canopy. Oddly, whilst the Up Inner Homes splitting bracket signal was renewed in 1955, no signal ladder was provided hence the makeshift arrangement shown here. COLOUR-RAIL

ABOVE: A short while later, No. 1455 heads off down the line to May Hill and ultimately to Ross. The rear Trailer coach is an interesting vehicle, one of four Suburban Brake Thirds with a driver's compartment in the van end, built in 1938 to Lot No. 1600 and numbered 1668-1671 by the GWR. As Trailer cars, their Diagram was A.34. Note the two different shades of red in which the coaches are finished, even allowing for some weathering on the leading vehicle. COLOUR RAIL

RIGHT: This study of the SLS Special at Monmouth Troy on 4th January 1959 is included for the detail of the goods yard and shed in the right background. There was one through road for goods wagons, on the left side of the shed in this view, whilst on the right an awning protected road vehicles from the worst of the weather when loading or unloading. The road entrance to the station lay behind the shed. BILL POTTER/KRM

Monnow Street, Monmouth in 1970, slightly later than the period of the views of the town's railway station within these pages but with a fine mix of 1960s cars on show, and the shops and signs probably having changed little over the decade since 1960. I used to own one of those Cortinas – it was my very first car. DEREK KNIGHT

On the same day, with the dreaded double yellow lines now a feature of modern life, this is Monmouth's most celebrated monument, the Monnow Bridge. It is the only remaining mediaeval fortified river bridge in Great Britain still with its gate tower, although this was added some years after. The bridge may date from 1272 but is certainly late 13th century and replaced an earlier wooden bridge. The tower was added some 20 or 30 years later. Its defensive qualities are questionable, because the river is here quite shallow but it was most useful for collecting tolls. The bridge is built of local red sandstone and has three arches. In 1923, it was scheduled as an Ancient Monument and it has also since been granted Grade I listed status. The increasing demands of 20th century road traffic through the town and especially on this severely hump-backed bridge, lead to calls for the construction of a new bridge, which only came to pass when the new A40 dual carriageway by-passing Monmouth to the east – between the town and the River Wye – was built. This also had an impact on Monmouth's railway history, because the new road obliterated much of the track bed of the old line to Pontypool Road, between Troy Tunnel and Usk but it did take all the heavy traffic away from the town centre. More recently still, in 2004, a new road bridge for the town was opened, situated to the right of the Monnow Bridge as seen here, which means the latter is now pedestrians only. However, the old cattle market, part of which features in the right background, had to be demolished to make way for it. DEREK KNIGHT

SECTION 7
MONMOUTH to PONTYPOOL ROAD

The industrial revolution in South Wales had seen much of Monmouthshire to the west of Pontypool grow and develop in importance. As a result, the county town of Monmouth, situated hard on the eastern boundary, was left in a rather isolated position but its status, nevertheless, ensured that it attracted the attention of Victorian railway promoters. We have already explored the route of the Ross & Monmouth Railway and will soon be travelling down to Chepstow but first we will stretch the boundaries of west Gloucestershire again

The Pontypool Road to Monmouth Troy Branch, as shown on a Bartholomew's 1961 edition half inch series map. Passenger services had been withdrawn by this date, although the intermediate stations – Glascoed Halt, Usk, Llandenny, Raglan and Dingestow – are still marked, whilst goods trains still ran as far as Usk. As was the case with such establishments, ROF Glascoed is not shown, nor are the intermediate halts at Cefntilla, Elms Bridge and Raglan Road Crossing. The very rural and sparsely populated nature of the countryside traversed is clear.

by tracing a line which not only started outside the county but then proceeded to travel even further off in the opposite direction. However, it would seem slightly perverse, in railway terms, not to also document the third line which served Monmouth, particularly as colour views of the branch to Pontypool Road are so few and far between in any case.

In point of fact, Monmouth's very first railway was the aptly named Monmouth Railway a 3ft 6in. gauge horse-drawn plateway, authorised in 1810 and opened in 1812. Running from deep in the Forest of Dean to Coleford and Monmouth, it was built to carry coal. The Coleford, Monmouth, Usk & Pontypool Railway was authorised on 20th August 1853 and was promoted with the intention of transporting Forest of Dean iron ore and timber to the hungry furnaces and mines of South Wales. It had grown out of an earlier scheme, the Dean Forest, Monmouth, Usk & Pontypool Railway, which was intended to link up with the South Wales main line near Blakeney but which had been modified in the face of opposition from the Severn & Wye Railway. Truncated back to Coleford, the name was changed as a result and the Monmouth Railway was purchased to use as a basis for the section into the Forest of Dean.

Initially, all went well, with 4¼ miles of single line railway opening from Little Mill Junction,

north of Pontypool Road, to Usk on 2nd June 1856. Sixteen months later, a further 12 miles were completed to Monmouth Troy and this section was opened on 12th October 1857. However, with little traffic available along the route, the company was now struggling to reach its destination at Coleford. The next major obstacle, the crossing of the River Wye east of Monmouth was achieved with the completion of the viaduct in February 1861 but thn money ran out. The line was built as far as Wyesham, to an interchange wharf with the tramroad but the money to improve this enough to allow locomotive working could not be found and the ambitions of the CMU&PR finally petered out. On 1st July 1861, the branch as it stood was leased to the West Midland Railway, a company which owned a sprawling collection

At Troy station, enthusiasts gather to study a display of photographs and memorabilia about the line as the SLS Usk-Monmouth Centenary special awaits departure on 12th October 1957. This was the natural viewpoint from which to photograph the station but spoilt by the telegraph wires running right across in the foreground. Pontypool Road's '57XX' Class 0-6-0PT No. 4668 was in charge of the train. The engine was later transferred to Llanelly shed and was withdrawn on 21st July 1965. MICHAEL HALE

LEFT: A slightly different angle for this second view of the SLS Special at Troy, with a two-coach auto train alongside probably from Ross. The special had started from Pontypool Road, so was actually waiting to make the return journey and, in so doing, became the very last train to depart westwards through the tunnel from Monmouth Troy. DEREK CHAPLIN

BELOW LEFT: Just over two years later but in a recreation of earlier times, the SLS Last Train Special of 4th January 1959 ran a short distance through the tunnel so that the photographers on board could capture this shot of it framed by the western portal. Note that the train has begun to reverse back through. DEREK CHAPLIN

BOTTOM: There was a small yard at this end of the tunnel, the track on the right in fact being a siding, where timber had been loaded when the line was operational (see GWR Rates Notice below) by means of this 10-ton capacity crane. The crane was normally kept padlocked and also electrically locked out of use and could only be unlocked from Troy signal box. It had its own ground frame with telephone connection to the signalman and due to its proximity to the running line, the lever in the box which unlocked it also locked the running line out of use whilst the crane was operational. Seen here in 1961, it may have been used to unload the agricultural machinery alongside it. PETER BARNFIELD

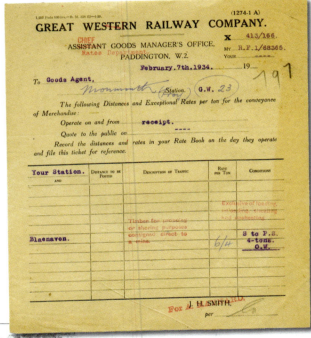

of disparate lines, which had little intention of expending money on extending the route from Wyesham to Coleford. This last section was finally completed over twenty years later by another company, the Coleford Railway, opening on 1st September 1883, by which time the local railway scene had changed considerably.

The West Midland Railway was absorbed by the GWR on 1st August 1863 and with the opening of the Ross & Monmouth Railway in 1873, the line was operated as a through route between Pontypool Road and Ross. Thereafter, it settled down to an uneventful existence, with a service of six trains a day each way for many years through the GWR era, supplemented by a number of extra trains between Pontypool Road and Usk, along with a couple of daily goods trains. After the Second World War, plans were published in the Forest of Dean for three large new industrial estates, one of which was to be at Coleford. To serve the latter, the line from Coleford to Wyesham, which had closed during the First World War was to be resurrected and become part of a major new rail artery to South Wales via Monmouth and Usk, echoing the unrealised ambitions of the CMU&PR over eighty years (*Continued on page 248*)

Right: The first station west of Monmouth was Dingestow (now converted to a private residence), of which no colour view has been found, so we move on to the next stop at Raglan. Looking towards Monmouth, the guard of the 1957 SLS Special chats to the footplate crew of No. 6417 during the stop here. The A449 dual carriageway now runs to the right. DEREK CHAPLIN

Below: An overall view of the disused station looking west on 26th May 1958, showing the main building, pagoda style corrugated iron goods lock-up and cattle dock. The loop here was for shunting purposes; there was no signal box and trains did not cross. After the track had been lifted, the station site became a council depot and the main building was retained, being visible from the main road still in remarkable condition. In recent years, it once again fell out of use and Monmouthshire CC offered it to the Museum of Welsh Life at St. Fagans. In late 2012, work began on dismantling it, so it could be moved and re-erected at its new home. Whilst it is sad to see the building leave its original location, its future is now assured. MICHAEL HALE

There were two tiny halts either side of Raglan, Elms Bridge to the east, opened on 27th November 1933, and Raglan Road Crossing to the west, which had opened on 24th November 1930. Both comprised short wooden platforms which were apparently not provided with shelters. The next station west was Llandenny, which had a red brick main building that had been extended at some stage and a small signal cabin controlling the level crossing. A goods loop with cattle dock was situated just the other side of the crossing to the right, whilst a siding branched off on the opposite side of the line and ran across the road, before splitting in two in the small goods yard behind the station building. Photographed again on 26th May 1958 and looking north east, the section of line between here and Raglan was used for wagon storage after 1957. This section of trackbed was paralleled by the new dual carriageway (which from Raglan is the A449, as the A40 heads away to Abergavenny), rather than obliterated by it, and the remains of the station building, signal cabin and platform could be seen from the road for many years afterwards. Apparently in use by a local farmer and standing in the middle of what had become a field, they have now gone. MICHAEL HALE

The shortest lived of any of the halts on the line was Cefntilla, opened on 14th June 1954. With the line closing officially twelve months later to the day but the last trains running two weeks earlier because of the national rail strike, its period of use was just 50 weeks. Seen here on 26th May 1958, it was similar in appearance to halts later opened on lines such as the branches from Kemble to Tetbury and Cirencester, being designed for railcar use. A single oil lamp in a traditional lantern provided lighting after dark, whilst the platform was too small for the nameboard which was instead positioned on the bank behind. There was no village by the name of Cefntilla but the halt, which was promoted by Lord Raglan, attracted good patronage from nearby hamlets during its short life, although not sufficient to save the line from closure. MICHAEL HALE

LEFT: The SLS Usk-Monmouth Centenary Special seen entering Usk station on 4th October 1957, on the outward journey. The two-coach train comprised an ex-GWR 'B' Set, although with the carriages in contrasting liveries. Just visible above the train is the roof of the signal box, which had a wooden upper section on a brick base, and there was a cast iron water tank on stilts positioned opposite. On the left, the green liveried DMU parked on the bridge carrying the line across the River Usk was freshly allocated to Cardiff Canton but not yet in service, the line to Usk being used for driver training on these new trains. DEREK CHAPLIN

ABOVE: Usk station, seen here looking to Monmouth on 26th May 1958 through the 256 yards long Usk Tunnel, was beautifully sited and with attractive red and blue brick buildings. The distinctive nameboards were also still in place, decorative wooden posts holding enamelled signs with dark blue letters on a white background. Whilst the buildings have all gone and the site is now heavily wooded, it has never been built on, so is still accessible. MICHAEL HALE

RIGHT: A member of a class of locomotive seen for the first time in these pages, 0-6-0PT No. 8461 shunts the goods yard at Usk on 18th April 1962. The '94XX' Class were a Hawksworth design introduced right at the end of the GWR in 1947 and No. 8461 was actually a BR era build, by the Yorkshire Engine Co. in June 1950. It had a short life, being withdrawn from Pontypool Road shed during the week ending 9th November 1963. The goods yard at Usk was across the river from the station, the embankment in the background leading onto the bridge. The bridge still stands and now carries a footpath, whilst the goods yard buildings survive in light industrial use. DEREK CHAPLIN

(*Continued from page 244*) earlier. However, with the country's finances devasted by the cost of fighting the war, the scheme came to nothing.

Following Nationalisation in 1948, under BR the passenger service dwindled further to just four trains a day each way and a single goods working from Pontypool Road to Monmouth Troy and back. In 1953, BR indicated that the section from Usk to Monmouth was likely to close but this provoked such a storm of protest that they agreed to a six month trial period with an enhanced train service. What ensued seems incredible now but this sleepy little country byway suddenly found itself with a new train service comprising eleven trains a day each way, with an extra each way working on Thursdays and Saturdays. Needless to say, passenger numbers rose dramatically to almost double what they had been. However, so did the running costs, with an extra railcar and crew now being required to maintain this intensity of service. Accordingly, BR took the decision that the line could never be made to pay and, following a TUCC inquiry in spring 1955, the line was slated for closure. There was much bitterness about this, as local people felt that BR had deliberately put on too many trains to inflate the costs. However, even if this was the case – and BR certainly developed a reputation over the following decade for nefarious accounting practices in regard to lines they wanted to close – with the benefit of hindsight nearly sixty years later, it looks a difficult decision to argue with.

In the end, the line went out with barely a whimper. The closure date was set for 13th June 1955 but an ASLEF-called national rail strike began on 28th May and ran through to 14th June. As a result, the final trains ran on Friday 27th May and there was to be no last train special or commemorations as there was for so many other lines. Pontypool Road to Usk was retained for goods but from there to Monmouth closed completely. A short section of track was lifted but otherwise the line was left derelict. Two years later, the Stephenson Locomotive Society contacted BR and asked if they could run a special over the line, to celebrate its centenary. Not only were they given an answer in the affirmative but BR also agreed to relay the short missing section (it was only a few yards). The train ran on 12th October 1957, after which Monmouth to Usk closed for good. Usk remained open for goods traffic until 1965, whilst the Royal Ordnance Factory at Glascoed, opened in 1938 near the western end of the line, ensured that a short section of it remained in use. However, although the factory remains today, now as BAE Systems Global Combat Systems Munitions, Glascoed, the railway does not, last section of the CMU&PR finally closing in 1993.

ABOVE: The establishment of the Royal Ordnance Factory meant that Glascoed became quite an important railway location, although the halt pre-dated it. This first opened on 16th May 1927 but was originally on the opposite side of the line. The new halt, opened on 22nd April 1938, was on the inside of the curve, which allowed room for a loop to be laid for trains accessing ROF Glascoed. The signal box was brought in to use on 21st August 1938, the line running in to the depot curving off to the right just beyond the signal. From 6th November 1940 to 24th April 1961, a separate line also ran into the depot to terminus platforms provided for the workforce. Alongside was a fan of transfer sidings, from which a line branched off to connect with the extensive railway system running round the depot. The halt is seen here on 8th August 1961, by which date goods trains to Usk were running via the loop, the running line being partially lifted. The signal box was still operational, closing on 25th June 1962. MICHAEL HALE

RIGHT: The SLS Usk-Monmouth Centenary Special waiting to depart from the bay platform at Pontypool Road on 4th October 1957. MICHAEL HALE

SECTION 8
MONMOUTH to CHEPSTOW
The WYE VALLEY LINE

The Wye Valley Railway Company was incorporated on 10th August 1866, with the intention of building a railway along the lower Wye Valley from the South Wales Railway's main line at Chepstow to Monmouth. In so doing, with the CMU&PR line already open and the Ross & Monmouth Railway having been authorised a year earlier, it would become the third railway to serve Monmouth. However, the collapse just a few weeks earlier in 1866 of the country's second largest bank, Overend & Gurney, meant that raising money to build the line was difficult. As a result, it was not until 1874 that work actually began on building it. The hiatus allowed time for the route to be modified, particularly at Tintern where the original plan was to take the line high above the village on the Welsh side of the river. However, although the new route was considerably easier, it now did not connect closely with Tintern or with its wireworks, the main local industry. Consequently, under pressure from local people, a branch was added crossing the river near the famous abbey and running up the valley to serve the wireworks. The re-sited Tintern station, meanwhile, was around half a mile outside of the Monmouth end of the village and a mile from the abbey, and was in fact closer to the tiny Wye port of Brockweir, albeit on the opposite side of the river.

Construction finally commenced in the late summer of 1874 and proceeded fairly straightforwardly, apart from a landslide near Redbrook in 1875, which blocked the partly built line. The railway was able to make use of the CMU&PR viaduct at Monmouth Troy and their alignment as far as Wyesham but south from there involved some major challenges. The Wye was bridged twice more, at Redbrook and Tintern, with a third bridge required for the Tintern Wireworks Branch. There were also tunnels at Tintern and Tidenham. The engineers announced that the Wireworks Branch was ready in August 1875 but it was not until October 1876 that the whole line was finished and the opening

RIGHT: *The Wye Valley Railway from Monmouth Troy to Chepstow, as shown on the Bartholomew's 1961 edition half inch series map. The stations are all marked, although passenger services had been withdrawn.*

RIGHT: Auto-fitted No. 6409 waits to leave with a Wye Valley train for Chepstow and Severn Tunnel Junction on 5th October 1957. The Ross auto can be seen in the tunnel entrance in the left background. BILL POTTER/KRM

BELOW RIGHT: Classmate No. 6439, in smart lined green passenger livery, on a similar working in the summer of 1958. Just glimpsed in the far right background is the mouth of the part constructed tunnel which heralded the start of the Monnow Valley Railway. This little known concern was promoted by the contractor Thomas Savin in the 1860s to link Monmouth with Pontrilas on the Newport to Hereford main line. It got no further than the construction of this very short tunnel in 1866, at which point Savin went bankrupt and work ceased, never to be restarted. It was used as a store by the railway or sometimes as a garage for the local deliveries lorry and still survives today, although now in the back garden of a newly built house. DEREK CHAPLIN

date was set for 1st November. The inaugural train, loaded with delegates and sketched for posterity by an artist working for the *Illustrated London News*, travelled from Chepstow to Monmouth and back, with a stop at Tintern so that the worthies on board could take lunch with the Duke of Beaufort. The only dampener was that the wireworks had gone out of business in the interim, although it did eventually reopen.

The initial passenger service comprised four trians a day each way, whilst significant goods traffic – why the line had originally been promoted – was expected from Redbrook Tinplate Works, Whitebrook Paper Mills, Tintern Wireworks and quarries near Tintern. Much of the anticipated goods traffic failed to materialise, with the exception of the tinplate works at Redbrook and stone from the quarries near Tintern and Tidenham, the latter ultimately being responsible for the survival of the southern end of the line many years after the rest of the branch had closed. Intermediate stations were provided at Tidenham, Tintern, St. Briavels and Redbrook, with halts later being added at Netherhope, Brockweir, Llandogo, Whitebrook, Penallt and Wyesham. Surprisingly, perhaps, given the impecunious nature of the concern, the WVR remained independent until 1905, when the GWR finally purchased the Company on 1st July.

The line had never made a profit and this situation did not change under the GWR. Little effort was made to promote it to tourists and the basic service of four or five trains a day each way remained until the end, even with the introduction of diesel railcars to the route. The Wireworks Branch, a thorn in the side of the WVR who had been forced to operate it at their own expense – they could only charge for use of the weighbridge – finally closed in 1935, the rails being taken up in 1940. The auto trains serving the Wye Valley generally started from a short terminus bay at Severn Tunnel Junction station, although a bay platform had also been provided at Chepstow. However, these trains could also serve the intermediate halts and small stations south of Chepstow, allowing some main line services to miss out these calls. Closure proposals for the passenger service first surfaced in the early 1950s and once the CMU&PR line had gone, it was clear that the writing was on the wall for Monmouth's other two branches. Despite the GWR having placed a Camp Coach at Tintern from 1937, which reappeared after the war and was continued by BR, the tourist potential of both routes was never properly exploited and the passenger service was withdrawn on the same day as the Ross-Monmouth line.

Goods traffic continued for another five years to Monmouth Troy but that too finally succumbed on 4th January 1964, with the line north of Tintern Quarry being closed completely. Traffic from the quarry continued until it too closed in 1981. Meanwhile, Tidenham station had been turned into a stone loading site for Dayhouse Quarry in 1968 and this now became the limit of operations, just a half mile up the branch from Wye Valley Junction. The last train to here ran in September 1992, when the quarry closed and has since been re-established as the National Diving Centre. Although the junction with the main line has been taken out, the heavily overgrown rails still remain in situ all the way to the disused Tintern Quarry and there are periodic calls for the reopening of the line, at least as far as Tintern, to carry tourists. Despite the poor state of the main road along the valley, which is often affected by rock falls and which climbs, twists and turns its way along much of the route, there seems little enthusiasm locally for such a line, with many being vehemently opposed to the idea of trains running past again. Significantly, even a recent Sustrans proposal to reopen much of the route as a cycle path foundered against the rock of similar opposition and so, for the time being at least, there is little chance of trains ever running along even a short section of this highly picturesque valley ever again. The station at Tintern survives today, operated as a tourist site by Monmouthshire County Council, whilst St. Briavels station site is privately owned by a local angling club.

Lots of human interest in this view on 28th May 1958; whilst the driver calls over to the signalman as he waits for the tanks of auto-fitted Class '64XX' No. 6431 to fill up, the fireman uses the pet pipe to wash out his tea cup. There were water columns on both platforms, served by the cast iron tower on the right. The starting signal is off but it will be a few minutes yet before the crew are ready to set off on their journey over the viaduct in the background to Chepstow. T.B. OWEN

This auto trailer was photographed in the yard at Monmouth Troy on a siding alongside the goods shed in 1963. Numbered W118W, it was a vehicle of considerable historic rarity, which had begun life as one of the GWR's steam railmotors, No. 22, built at Swindon in July 1904 to Diagram G, one of the earlier type with matchboard sides. It was withdrawn from service in February 1920 but was immediately converted to an auto trailer, to Trailer Diagram A9, 49ft 8ins in length and with seating for 62 passengers. Conversion entailed removal of the steam powered engine unit and its replacement with a coach bogie and additional seating. Renumbered W118W by BR, it was also repainted with the red/brown livery seen here. Where this vehicle worked on the system is not known but it was eventually condemned in November 1957, being the last of the trailers converted from steam railmotors to go. However, it was not scrapped and it next resurfaces in official records in June 1961, when it was recorded as being renumbered into internal use service stock as DW079044 and made into a classroom stationed at Monmouth. These details are taken from *Great Western Auto Trailers, Part One: The Pre-Grouping Vehicles* by John Lewis (Wild Swan 1991) and in the text John speculates that W118W had been at Monmouth since being condemned. This may mean that its final duties were on the Wye Valley branches. It would be interesting to know what was taught in the coach, as it seems an odd place to site such a facility. This second career was relatively short-lived, with the trailer finally being condemned in March 1963 and sold in February 1964 to Birds of Morriston for breaking up; '*Cond*' can be seen painted on the side at the far end. The goods shed, after surviving mostly in commercial use for nearly another three decades, was demolished in 2002 so that the site could be used for housing. DEREK CHAPLIN

The only member of the '74XX' Class to feature within these pages, No. 7437 is seen shunting wagons in Troy yard in typical British summertime weather in 1963, as the sun makes a weak attempt to drive away the clouds after a burst of rain. The '74XX' Class were a development of the '64XX' but without the control apparatus for auto working. No. 7437 was built at Swindon in September 1948, so was actually a BR engine. Its first shed was Worcester but it was based at Severn Tunnel Junction at the time of this photograph and was withdrawn from Llanelly shed during the week ending 13th March 1965. With the construction of the small Troy Gardens housing development on part of the station site from 2002, all remaining railway structures were demolished, with the sole exception of the little brick yard hut just glimpsed behind No. 7437. Roofless and unloved, it stands hidden amongst bushes. NPC

Troy station awaits its fate in late 1963, although there are still wagons in the yard and a crimson & cream parcels lorry by the main building. The polish on the rails indicates the lines that were still in use, with the Up line heading on to the viaduct appearing very rusty. The signal box had closed on 27th March 1960, officially being replaced by a new ground frame, although in reality this meant reducing the box to ground frame status and removing all the signal arms. Those levers not required were locked out of use, hence the simplified layout operationally. In the distance, the single line width of the metal span of the viaduct, as compared to the wider approach arches, is noticeable, whilst in the foreground note the decorative tiles on both platforms beneath the awnings. In the background, the Kymin rises to 800 feet, providing a viewpoint over Monmouth and into Wales. A local gentlemen's dining club built the famous Round House up here in 1794, where Lord Nelson and Lady Hamilton once took breakfast in 1802. It is today a National Trust property. NPC

After completing the shunting at May Hill, the 1961 BLC brake van trip made its way round to Troy station, where a photographic stop was made. The signal box dated from 1916 and housed a 38 lever frame. Goods traffic was still quite healthy at this date, with a large number of new agricultural machines freshly delivered in the goods yard. Perhaps the 8-wheeled flatbed lorry on the road above the tunnel mouth is on its way down to carry some of them to their final destination. Incidentally, the Birmingham Locomotive Club later changed its name to the Industrial Locomotive Society. PETER BARNFIELD

Looking from under the canopy of the Down platform waiting shelter, the closed Refreshments building still carried its nameboard. PETER BARNFIELD

G. W. R.

Monmouth (TROY)

ABOVE: Troy station on 9th May 1964, after final closure. ALAN JARVIS

RIGHT: Just a couple of months after the view above, the sun shines down on a sad scene, with the demolition men part way through their task. Slightly bizarrely, having partly pulled the water tower down, the legs have parted company with the tank which is still being held up by the water pipe. DAVID BICK/NPC

BELOW: The station and SLC brake van tour seen from just inside the tunnel, showing the water column on the end of the Down platform. Note also the telephone box on the wall on the left, which connected to the signal box and is believed to have been for the use of train crew when using the crossover just inside the tunnel, the rodding for which can just be made out. PETER BARNFIELD

MONMOUTH to CHEPSTOW: The WYE VALLEY LINE

This looks like something of a chance shot, no doubt the photographers having chased the train up the Wye Valley in their Morris Minor and then making a quick stop on the A466 coming in to Monmouth to just catch the train as it pulls away from Wyesham Halt. Opened on 12th January 1931, the halt comprised a short wooden platform with a corrugated iron hut as a waiting shelter. There is a PW hut at the end of the platform but the purpose of the larger hut on the other side of the bridge is unknown, with no mention of it being found elsewhere; was it the lamp hut perhaps? The signal was the Monmouth Troy Outer Home, which had to be situated at least 440 yards away from the points and allowed the Troy signalman to accept a train from Chepstow under line clear, when he also had a train approaching from May Hill. Not only does this picture record the halt in colour for posterity, it also shows the bridge spanning the road which is also now just a memory, the road having since been widened at this point. The embankment on the left remains but the site of the halt and much of the trackbed on the right for about 500 yards has been built on. The white house seen through the bridge was Wyesham Toll House, which collected the tolls at this end of the Monouth to Chepstow turnpike road. Opened in 1829 by the Monmouth Turnpike Trust, the road provided the first full length access to the Wye Valley but, regrettably, the toll house has also been demolished since this photograph was taken, a modern bungalow now occupying the site. DEREK CHAPLIN

As this wonderful view shows, Redbrook station's situation was every bit as picturesque as that of Symond's Yat but without the cachet of the former, which drew tourists to take the Wye Valley Tour from the beginning of the 18th century, long before the coming of the railway. This may in large part be due to Redbrook's industrial pre-eminence, with the first copper smelting works in Britain having been established here on the banks of the Wye in 1690. By the 19th century, this had become a tinplate works, although this was closed at the time the railway was built, only re-opening several years afterwards but which was still open at the date of this picture in November 1958; it did not finally close, in fact, until 1961. Redbrook Signal Box dated from the opening of the Wye Valley Railway, the signalling and cabins for the line being provided by McKenzie & Holland of Worcester. However, it was reduced to ground frame status on 11th January 1927, which meant it had no regular signalman but was opened for use as required. It is thought that the box may have been equipped with a 10 lever frame. The goods yard, behind the photographer, had a small stone-built goods shed on a loop siding, another siding and a 5-ton capacity yard crane. DEREK CHAPLIN

ABOVE: Two views of the SLS Special at Redbrook on 4th January 1959, both taken on the outward run. The picture top left, which is looking towards Monmouth, also shows the red sandstone-built goods shed, which was very similar to the ones provided at Tintern and Bigsweir. The view above is looking back towards Chepstow. DEREK CHAPLIN; COLOUR RAIL

LEFT: The view from the train as it crossed over the A466, looking up the river towards Monmouth. Since the closure of the line, the landscape of this part of Redbrook has been considerably altered, with the station site, embankment and road bridge all obliterated to allow for realignment of the road and other developments. Coupled with tree growth, this view of the river is therefore no longer possible. BILL POTTER/KRM

LEFT: A similar view but from slightly further back down the line, taken from the SLS Special just after it had crossed the river bridge and was standing in the station. The mid point of the river just here forms the boundary between England and Wales but around 100 yards further on, the boundary turns right, following the B4231 road to Newland up the hill. The station, therefore, was just in England. The hut near the river was within the railway's boundary but its purpose is not known. The treeline in the centre distance marks the course of the line towards Monmouth, with the route of the old line to Coleford from Wyesham Junction, closed in 1917, just about discernible around 50 yards further up the hillside as it rounds the promontory. This then curved to the right towards the Forest of Dean, passing through Redbrook Tunnel, cut through the solid limestone of the hill above the train. COLOUR RAIL

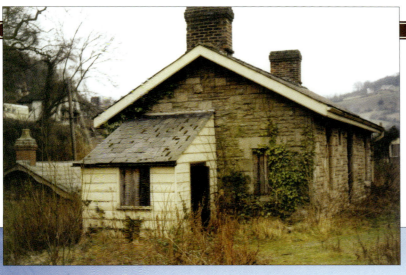

LEFT AND BOTTOM: Two views of Redbrook station building in 1967, which provide useful detail for modellers. Again built of local red sandstone, it was similar to the other original Wye Valley Railway Company stations at Tidenham, Tintern and Bigsweir. As can be seen, however, Redbrook had gained wooden lean-to extensions at either end. When the station opened, it was named simply Redbrook but, from 1933, the GWR renamed it Redbrook on Wye, perhaps in a half-hearted attempt to attract tourists, with new station nameboards being provided. IAN POPE COLLECTION

ABOVE: The demolition men at work at Redbrook in the summer of 1964, just a few months after the final goods services to Monmouth had ceased, the line having closed completely north of Tintern Quarry on 6th January. The rails are being cut into short lengths to aid removal and the remains of the rail built buffer stop at the end of the short headshunt can be seen on the right. The tinplate works had provided the bulk of rail-borne traffic here in the late 19th and early 20th centuries, with deliveries of coal coming inwards, much of it from pits in the Forest of Dean, and sheets of tinplate being shipped outwards. A siding was originally provided into the works, running back from the yard, through a gate and then on a low embankment to cross the Chepstow to Monmouth road. However, this seems to have been lifted just after the First World War and goods traffic dwindled considerably as a result. Electric Train Staff working, coupled with the use of tablets had been introduced in 1907 to allow Redbrook and Tidenham signal boxes to be switched out when not required. With the reduction in goods traffic, from 1925, the box was opened daily as required, being reduced to ground frame status two years later, the block section then becoming Bigsweir to Monmouth Troy. The nameboard on the front of the box indicates its ground frame status. DAVID BICK/NPC

RIGHT: The shell of Redbrook North Ground Frame in 1967. As the name indicates, there was also a Redbrook South Ground Frame at the other end of the yard – beyond the goods shed in the right background – which was provided in 1927 when the box was reduced in status. The station site was cleared completely a year or so after these photographs were taken. Incidentally, whilst most of the images in this volume are from colour slides, these three views of Redbrook in 1967 exist only as colour prints. IAN POPE COLLECTION

ABOVE AND LEFT: Whilst I have so far kept to the mid-1970s cut-off date for the pictures within these pages, that rule is being broken here to illustrate the viaduct spanning the River Wye at Redbrook, taken on 25th July 1989. Built on a gentle curve, it comprises five plate-girder spans supported on four pairs of cylindrical cast iron columns filled with concrete. On the left (Welsh) bank of the river is the Boat Inn, the roof of which can just be seen above the railway embankment. It has long been a popular hostelry which, when the railway was open, recived its barrels of beer by rail. The GWR gave a special dispensation for trains to stop just before the viaduct so that the beer could be unloaded virtually straight into the inn. From 1st August 1931, a new halt was opened just a little further along the line to the left and the beer barrels were subsequently unloaded on the platform here. Named Penallt Halt, it was almost identical in appearance to Wyesham Halt. In 1955, a walkway was added to the viaduct for the benefit of pedestrians who had presumably just walked along the rails previously. Seen here in the picture on the left, it consisted of sections of pre-cast concrete decking, with concrete posts supporting wire fencing. The footbridge is today part of the Wye Valley Trail. BILL POTTER/KRM

RIGHT: This view from the Welsh bank of the River Wye was taken in 1965. Looking through one of the spans of the viaduct, it shows the site of Redbrook Tinplate Works, closed four years earlier, with the gable ends of a couple of the then remaining buildings visible in the background. Today, the site is covered by the Tinman's Green housing estate. In the foreground, on the river bank, is the old stone warehouse used by the works originally to store the tinplate until it could be shipped down the Wye, prior to the coming of the railway. Believed to be at least 200 years old, this historic building was taken down in 1999 to make way for the Millenium Green and is currently in store awaiting re-erection somewhere else. NPC

ABOVE: Redbrook viaduct in 1985. DENNIS PARKHOUSE

LEFT: A brief glimpse of Monmouth's first railway, this is Redbrook Incline bridge on the Monmouth Tramroad in 1965. This horse-drawn plateway, which ran from various industrial concerns in the Forest of Dean near Milkwall and Broadwell, through Coleford, down the Newland Valley to Redbrook and then along the Wye to Monmouth, opened to traffic on 17th August 1812. The main line of the tramroad ran around the top of the hill seen behind the viaduct in the view above (the later Coleford Railway cut off the corner by tunnelling through), with Redbrook being served by a line which branched off at the apex of the bend. This ran down a steep, rope-worked, twin track, self-acting incline, over the bridge shown in this picture, to serve the Wye Valley Cornmills, Upper Redbrook Tinplate Works and Redbrook Brewery just below the arch, and then running on to the larger Lower Redbrook Tinplate Works. The Monmouth Tramroad had largely fallen out of use by the 1870s, when the Coleford Railway was being proposed. The incline bridge is today Grade II* listed. DAVID BICK/NPC

RIGHT: A view from one of the brake vans on the summer 1961 trip, looking down river shortly after leaving Redbrook. The train has just passed Penallt Halt, which was on the other side of the line, facing the river. The scattered community of Penallt which it purported to serve was actually situated nearly a mile away, up on top of the hills on the Welsh side of the valley. Whilst neither the will nor the means seems to exist to re-open the line, despite continued interest in the idea from certain quarters, this view well illustrates what has been lost – the chance to enjoy the unspoilt beauty of the Wye Valley from the comfort of a railway carriage. PETER BARNFIELD

LEFT: A beautiful autumnal view up river from just above Bigsweir Bridge, looking towards Whitebrook, in 1964. The railway is on the far side of the field on the left and Whitebrook Halt, opened on 1st February 1927, was situated a few hundred yards along, just past where the river turns first left and then right. ANNE BEAUFOY

RIGHT: Bigsweir Bridge on 15th October 1937, looking up river. The photographer was standing on the river side of the railway and St. Briavels station is (sadly) just out of view on the left. The village it served lies a mile up a long steep climb to the right. This was among a batch of lantern slides acquired, mostly dated and obviously produced from colour film similar to the Dufaycolor slides featured elsewhere in these pages. The cast iron bridge was built in 1827 by the Monmouth Turnpike Trust, to the design of Charles Hollis and manufactured in Merthyr Tydfil. Now Grade II listed and with traffic crossing it controlled by traffic lights either end, a major programme of repair works to the bridge and repainting was completed by Gloucestershire CC in 2011. The toll house, which stands at the Welsh end of the bridge, has also been restored and the house seen here on the right of the picture still remains. NPC

A two-coach train for Monmouth pauses at St. Briavels station on 2nd January 1959 on what was to prove the penultimate day of regular passenger services on the branch. The signal box here, hidden by the open wagon, was retained to operate the level crossing over the A466 road, the gates of which can just be seen. Note that the goods yard was still busy, with a selection of open wagons in the siding on the right loaded with containers. The station was also the permanent way depot for the line, the inspection trolley and other equipment being housed in the huts in the left foreground. St. Briavels opened as Bigsweir but was then renamed St. Briavels & Llandogo (as shown on the GWR ticket, inset), the latter name being dropped in 1927 with the opening of Llandogo Halt. St. Briavels was the nearest community of any size but the village actually lies over a mile away at the top of hills to the right, on the edge of the Forest of Dean. The site is today privately owned by a fishing group, the Wye being popular with salmon fishermen and the station building survives in reasonable order. The goods shed, which was very similar to those at other stations on the line, also still stands but is in a parlous state. It is now a historic building which would benefit from some immediate attention. DEREK CHAPLIN

Post closure views are rarely as satisfying as pictures taken when the lines were still open but these two excellent studies of St. Briavels station – so rarely photographed in any case – could not be omitted. They were taken in late summer 1964, with the vegetation already growing wild and the rails heavily rusted, despite the goods service having only been withdrawn at the beginning of that year. Looking towards Monmouth, they provide good detail of the buildings here, including the signal box by the level crossing. Very sadly, since the previous caption was written for the first edition, the goods shed has been demolished. BOTH NPC

LEFT: Relics such as this abounded on the railway system in the 1960s but many were lost after lines were closed and the scrapmen descended. This Wye Valley Railway cast iron notice of 1876 would undoubtedly command a healthy sum at auction today, as an unusual and sought after piece of railwayana. It was photographed still in situ near Llandogo on 30th August 1960. Although shown upright here, it will be noted from the angle of the field behind that, in actuality, the post holding it was on rather a tilt! One of these signs survives in the Vintage Carriage Trust Museum at Ingrow station, on the Keighley & Worth Valley Railway. ALAN JARVIS

RIGHT AND BELOW: Two views of the afternoon goods train to Monmouth near Llandogo on 30th August 1960. Despite the presence of a second brake van, this is not believed to be another, earlier, photographers trip, although at least three gentlemen with cameras were positioned at this point. This is the only location at which pictures of this train have been seen, however, so perhaps it performed a special photographic stop. The chap standing by the engine, right, looks to be a railway official, whilst the gentleman bottom right below is believed to be the photographer R.C. Tuck, whose black and white shot of the train features in the Oakwood Press volume on the Wye Valley Railway. ALAN JARVIS; DEREK CHAPLIN

Another snapshot from the brake van of the summer 1961 BLC trip, as the train rattles through Llandogo. The valley is quite wide here and the village is spread across the crescent shaped hillside on the Welsh side of the river. Just ahead of the train is Llandogo Halt, which opened on 9th March 1927, saving villagers the one mile walk to St. Briavels station, which dropped the 'and Llandogo' suffix at the same time. Apart from the halt and despite its size, Llandogo had little to do with the railway, having been very much a river community. Several trows, the wooden flat bottomed sailing vessels of the Severn and Wye rivers, were built and worked from here, carrying bark to tanneries in Bristol, as well as timber, tinplate and other commodities, a trade which carried on until the early years of the 20th century. This trade is remembered in the names of two public houses, the Sloop Inn in Llandogo and the Llandoger Trow on the Welsh Back near the old docks in Bristol. The course of the railway and the site of the halt are still clearly distinguishable today. PETER BARNFIELD

LEFT: The village of Brockweir, looking across the River Wye towards the hills of the Forest of Dean, circa 1937. This is again a Dufaycolor slide from the visit to the Wye Valley by our unknown family heading from Hampshire to North Wales. Brockweir bridge was built in 1905-06 by Finch's of Chepstow and replaced a pedestrian ferry. Note the Royal Arms Hotel in the centre of the picture, selling Stroud Brewery Ales. NPC

RIGHT: The identical view but taken about thirty years later, in summer 1968. Brockweir was an important Wye port with wooden sailing trows trading from here until the early years of the 20th century, whilst the little steam barge *La Belle Marie* offered a fortnightly service across the Severn Estuary to Bristol up until just before the First World War, carrying market garden produce to sell and bringing back cargoes of coal and general goods. She was broken up at the quay here between the wars. In 1967, a Mr Barrett from Tintern began clearing the old quay of mud and silt, and the results of his efforts can be clearly seen in this picture, with the stones of the quay, then around 180 years old, exposed to view (as it still is today). The railway ran through an arch at this end of the bridge, which has been filled in since closure. Note that the Royal Arms Hotel had also closed and was now a private residence. NPC

LEFT: A circa 1965 picture postcard view of Brockweir, looking across the river from downstream of the bridge and showing the arch through which the railway ran. The support pillar visible in the centre of the span (there were probably two or three more) suggests that this view was taken after the railway had been lifted. Note that the wrought iron lattice railings matched those on the main bridge. On the far bank, a couple sit in deckchairs next to their Morris Minor and enjoy the view. NPC

Brockweir Halt, opened on 19th August 1929 for the convenience of villagers who were only just over the other side of the river, lay just 500 yards north of Tintern station. On the left is the A466 road from Chepstow to Monmouth, which has been widened and realigned slightly since the railway closed, obliterating the site of the halt. This highly picturesque view, looking north towards Monmouth, was taken on 16th August 1958 and the photographer was standing on the stone arch at the western end of Brockweir Bridge, from which steps led down to the halt. In an increasingly frantic world, our leisure time has become ever more important and it is difficult, when looking at a view such as this, not to ponder just what could have been made of this line if it had just survived a little longer. Sadly, patronage in the 1950s was not enough to keep it open. DAVID SOGGEE

A visit to Paul Chancellor of Colour-Rail looking for pictures of the Midland lines for Volume 3 also produced this breathtaking, recently acquired view of the Wye Valley motor train heading away from Brockweir Halt circa 1955. Hauled by a pannier tank, the train comprises an ex-GWR Diagram A31 59ft 6ins auto trailer (converted from one of the steam rail motors in the number series 73-83 in 1934-35) and another of the Suburban Brake Thirds with driving compartment in the van end (as previously seen at Monmouth Troy); both are in the unlined BR crimson livery of the early to mid 1950s, with the bright paintwork of the latter vehicle suggesting it had recently been outshopped. The view is looking from the Brockweir village side of the River Wye and the train is approaching the Tintern Home signal, the station being just out of sight around the curve. COLOUR-RAIL

No, it's not a model railway! Of all the Dufaycolor slides that were in the collection I bought – thirty-six in total – this was undoubtedly the one I was most pleased to acquire. Quite simply, it took the breath away and in my opinion ranks amongst the best railway colour views I have ever seen. The dating of these slides as circa 1937 is based on the Camp Coach positioned at the end of one of the goods sidings. The GWR first instigated the Camp Coach scheme in 1934 and it was deemed such a success that the number of sites where coaches were positioned was doubled from 19 to 38 the following year, Tintern being one of the new sites, although certainly for the first year a bogie clerestory coach was used here. These photographs were therefore taken sometime between 1936 and 1939. Apart from the Camp Coach, of which more overleaf, there is much else to study and enjoy in this picture, which was taken from on top of the small hill that the line tunnelled through after crossing the river; the start of the bridge parapets can just be seen at the bottom of the picture. A straight tank '45XX' Class 2-6-2T is about to gather some wagons from the yard, having arrived with the branch pick-up goods. Brian Handley's book on the Wye Valley Railway makes no mention of engines of this size or class appearing on the line in its motive power chapter but this photograph confirms that they appeared on goods workings, probably quite regularly at this time. Locomotives working the

branch were rostered from the shed at Severn Tunnel Junction. The third rarity in this view is the private owner wagon, which has come from Crawshay's Lightmoor Colliery, near Cinderford in the Forest of Dean. This colliery closed in 1940, whilst colour views of pre-war PO wagons are very rare because they disappeared from the scene after Nationalisation of the railways. This wagon looks in good condition with the lettering clearly visible; the livery was overall black, with white lettering shaded red. The GWR dark stone colour paint on the timberwork of all the buildings is also noticeable, whilst the 5-ton capacity yard crane appears to be painted a deep rusty red. There were a couple of cattle pens alongside the short bay siding by the station building, whilst the siding on which the Camp Coach is standing ran through the goods shed. The weighbridge hut is next to the road entrance into the yard and the small stone cottage where the stationmaster lived is by the station entrance from the road. note the extensive and neatly kept vegetable garden behind it. The cottage still stands but has acquired an extension at right angles at the far end. Brockweir village can be seen in the right distance, whilst almost hidden in the trees up on the left is Meadow Farm, which today is the home of Kingstone Brewery, a micro-brewery producing some very drinkable ales. Now stop reading and take a few moments to enjoy this magnificent scene. NPC

RIGHT: Tintern station in 1931, with two of the station staff posing and several passengers waiting for the next train. This photograph was taken by Mr Bernard Wakeman of Minehead and published as a postcard in the late 1960s by a printing firm in Derby. They are no longer in business, whilst an internet search for Bernard Wakeman turned up references to a number of colour photographs that he took in the 1930s, which are now in the National Geographic collection in the USA. However, there was no sign in their collection of the original for this image, which was presumably also a Dufaycolor slide. Reproduced here from the 1960s postcard, the image is by no means sharp but it merited inclusion due to its early date and also because it is contemporary with the other Dufaycolor slides. Incidentally, if anyone knows of the whereabouts of the original slide, I would be most interested to hear. BERNARD WAKEMAN BSc/NPC

ABOVE: A view towards the station from track level, looking north towards Monmouth circa 1937. It is my belief that the person who took these pictures was not interested in railways particularly, rather I think he was trying to capture the landscape around Tintern and the station happily featured in several of the views. It had an unusual layout, which reflected the belief that it would be the most important intermediate station on the line when it was first built, with tourists visiting Tintern Abbey. There were three platform faces, with the platform on the Down side being an island and the secondary arm of the bracket signal in the foreground was to permit Up trains to run into the Down loop in front of the signal box. As can be seen, with the each way passenger service having never got beyond five trains a day, it was largely used for extra wagon storage. However, excursions from Paddington regularly arrived here, which did use the island face. Although northbound trains could run directly into the loop, Monmouth-bound trains were not permitted to leave from it. The island platform canopy was a particularly graceful structure, as can be seen. On the far side of the valley, what looks to be a road running along just above the river is no longer shown on maps, although on Google Earth it appears as a tree lined track running from Brockweir and ending in what is now woodlands just on the right here. What I initially believed to be a bus, just to the left of the telegraph pole, is therefore likely to be a hut of some sort, with another visible to the right. NPC

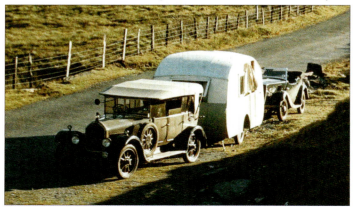

RIGHT: Having previously mentioned the vehicles in which the party travelled, I have included a picture of their little convoy somewhere in North Wales. The car in front, registration number KO 6367, is a Humber, almost certainly a 1928 four-cylinder 14/40. This was a high quality car, intended to lure those motorists wanting Rolls-Royce quality at a lower price. The car behind, Registration DLR 633, is a Series 1 Morris 8 4-seater Tourer, which was launched in time for the 1934 Olympia Motor Show for the 1935 season. The caravan could be one of the Eccles models. NPC

Our unknown photographer chose quite an unusual angle for this shot but one which once again lends credence to the idea that the railway just happened to feature in some of the pictures. The viaduct spanning the river, carrying the railway into Tintern Tunnel, was just to the left. It comprised a single lattice girder 60 yards long, supported on stone abutments either end and two pairs of cylindrical cast iron columns standing in the river. The spans were removed shortly after closure and only the abutments now remain. Incidentally, it is quite noticeable with these Dufaycolor slides that the focus gradually blurs out towards the edges of the picture. The charms of this part of the Wye Valley are well illustrated here and, in a gentler age, the attraction of camping here for a week in a railway carriage were considerable. A lovely account of a stay here in 1937, contemporary with these pictures being taken, appears in Mike Fenton's book *Camp Coach Holidays on the GWR*; during this week, the train was taken up the line to St. Briavels station and then a walk up the mile or so steep climb to visit St. Briavels castle, whilst an evening visit was also made to Tintern Abbey at the time of a full moon. The passenger service at this time was provided by a GWR railcar, which then station master Andrew Muldowney referred to with obvious pride (despite the limited service) as '*our streamlined railcar*'. As at Kerne Bridge, a Camping Coach was positioned here again when the scheme was reintroduced by British Railways a few years after the war. One of the vehicles used was bogie compartment coach No. W9898W, which was recorded as being here in 1956. Interestingly, a BR Camping Coaches brochure for the 1961 season shows an 8-berth coach still being available for hire here, despite the passenger service on the line having been withdrawn two years earlier. A week's stay cost between £7 10s and £12; Kerne Bridge was not shown, however. No photographs showing the Camping Coach here at this late date have yet been seen to confirm this and it would be useful to know if one actually was stationed here in the early 1960s. NPC

ABOVE: Is this the first known view of a GWR 6-wheeled Camp Coach in colour in its original livery? There is no evidence that our unknown family stayed in the coach – why would they, when they had a caravan with them? – but they certainly spent some time around the station at Tintern photographing the surrounding landscape. This view is looking across the Chepstow to Monmouth road, in the middle distance, over to the start of the narrow Trelleck Valley. Coach No. 9988 was stationed here probably from the 1936 season but was certainly here in 1937. A 6-wheeled Composite built in October 1884 to Diagram U19 and numbered 794, it was renumbered 6794 in 1907 and condemned in November 1931. As built, it was 31ft long, 8ft wide and 7ft 6ins high, with axles 9ft 6ins apart and five compartments arranged in order Third, Second, First, Second, Third Class. It was condemned at Barry, so is likely to have been working in South Wales at the end of its first career. However, it was not broken up and in March 1934 was converted to a Camp Coach. The Camp Coach scheme was suspended during the Second World War and No. 9988 was recorded at Reading Signal & Telegraph Dept in 1941 and subsequently, staying with the S&T, at Slough in 1948, Chippenham in 1949 and Carmarthen in 1950. Its life finally came to an end after it was condemned for the second time in July 1954, by which time it was seventy years old. Newly repainted at the start of the season, note the curtains and the GWR monogram on the side. NPC

BELOW: Tintern village circa 1937 from the Wireworks Branch viaduct, which spans the Wye part way round what is referred to as the 'Tintern Loop'. This is another of the slides which suffered from light incursion to the camera and the image has therefore been 'Photoshopped' to 'repair' it (bottom left). NPC

BELOW: An unidentified Class '57XX' pannier tank shunts the daily goods train on 16th August 1958. On the journey up to Monmouth, the task would involve mostly dropping off empties, with loadeds being collected on the way back down, unless there were any laden wagons in the yard destined for points north of here. Note the two wagons loaded with stone on the far side of the island platform, which were presumably for collection on the return journey, whilst on the platform is another local cargo – canoes for use on the river. At this date there was still a Camping Coach stationed here at Tintern, although out of site here in the goods yard. DAVID SOGGEE

LEFT: The cover of the 1961 season BR Camping Coaches leaflet, with the extract mentioning the Tintern coach. NPC

RIGHT: No. 6439 at the head of the SLS Special on 4th January 1959 on its way up the valley to Monmouth and Ross. The engine is standing next to the water tower, a cast iron tank mounted on a stone tower. BILL POTTER/KRM

BELOW: Looking the other way, showing the north end of the loops and also just how close the station was to the village of Brockweir, in the background, which was always something of a gripe for Tintern residents. I think the smartly dressed gent chatting to the train crew in the foreground was probably the railway inspector in charge of the special. Note that the panels on the side of the water tank appear to be still in GWR colours of light and dark stone. DEREK CHAPLIN

BOTTOM: A view from the train on the approach to Tintern from the south. The abbey ruins are prominent on the left and the bridge which carried the Wireworks Branch across the river can be seen in the centre. Given that a halt was provided for Brockweir, it was somewhat perverse that the GWR never built one near the Wireworks Branch junction, which would have been much handier for the villagers of Tintern. NPC

BOTTOM LEFT: The Tintern Abbey bookmark from the Holiday Haunts Bookmarker series issued by the GWR. NPC

LEFT: A glimpse through the trees of the pannier tank seen in the main view below running round its train in the station at Tintern. JOHN THORN

G.W.R.

TINTERN

RIGHT: This April 1963 view from above the entrance to Tintern Tunnel makes for an interesting comparison with the 1930s picture (which was taken from a similar position) but is looking in a more westerly direction and, as a consequence, shows the river viaduct in the foreground. The train is clearly a ballast working with the five 'Dogfish' hoppers and four open wagons loaded with crushed stone from Tintern Quarry. Looking at the *Appendix to the WTT* for 1960, it would seem that stone trains had to work down to Tintern station from the quarry, in order that the porter here could telephone the Wye Valley Junction signalman to advise him of the time of departure, this being the nearest place where communication with the box there could be made. Otherwise, the signalman would have no idea when to expect the train back, whilst he could also advise if it needed to be held at Tintern for a time first. The engine would run round the wagons before heading back south. The mineral wagon in the yard indicates that coal deliveries were still being made whilst the box vans may have been for early season market garden produce or for parcels. The demolition of the viaduct after closure of the branch has made all proposals to reopen part of the line as a tourist route or even as a cycle route difficult, due to the added expense of replacing it. This has combined with local opposition to reuse of the line as any sort of through route to stymie all plans so far, with even Sustrans deeming it too difficult to proceed with their cycle route plans at the current time. JOHN THORN

The BLC brake van trip making a photographic stop at Tintern in summer 1961. Note that the woodwork of the station building and signal box had been repainted in Western Region chocalate and cream but the island platform canopy had been removed. The signal box was particularly attractive, built on a stone base with two arched windows to the front and again being a product of McKenzie & Holland. The box was closed on 27th March 1960, with new North and South ground frames being provided to operate the points thereafter. PETER BARNFIELD

A desolate scene, as the half demolished station quietly awaits its ultimate fate in 1968, the tracks having been removed in 1964. Happily, all was not lost, however. In the early 1980s, the site was bought by Monmouthshire County Council and the buildings seen here refurbished. The water tower was also saved, although the trackbed in between the platforms was infilled. Today, the site is a popular destination for tourists, with a shop, cafe, picnic area and a short length of track on which stand two coaches and a goods van containing a model railway, whilst the signal box is used for art exhibitions – all in all, a fitting memorial to the Wye Valley Railway. MICHAEL HALE

RIGHT: Having crossed the River Wye and passed through Tintern Tunnel, the line began a gentle climb towards Netherhope, its highest point, first passing the junction for the Wireworks Branch. Hugging the side of the valley just above the Gloucestershire bank of the river, the branch crossed the three arch Black Morgan Viaduct before arriving at Tintern Quarry. After withdrawal of the Monmouth goods service in late 1964 this became the terminus of the line. The quarry had a fifty year life, commencing operations in 1931 and ceasing in 1981. This view, taken on 5th May 1971, is looking north, with BR blue liveried 'Hymek' diesel-hydraulic No. D7094 shunting a rake of empty Dogfish wagons into place for loading. Just beyond the locomotive on the right was the site of the short-lived and unadvertised Tintern Quarry Halt, which was provided in 1931 but fell out of use after the Second World War. A rake of loaded 'Dogfish' wagons can just be glimpsed ahead of the engine.

LEFT: Rail facilities here comprised a simple run round loop with a short stub/headshunt at the north end (which looks as though it may have been taken out by the date of these views) and a longer siding for loading running off at the south end. The remaining stub of the branch was also used. Here, having deposited the empties beneath the hoppers for loading, D7094 heads back down the loop to collect the train of loadeds waiting at the end of the branch.

BELOW: A short while later, the 'Hymek' departs with the train of loaded 'Dogfish' wagons past the loading siding. The Western Region diesel-hydraulics were all 'lookers' and the 'Hymeks', with their distinctive swept-under nose ends, were certainly no exception. Due to their non-standardisation, their lives were all short, however, with the last few going in early 1975. New into service in 1964, D7094 was withdrawn in 1972, having given just eight years of service. ALL BILL POTTER/KRM

LEFT: Bill Potter climbed up into the woods above Tidenham Tunnel to get this view looking down on Tintern Quarry on 17th October 1974. The main part of the quarry is beyond the bare rock face, behind, below which it burrowed down into the earth. The cramped nature of the loading site is evident and the rails of the branch can just be glimpsed through the trees, curving away from the quarry in the foreground. Since closure in 1981, the quarry has largely reverted to nature and is today used as an unofficial climbing site. BILL POTTER/KRM

RIGHT: The trackbed of the branch at Shorn Cliff, between the quarry and Tintern, looking north on 10th December 1964. It would appear that track lifting had been carried out using a tracked vehicle, with the sleepers left lying against the bank. B.J. ASHWORTH

ABOVE: D7094 threads its way cautiously past the remains of Netherhope Halt on 5th May 1971, with the crew looking back to check that their train had safely cleared the tunnel. There are three men in the front cab and at least one in the rear, so perhaps there was an element of enjoying a day out in picturesque unfamiliar territory in glorious sunshine for the crew on board. Netherhope Halt was opened on 16th May 1932 and was situated in a shallow cutting just to the south of Tidenham Tunnel and the stone-built overbridge carrying Netherhope Lane across the line. After withdrawal of the passenger service, the halt was simply left for a time, with the corrugated iron hut that sufficed for waiting accommodation finally disappearing sometime in the late 1960s. Everything else, including the nameboard posts, was simply left to rot. D7094 was allocated to Cardiff Canton depot, certainly for much of its later life, but the ballast trains were generally worked to Gloucester. This one could have been destined for South Wales and that may explain the number of train crew involved. Originally introduced into service in an attractive two tone green livery, with white window surrounds and the later addition of a yellow warning panel on the ends, this is the BR corporate blue livery of the late 1960s/early 1970s. The numbers were cast in aluminium and then fixed to the body sides, an unusual and nice touch clearly distinguishable here. DAVE COBBE/RAIL PHOTOPRINTS

RIGHT: Looking north towards the road overbridge and the southern portal of Tidenham Tunnel in the early 1980s, shortly after traffic on this section of the branch had ceased following the closure of Tintern Quarry. Over twenty years after the passenger service had finished, the platform is still in existence and even one of the nameboard posts still stands. Today, trees and bushes have grown to hide the cutting and tunnel mouth but the track was never lifted so, beneath it all, the heavily overgrown rails and rotting wooden sleepers remain in place. DENNIS PARKHOUSE

Two rare views of '14XX' Class 0-4-2T No. 1421 near Netherhope with the Wye Valley Branch train circa 1957-58, which, since the publication of the first edition, I have now been informed were taken by Hugh Crowther, an accomplished artist who lived at Netherhope. They make an interesting comparison with the two pictures opposite, which were taken from roughly the same location. The photographer was standing alongside of and just down from the overbridge carrying Bishton Lane across the railway, which makes a junction with Netherhope Lane, seen running across in the background from left to right, just off the right edge of the picture. Behind the auto train, the line curves to the right, past a PW hut sited on top of the cutting side and then heads for Netherhope Halt and Tidenham Tunnel, just to the right of the white house. Note that this property was later modified with the addition of three dormer windows, as seen in the picture on the previous page. Like the auto coach seen earlier at Monmouth Troy, Trailer W211W next to the engine had also been modified from a steam railmotor, No. 81, originally built at Swindon in 1907. It was converted to a 59ft 6ins trailer in 1934, to Diagram A31 and photographs indicate that several of the trailers converted under this diagram worked on the branches to Monmouth. Seen here in the brick red livery, Trailer W211W was condemned in March 1959. NPC

The photographer quickly nipped up the bank and across the lane to then take this view of No. 1421 as it headed away from under the bridge towards Chepstow. This part of the trackbed is also now heavily overgrown. No. 1421 was new in November 1933 and its first allocation was to the tiny shed at Pontrilas, for working the Golden Valley Branch to Hay on Wye. This was a short stay, however, and by March 1934 it was at Newport Ebbw Junction, where it stayed until September 1949, apart from the occasional sojourn out for works visits. Three years at Llantrisant was then followed by further stays at Ebbw Junction in 1952 and 1956, the latter until 1958; it is presumed these photographs were taken therefore sometime in those final two years at Ebbw Junction, for the passenger service ceased at the end of 1958 and the next allocation was Laira in June of that year. No. 1421 was finally withdrawn from Gloucester Barnwood shed on 28th December 1963 and sold to birds of Risca for cutting up the following year. NPC

RIGHT: With recently dropped ballast evident but the track showing distinct signs of the lack of maintenance as tufts of grass grow round the sleeper chairs, 'Hymek' No. D7068 makes its way up the branch light engine on 2nd August 1972.

BELOW: Some time later, the 'Hymek' makes its way back down the branch with a train of loaded 'Dogfish' hoppers. The viewpoint is almost identical to the picture opposite page top. BILL POTTER/KRM

LEFT: With steel tyres no doubt squealing on the curve, No. D7094 makes its way past Bill with its train of empty hoppers on 5th May 1971, whilst the driver leans out of his cab to be recorded for posterity. He slowed the train here so Bill could get a second shot slightly further along and then doffed his cap as they pulled away again. Bishton Lane bridge was a very lightweight looking structure in stone and wrought iron. It still stands today but is now supported by four sturdy metal props, as the iron support span has cracked and its continued survival must be in doubt. BILL POTTER/KRM

ABOVE: Coming from Chepstow, the first station on the branch was at Tidenham, opened with the line in 1876. Despite this, its rather isolated situation meant that it was never very busy and also that it was rarely visited by photographers. Facilities here comprised a loop with a short siding running off it at the south end, with the goods shed, practically identical in design to those at St. Briavels and Redbrook, positioned alongside the loop, facing the station. The station was closed for thirteen months from 1st January 1917 to 1st February 1918, presumably as a wartime economy, whilst the signal box was shut on 30th October 1928, after which Tidenham was reduced to the status of a halt, in common with Redbrook. New North and South ground frames were brought into use for operating the loop and siding as required. By the early 1950s, the goods yard was seeing only minimal traffic and the South Ground Frame and loop connection were taken out on 20th November 1952, leaving the North Ground Frame to operate what was now just a long siding. Even this proved too much, so it was removed on 13th February 1955, reducing Tidenham station to just a single line and platform. This view, taken on 2nd August 1971 looking south towards Chepstow, shows the station site after it had been taken over by Dayhouse Quarry, which seems to have begun operating circa 1968. All of the buildings had been demolished and the platform rebuilt for use as a loading bank, with tractor units and shovels in use to load the quarried stone into the wagons – a much more basic operation that that just up the line at Tintern Quarry. A new loop was laid, although much longer and on a straighter parallel course than the previous loop had been, so that locomotives could run round. This came into use on 22nd March 1968 and at the same time, a short section of the branch running north from here was slewed towards the Up side, although quite why is not known. In 1981, the loop was shortened, whilst at some stage an overhead conveyor was installed to facilitate loading of lorries and railway wagons. The quarry, operated by T.S. Thomas & Sons (Lydney) Ltd, ceased sending stone out by rail in 1990, the last train departing on 29th March. Quarried stone was still despatched by road for some years afterwards but production finally ceased in the late 1990s and the site is now home to the National Diving & Activity Centre, the deep quarry having filled with water after production ended. The station's position at the summit of the line is clearly shown here, with the track dropping sharply away just beyond the wagons, whilst the descent towards Tintern begins just in front of the photographer. The Wye Valley has always presented something of a geographical anomaly, as the land through which the river flows is at its highest just before it reaches Chepstow and its confluence with the Severn. A writer exploring the Wye Valley many years ago once pondered on this point whilst visiting a local hostelry, becoming the beneficiary of a piece of local wisdom from an elderly drinker sat in the bar: "Well 'er's a contrary old river, so p'raps 'er flowed up 'ill a bit once." BILL POTTER/KRM

LEFT: Wye Valley Junction as seen from the SLS Special of 4th January 1959. The train has just passed the site of Tutshill Halt, which closed with the branch. Wye Valley Junction Signal Box, which dated from 1875, was closed on 3rd March 1969 and replaced with a new ground frame. Note the point for the ash drag part way up the steep climb, to protect against runaways. COLOUR RAIL

'Hymek' No. D7068 waits up the bank beyond the ash drag, as two of the crew walk down to operate the ground frame to let their train out on to the main line on 2nd August 1971. By this date, with Chepstow Signal Box having closed, the crewman would first have to telephone Newport panel box for permission to operate the frame. If the line was clear, Newport would then press the release button for the frame, unlocking it so the points could be set. With the nearest crossover now at Chepstow following removal of the one here in 1969, the same procedure had be followed at the East Ground Frame there. Note that the train appears to have a brake van on the rear. Incidentally, in Section 36 of his *Track Layout Diagrams of the GWR and BR(WR)*, Tony Cooke notes the ash drag as being taken out by August 1963 but it is clearly still in place here. With the signal box having closed, was the point now kept in the 'safe' position leading into the drag for trains coming off the branch, to be opened by the train crew from the ground frame? With spring loaded points, trains heading up the branch would have been able to run through them without having to stop. Note the Plassermatic ballast machine coincidentally passing on the Down line. BILL POTTER/KRM

Three months earlier, on 5th May 1971, No. D7094 makes its way cautiously down the steep bank off the branch and onto the main line, past the ground frame as one of the train crew holds the point lever firmly in place. These two views were taken from Sedbury Lane bridge; behind the photographer, the view here today has changed dramatically following the construction of a by-pass which provided a new bridge across the river alongside the railway bridge, cutting out the route over the old Chepstow road bridge. The railway is now covered by a new tunnel approximately 1,000 feet long, with the by-pass running on top. The two overbridges in the distance carry a farm track over both lines, that on the Wye Valley Branch being identical in design to the one at Bishton Lane. Beyond, Sedbury Lane bridge can just be glimpsed through the main line arch but the lane then passed under the branch which is still climbing at this point, before curving away left on the horizon. Just the other side of Sedbury Lane bridge, on the Down side, was the site of Beachley Junction, laid in 1918 for the branch to the new National Shipyard No. 2 at Beachley, which was built using German PoWs as labour. However, the war ended before this 'white elephant' project could produce any ships. One vessel was eventually completed here, *War Odyssey* in October 1920 (renamed *Monte San Michele*, she was lost on passage to New York in February 1921), after which the Beachley site was closed. The route of the branch roughly paralleled Sedbury Lane, the connection with the main line being taken out in 1928. The Beachley site later became an Army Apprentices College and is now the home of 1st Battalion (The Rifles) but is now scheduled to be closed by 2027. BILL POTTER/KRM

Auto-fitted Class '64XX' 0-6-0PT No. 6426 waits at Chepstow with an auto working from Newport in the summer of 1960. Chepstow station was opened by the South Wales Railway on 19th June 1850 but was initially a terminus for trains arriving from South Wales, as Brunel's bridge across the Wye, seen in the right background, had not been completed. A temporary station, Chepstow East, was provided on the far bank for passengers arriving from Gloucester and a coach service ran between the two. It was a full two years before the bridge was ready for opening, on 19th July 1852, at which point the temporary station was shut and Chepstow became a through station. As originally built, the platforms here were very low and the situation apparently became worse after the rails were narrowed from broad to standard gauge in 1872, leading to complaints from passengers. Accordingly, in 1877-78, a delicate operation was begun, by local contractor C.W. Whalley, to raise the station buildings up 2 feet by means of jacks, after which the platforms were rebuilt at a more acceptable height. Wye Valley Branch trains had used Platform 3, on the far side of the station but once the services began running from Severn Tunnel Junction, they used the Up platform instead. Note the unusual shunting disc signal, gantry-mounted and jutting out from the station building to the left of No. 6426, for the crossover in the foreground. The footbridge, built by E. Finch & Co. in their yard just off to the right, still survives. ALAN JARVIS

SECTION 9
CHEPSTOW to GRANGE COURT JUNCTION

Whilst waiting for the autotrain seen opposite, Derek Chaplin took this shot of 'Dub-Dee' 2-8-0 No. 90188 as it clanked through with a train of empty mineral wagons returning to South Wales, with the fireman apparently hosing down the footplate. These highly functional but unattractive engines were regularly seen on this route in the later years of Western Region steam. Designed by R.A. Riddles for the War Department (WD – hence the nickname), the engine was built by the North British Locomotive Co. in Glasgow and was new into service in September 1943. In common with other wartime designs, they were also known as 'Austerities', because they were built without any of the refinements of earlier steam engines. Originally WD No. 7214 and then 77214, the engine became BR No. 90188 in February 1951 and was then allocated to Cardiff Canton shed. It spent much of the next decade at either Cardiff or Newport Ebbw Junction and was working from one of those sheds when photographed here. However, by 1962 it had gravitated north to Yorkshire and then to Staveley Barrow Hill shed in Derbyshire. Withdrawn on 11th April 1963, it was scrapped by John Cashmore Ltd at their Great Bridge yard later that year. DEREK CHAPLIN

The history of the South Wales Railway's line between Gloucester and Chepstow was largely covered in the introduction to Section 1. Despite appearing today to be one seamless route, the line was opened in stages and involved three different companies – the SWR, the GWR and the Gloucester & Dean Forest Railway (G&FDR). Gloucester to Chepstow East temporary station opened on 19th September 1851 and then into Chepstow station from 19th July 1852 when Brunel's tubular bridge spanning the River Wye was finally completed.

Having reached Chepstow we complete the circle by travelling north east back towards Gloucester, finishing our journey at Grange Court Junction. Today, the only station between Chepstow and Gloucester is Lydney, with Woolaston, Awre, Newnham, Westbury Halt, Grange Court Junction, and Oakle Street all having gone. The main line not having the attractions of the various branches for most photographers, finding colour pictures of several of these locations has been challenging and, in some instances, fruitless. The junctions have also gone – at Lydney for the Severn & Wye line and for the line across the Severn Bridge to Sharpness; at Awre for the Forest of Dean Central Branch; and at Bullo Pill for the Forest of Dean Branch and the Bullo Dock Branch. In 2012, the line was brought under the control of the new Cardiff signalling centre, which saw the abolition and demolition of Lydney gate box, the old Lydney West Signal Box. This now leaves Awre Junction as the only surviving signal box along the line, albeit in use only as a PW storage base.

Whilst after Nationalisation the Gloucester to Severn Tunnel Junction line remained a haven for ex-GWR steam, with everything except 'King' Class locomotives likely to be seen, ex-LM&SR classes such as 'Black 5's and '4F's also began to be seen venturing south along the banks of the Severn whilst, from the later 1950s, BR 'Standard' types began to feature regularly too, particularly '9F's on heavy South Wales freights (and occasionally on passenger workings too), as well as ex-WD 2-8-0s. When the diesel era arrived, the line continued to enjoy a variety of motive power, with Class '14' 'Teddy Bears' on regular visits to Tintern, Coleford and Cinderford, 'Hymeks' and English Electric Type '3's (later Class '37') on branch and main line workings, 'Warships', Class '52' 'Westerns', Class '24's, Class '44' 'Peaks', Brush Type '4's (later Class '47') and Class '50's, whilst local passenger trains were in the hands of DMUs. Some of this variety will be illustrated over the following pages.

The signal box and goods shed, looking towards Severn Tunnel Junction on 6th May 1967. Note that the former carried a non-standard Western Region replacement nameplate, proclaiming it as Chepstow Station Box. Quite why the WR felt the need to name it thus is not clear, as there were no other Chepstow boxes from which to distinguish it. The box dated from circa 1894, when it was built as a replacement for East and West signal boxes positioned at either end of the station. The West box had been situated just the other side of the goods shed and straddled the siding running through it. A second West box, positioned further down the line round the curve, was in operation for just four years after WW1 in conjunction with the newly established shipyard. The station nameboard was also a WR replacement, with the panels advertising the need to change here for Wye Valley line trains having been removed. Like its counterpart at Ross-on-Wye, the wide aperture for the line running through the goods shed betrays its broad gauge origins. MARK B. WARBURTON

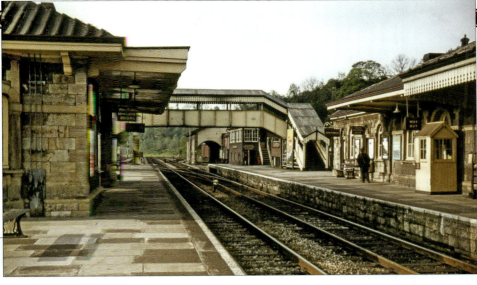

LEFT: The first of three further views of the station taken on the same occasion as the previous one. Here, the photographer has moved back along the Down platform a short distance and has this time included the footbridge steps and the small wooden hut used by the member of the station staff whose job it was to collect the tickets. Chocalate and cream abounds and the signage is all BR (WR). Change was not far away, however. On 3rd March 1969, the signal box was closed, following closure of the goods yard the previous year, the sidings being taken out from 28th April 1969. MARK B. WARBURTON

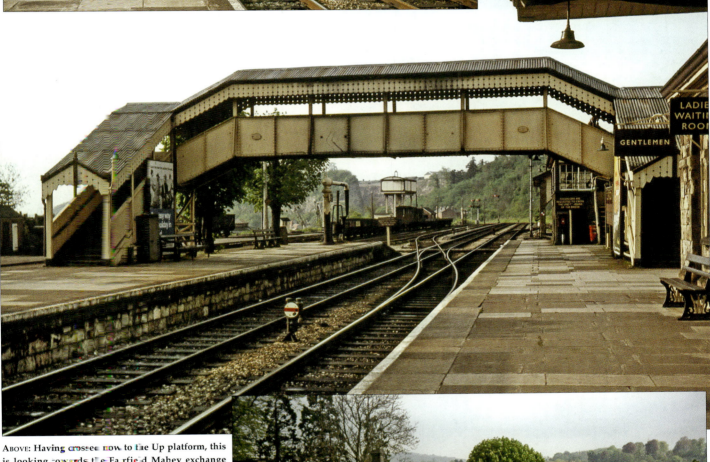

ABOVE: Having crossed now to the Up platform, this is looking towards the Fairfield Mabey exchange sidings. There is a hint of the new corporate blue era from the poster on the side of the bridge steps but otherwise, some seventeen months after steam had ceased on the Western Region of British Railways, this is a pure steam era scene, with the water tower still in place, a water crane at the end of the Down platform and another just visible at the far end of the sidings. MARK B. WARBURTON

RIGHT: Looking in the Gloucester direction from the footbridge. The platforms were extended northwards in 1927 (the Up platform extension, on wooden stilts, is clearly visible here) but they were subsequently removed in 1970, returning them to their 1878 length. All of the accoutrements that went to make up a steam age British railway station are here in these views and together they form that indefinable something that is missing from the railway today. MARK B. WARBURTON

ABOVE: Photographed from the footbridge, No. 6158 arrives at Chepstow with a two coach stopping train. New in 1933, the engine was at Severn Tunnel Junction shed from August 1961 to October 1963 (so the picture is within this date range), when it was transferred away to Aberdare, from where it was withdrawn in June 1964. There is a glimpse inside the signal box through the open window and plenty of traffic on view in the goods yard. NPC

BELOW: A nice study of the Down side shelter from a train in the Up platform circa 1962, with coaching stock also standing in the erstwhile Monmouth Branch platform. Sadly this fine Brunellian building was demolished in 1970. The lamppost was a recent installation, the older GWR lamps still featuring in the 1960 views. NPC

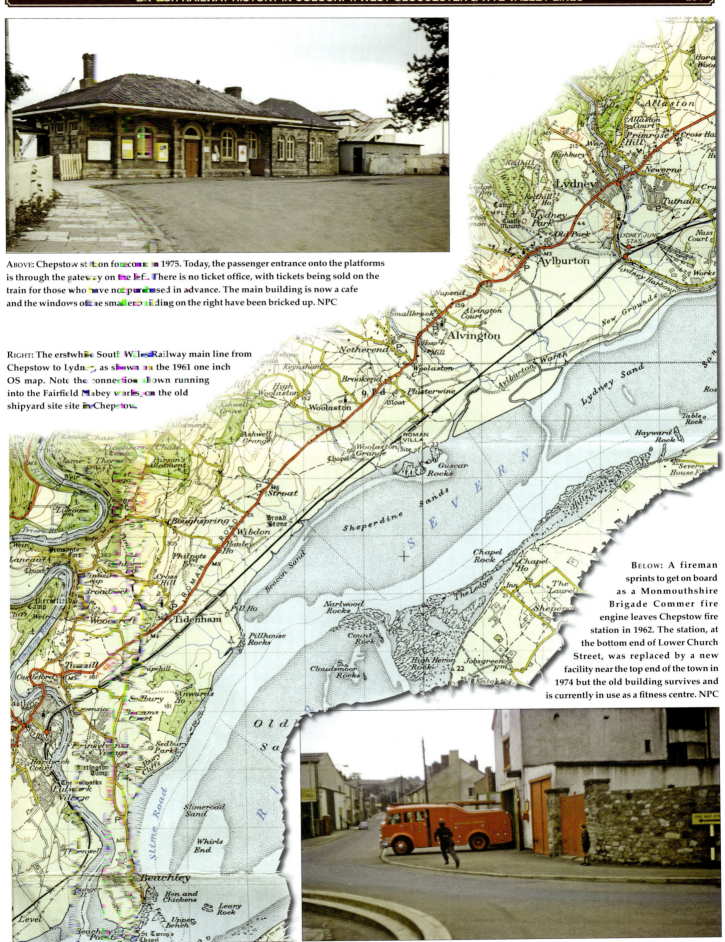

ABOVE: Chepstow station forecourt in 1975. Today, the passenger entrance onto the platforms is through the gateway on the left. There is no ticket office, with tickets being sold on the train for those who have not purchased in advance. The main building is now a cafe and the windows of the smaller building on the right have been bricked up. NPC

RIGHT: The erstwhile South Wales Railway main line from Chepstow to Lydney, as shown on the 1961 one inch OS map. Note the connection shown running into the Fairfield Mabey works on the old shipyard site site in Chepstow.

BELOW: A fireman sprints to get on board as a Monmouthshire Brigade Commer fire engine leaves Chepstow fire station in 1962. The station, at the bottom end of Lower Church Street, was replaced by a new facility near the top end of the town in 1974 but the old building survives and is currently in use as a fitness centre. NPC

LEFT: Looking north through the platforms at Chepstow in 1970, before the Down side waiting rooms had been demolished. The Up side buildings survive in their entirety, including the canopy jutting out from the waiting shelter but all the platform side doors and windows are now blanked off. When the platforms were raised in 1877-78, the opportunity was also taken to widen them, so there is not the extra width here between the rails that you see at many ex-broad gauge stations. NPC

RIGHT: The history of the National Shipyards is complicated and well documented elsewhere (see Bibliography). National Shipyard No. 1 was at Chepstow, alongside Finch's yard, between the station and the River Wye. Soon after the shipyard was first set up in 1918, Finch went into liquidation and their yard was also absorbed into the site, although was initially operated as a separate concern. With the Government looking for a buyer for the yards after the war had ended, and with not a single ship having being completed, in 1920 the No. 1 Shipyard (including Finch's yard) was sold to a new company, The Monmouth Shipbuilding Co. Ltd. It was under their auspices that the five ships on which work had started were completed, four of them – *War Glory*, *War Iliad*, *War Genius* and *War Epic* – in 1920, with the fifth – *War Idyll* (did no-one see the irony in that name?) coming off the slips in 1921. The post war slump saw the Monmouth Co. fail in 1925 but the yard was then taken over by the Fairfield Shipbuilding & Engineering Co. of Govan, who used it to build small vessels, railway rolling stock and steelwork for bridges. When the Admiralty had been building the Chepstow and Beachley yards, they had brought in locomotives to work on site. Two of them passed with the yard to the Monmouth Co., then to the Fairfield Co., who went into liquidation in 1966. Both were still on site in the late 1960s; top and seen here on 28th March 1969, is the ex-GER 'coffee pot' 0-4-0ST No. 229, built by Neilson & Co. in 1876 and bought by the Admiralty in 1917. The second locomotive, below, photographed on 4th February 1967, is Kerr Stuart 0-4-0 well tank Works No. 3063 of 1918, which went new to the Beachley shipyard. Both engines remained here on site until the early 1980s, when they were bought by Bill and Richard Parker. Cosmetically restored, the ex-GER engine was put on display at the North Woolwich Railway Museum in London. That facility closed in 2008 and the locomotive is now back at Bill Parker's Flour Mill Colliery railway workshops in the Forest of Dean, where it is planned to restore it to full working order. Meanwhile, Bill has already fully restored the Kerr, Stuart, which is currently on a tour of preserved lines and sites. BOTH BILL POTTER/KRM

No. 5927 *Guild Hall* coasts across Brunel's tubular bridge spanning the River Wye at Chepstow in 1959, with train No. 710, an express bound for Swansea. A 15mph speed restriction was placed on the bridge in the 1950s, as some of the girders had become distorted. Whilst the 'blood & custard' coach livery proved less than durable in use, with the red in particular showing a tendency to fade, a mixed rake of red & cream and maroon liveried stock always looked attractive and places pictures such as this firmly in their period. The second and third coaches look to be ex-GWR 'Cornish Riviera' stock built in 1929, both 60 foot full Thirds but showing the compartment and corridor sides respectively. *Guild Hall* was a little younger, being new into service at the end of June 1933; it was withdrawn from Tyseley shed during the week ending 24th October 1964. T.B. OWEN

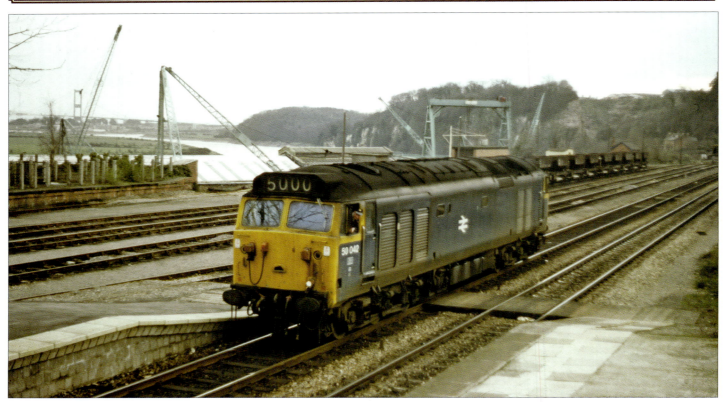

Class '50' No. 50042 runs light engine through the station on 27th February 1977. The locomotive may have just arrived back from Tintern Quarry and be running round its train prior to heading back to Gloucester, although a 'Hoover' on this duty must have been quite rare. A rake of empty 'Dogfish' hoppers in the background await taking up to the quarry and note the overgrown cattle dock on the left, with some of the cranes in Mabey's yard behind. BILL POTTER/KRM

The green BR diesel liveries are associated with the 1960s but here is Class '47' No. D1735. passing through Chepstow hauling a lengthy train of steel billetts and still wearing two tone green on 2nd August 1971. Note that the Down side waiting rooms had gone by this date, although fairly recently looking at the clean stonework of the replacement shelter. New into service in May 1964, under the 1970s BR TOPS renumbering scheme, this locomotive became No. 47142 from April 1974, was named *The Sapper* on 3rd October 1987 and was withdrawn in April 1998, being cut up by Berry's of Leicester the following year. The building behind the engine has a long and interesting history. Built as a steam powered flour mill in 1851, it was converted to maltings in 1890 and two malt kilns were erected nearby. Used by the shipyard during the First World War and subsequently as a barracks by the Royal Engineers, it latterly became offices for Fairfield-Mabey Ltd until severely damaged by fire in January 2002. Grade II listed, it has since been restored for use as offices. Chepstow station building is also now Grade II listed. BILL POTTER/KRM

'Peak' Class '45' No. D128 drifts through the platforms with a train of blue and grey Mk 1 stock forming a Newcastle to Cardiff train, also on 2nd August 1971. New in to service on 8th November 1961, the locomotive was renumbered as No. 45145 on 17th December 1974 and fitted with electric train heating. It was unofficially named *Scylla* and was withdrawn from traffic on 9th September 1987 but then, a month later, was reinstated for another four months. BILL POTTER/KRM

On the same day, another Class '45', No. D94, heads north with a Freightliner container train, 4S88, bound for Scotland. The 'Peak' was renumbered as No. 45114 in September 1973 and was withdrawn on 17th February 1987. Whilst the 'Dogfish' hoppers were for Tintern Quarry, some of the other wagons in the sidings are likely to have been working to Fairfield-Mabey's yard, which was rail connected until 1985. Note the 'Hymek' also lurking at the back of the yard. Although not used since then, it is only within the last few years that the sidings have finally been taken out. The shipyard meanwhile is still used for the fabrication of bridges for export worldwide but the establishment of a new site out of the town for building wind turbines may see the company vacate the old yard. If so, it is likely to be redeveloped for housing. The four slipways which were laid in for launching ships are currently still clearly visible from passing trains. BILL POTTER/KRM

A spectacular side-on portrait of Brunel's bridge, as a northbound mixed freight rumbles across in this circa 1960 view are the two fishermen at work in the river below. They are fishing for salmon and are using traditional Wye stop boats, positioned broadside across the river and manoeuvred by sculling, using a sweep oar at the stern. Note the arrangement of poles on both craft. The net was suspended from the two jutting out at opposing angles from bow and stern of the boat, the poles being balanced on pivots and weighted at their other ends. With the net lowered into the water, they were then propped up at the other end to hold them in place and the fisherman then waited for the fish. Once he felt the salmon swim into his net, he would knock away the prop and the weights at the ends of the poles would take effect, causing them to drop and swiftly lifting the net out of the water, complete with his catch. Similar but generally slightly larger boats were also used out on the River Severn and the practice, which dated from the early 1600s at least continued into the early 1980s. A preserved Wye stop boat can now be found at the Dean Heritage Centre at Soudley, near Cinderford. COLOUR-RAIL

An unidentified Class '56XX' 0-6-2T trundles towards the bridge with a mixed bag of open wagons in mid 1959. Note the old abandoned vertical boiler steam cranes in the undergrowth on the right. T.B. OWEN

LOCAL INSTRUCTIONS.
BEACHLEY JUNCTION—ST. BRIDES
CHEPSTOW

WATER MAINS AND ELECTRIC POWER CABLES—CHEPSTOW RIVER BRIDGE

A water main is carried over the Up side of the Tubular Bridge. The water can be turned off at the valve at the Chepstow end of the bridge. The key is kept on the centre abutment wall near by, and a duplicate key is in possession of the Signalman at Chepstow Station signal box.

Two H.T. electric power cables 3 ins. in diameter are also carried over the bridge. Should an emergency arise which necessitates the electric current being cut off, this will be done on a telephone message being sent to the South Wales Electricity Board (Telephone Chepstow 2539).

LEFT: Brunel's railway bridge spanning the Wye, as viewed from the 1816 road bridge designed and built by Thomas Telford, also responsible for the bridge at Over seen much earlier in these pages. Taken in summer 1960, a freight train heads north. Note the slight bow in the tubular girders, providing extra tension and strength, and from which the bridge was suspended. DEREK CHAPLIN

ABOVE RIGHT: This extract from the *Newport Traffic District Sectional Appendix to the Working Time Table* of July 1961 indicates that it was not just the railway that the bridge carried across the river, there was a water mains and two electric power cables as well.

RIGHT: A fine view of Telford's and Brunel's iconic bridges at Chepstow, as seen from the Gloucestershire bank of the Wye looking east. It is difficult to believe now that the nearer bridge carried all the road traffic heading across the England-Wales border at this point up until 1988. In that year, the Tutshill by-pass was opened, which included a new road bridge spanning the river alongside the rebuilt railway bridge. Telford's old bridge is single lane, with access on to it controlled by traffic lights at each end and with a severe weight restriction. BILL POTTER/KRM

A superb study of the bridge taken in 1959 from the river bank below, at which time it was becoming clear that it would have to be replaced. Brunel's design, whilst revolutionary, also had an in-built weakness. The bow in the tubular girders was caused by stressing them with chains and bracing struts, whilst the light-weight bridge deck was rigid, as the chains clamped it in place. The structure was not only much lighter than Stephenson's box girder design, it was also much cheaper to construct. Although not immediately apparent, Brunel's design was actually a suspension bridge and its success led to the construction of the Royal Albert Bridge spanning the River Tamar near Plymouth, long recognised as one of his greatest monuments. This later bridge still survives largely as it was built, although it has been strengthened over the years. With the Chepstow bridge, however, Brunel, allowed for a slight movement of the suspension chains against supports on the bridge deck to relieve stress, which in turn led to a weakening of the structure and hence the eventual need for its replacement. The original support pillars did survive the rebuild, however. T.B. OWEN

Work under way on dismantling Brunel's bridge on 8th June 1962, as 'Mogul' No. 7314 steams carefully through with a typical mixed freight of the period. In fairly grubby condition the locomotive was to be withdrawn from Shrewsbury shed less that a year after this picture was taken, during the week ending 23rd February 1963. The photograph was taken from Beachley Road bridge, which now spans the new by-pass as well, running alongside the railway on the right. The original bridge was fabricated by the firm of Finch & Willey. Edward Finch, originally from Liverpool, stayed here after construction was finished and began his foundry business, specialising in bridges but later diversifying as well into ship building. Two of his railway footbridges can still be found in situ on the Dean Forest Railway at St. Mary's Halt in Lydney and at Parkend. COLOUR-RAIL

ABOVE: The new bridge, a welded underslung Warren truss girder span, was designed by P.S.A. Berridge (1901-80) and built at the adjacent Fairfield-Mabey yard, where Brunel's bridge had been fabricated over 110 years earlier. Of the original bridge, the cylindrical tripled Tuscan cast iron columns still survive and indeed support the new bridge, although they were filled with concrete for additional strength. The wrought iron approach deck is also original, along with the abutment at the Chepstow end. At the Gloucester end, the bridge was always simply 'hung' off the edge of the cliff, with the abutment being cut into the rock. An annular section of one of Brunel's wrought iron tubes is on display at Mabey Bridge's headquarters nearby. BILL POTTER/KRM

RIGHT: A panorama of the replacement bridge, showing a Cardiff-bound DMU crossing on 27th May 1977. A third generation Swindon-built Inter-City unit of Class '123', they were originally four car sets but had been reduced to three and all ten were transferred to Cardiff Canton in May 1976. This was one of only two of the sets still in use at Cardiff at this date, with all ten being transferred north to Hull just over a week later. This vista has now been lost following construction of the Chepstow by-pass bridge. BILL POTTER/KRM

WOOLASTON STATION

There are three or four of the halts on the lines covered in this volume that I did not manage to find pictures of but only one station proved totally elusive – Woolaston, on the main line between Chepstow and Lydney. Serving a very scattered community, most of which lay a mile or more from the station, which itself was situated at the end of a long narrow lane leading nowhere else, its appearance, operations and, indeed, existence went little recorded over the years by railway photographers. Closed some years before the Beeching Report, I would be hard pressed to find even half a dozen black and white photographs of it, so it was unsurprising that no colour view of Woolaston station has ever been seen. Opened a year after the line had been throughout, on 1st June 1853, usage of the station dropped sharply after the Second World War. Increasing car usage and the village's handy situation on the main A48 between Gloucester and Chepstow saw locals turning to road transport instead, with the result that passenger trains ceased to stop here from 1st December 1954. The small goods yard – two sidings, with cattle pens and a goods shed – was situated about 150 yards south west of the station, towards Chepstow and on the Up side. Cooke's T*rack Layout Digrams Section 36* shows the yard as being taken out of use in September 1956, along with the associated crossovers, with the redundant track all removed over Christmas 1957. However, the *Gloucester District WTT* for freight trains, editions for winter 1958-59 and for summer 1961, both show certain Down trains still calling here, for which I currently have no explanation.

BRITISH RAILWAY HISTORY IN COLOUR: 1. WEST GLOUCESTER & WYE VALLEY LINES

This view of Tutshill Halt, from a colour print rather than a slide, fills yet another gap in the first edition of this book. Taken on 14th April 1962 from the top of the cutting, ex-GWR '28XX' Class 2-8-0 No. 2857 trundles through heading back to South Wales with a long train of empty mineral wagons. Tutshill Halt had a short existence, being a late opening by the GWR, on 9th July 1934, whilst being served only by Wye Valley Branch trains, it closed with the service to Monmouth on 5th January 1959. Fortunately, over three years later, the sleeper-built platforms, shelters, lampposts and steps down each side were all still in place. No. 2857 had enjoyed a long career; built at Swindon Works in May 1918 and a resident of Aberdare shed at the date of this picture, the engine had just under a year left in traffic, being withdrawn from Neath Court Sart in late March 1963. NPC
INSET: A Chepstow-Wye Valley Junction temporary works electric token. These 'temp sections' were in vogue in the 1950s/early '60s for major track and structure works. Here it was provided for the stages of the Chepstow Bridge re-building in 1961-62, which necessitated closure of one line whilst the other remained open for traffic. JOHN JENKIN COLLECTION

ABOVE: 'Mogul' No. 6373 passes Lydney West Box on 15th August 1959, unusual motive power perhaps for this Cardiff to Newcastle express. The train is on the dual level crossing of road and railway branch line leading down to Lydney Docks; one of the rails for the latter can just be seen in the immediate right foreground. No. 6373 carries a Gloucester 85B shed plate on its smokebox door and was withdrawn from Severn Tunnel Junction on 28th December 1963. It appears as though some drainage work is underway on the track and a temporary 'Commencement' signal (a black 'C' on a white disc) has been put in place to show Down trains where the work starts. Note, too, the Watts Tyres lorry waiting at the crossing. The company are still based in Lydney, although have closed their manufacturing facility. T.B. OWEN

LEFT: A study of the steam age facilities at Lydney Junction, with ex-GWR '28XX' Class No. 3805 just creeping into the picture on the right. New in 1939, the 2-8-0 spent much of its life working from Newport Ebbw Junction shed, from where it was withdrawn on 28th September 1964. There was an extensive wagon repair works here at the Junction, which dealt with repairs to all the coal wagons used in the Forest of Dean. The easternmost building of the works is in view beyond the brick built toilet block, whilst in the left background, over the station nameboard, part of the white-painted, corrugated iron main workshop building can be seen. DEREK CHAPLIN

RIGHT: A three-car Swindon Cross-Country DMU of Class '120', with the Motor Brake Composite coach leading, arrives at Lydney Junction on 26th April 1967, with a service to Cardiff Central. The two pitched roofs visible above the trees on the left are again part of the wagon works but this had shut in 1964, following the closure of all the remaining coal mines on the old Severn & Wye system – Cannop in 1960 and Princess Royal in 1962, although the latter continued to deal with screened coal from Pillowell drift until 1965. The adjacent Lydney tinplate works had also ceased operations in 1960.

BELOW: The same train waiting at the Down platform a few moments later. The waiting shelter survives, albeit in much altered form, but the main station building, which had the distinction of being almost totally surrounded by track for most of its existence, was demolished circa 1970. The brick building further along, which housed the Gents toilets, survived into the 1990s.
BOTH BILL POTTER/KRA

SECTION		WORKING LOADS Maximum number of wagons to be conveyed except by Trains specially provided for in the Service Books or by arrangement	MAXIMUM ENGINE LOADS																
			For Group A Engines				For Group B Engines				For Group C Engines				For Group D Engines				For Group E Engines			
From	To		Class 1 Traffic	Class 2 Traffic	Class 3 Traffic	Empties	Class 1 Traffic	Class 2 Traffic	Class 3 Traffic	Empties	Class 1 Traffic	Class 2 Traffic	Class 3 Traffic	Empties	Class 1 Traffic	Class 2 Traffic	Class 3 Traffic	Empties	Class 1 Traffic	Class 2 Traffic	Class 3 Traffic	Empties
DOWN TRAINS																						
Swindon	Coates	70	37	49	74	93	43	57	86	100	45	60	90	100	62	83	100	100	75	100	100	100
Coates	Chalford	70	17	23	34	43	20	27	40	50	22	29	44	55	29Y	39	58	73	35Z	47	70	88
Chalford	Gloucester	70	37	49	74	93	43	57	86	100	45	60	90	100	62	83	100	100	75	100	100	100
Gloucester	Bullo Pill	70	32	43	64	80	37	49	74	93	39	52	78	98	52	69	100	100	63	84	100	100
Bullo Pill	Lydney	70	33	44	66	83	38	51	76	95	42	56	84	100	55	73	100	100	66	88	100	100
Lydney	Chepstow	70	29	39	58	73	33	44	66	83	37	49	74	93	48	64	96	100	58	77	100	100
Chepstow	Caldicot	70	37	49	74	93	43	57	86	100	45	60	90	100	62	83	100	100	75	100	100	100
Caldicot	Severn Tunnel Jn.	70	37	49	74	93	43	57	86	100	45	60	90	100	62	83	100	100	75	100	100	100
UP TRAINS																						
Severn Tunnel Jn.	Caldicot	60	33	44	66	83	38	51	76	95	42	56	84	100	55	73	100	100	66	88	100	100
Caldicot	Chepstow	60	22	29	44	55	25	33	50	63	27	36	54	68	36	48	72	90	43	57	86	100
Chepstow	Lydney	60	33	44	66	83	38	51	76	95	42	56	84	100	55	73	100	100	66	88	100	100
Lydney	Bullo Pill	60	30	40	60	75	35	47	70	88	37	49	74	93	50	67	100	100	60	80	100	100
Bullo Pill	Over Junction	70	33	44	66	83	38	51	76	95	42	56	84	100	55	73	100	100	66	88	100	100
Over Junction	Gloucester "T" Sidings	60‡	22	29	44	55	26	35	52	65	28	37	56	70	37	49	74	93	45	60	90	100
Old Yard	"T" Sidings (See note A)	50	24	32	48	60	27	36	54	68	32	43	64	80	42	56	84	100	50	67	100	100
Gloucester "T" Sidings	Brimscombe	60	28	37	56	70	32	43	64	80	35	47	70	88	47	63	94	100	57	76	100	100
Brimscombe	Chalford	60	13	17	26	33	15	20	30	38	17	23	34	43	22	29	44	55	27	36	54	68
Chalford	Sapperton	60	12	16	24	30	13	17	26	33	14	19	28	35	19	25	38	48	23	31	46	58
Sapperton	Swindon	70	37	49	74	93	43	57	86	100	45	60	90	100	62	83	100	100	75	100	100	100

RIGHT: A close up of Lydney Junction Signal Box circa 1967, which is from a colour print rather than a slide and hence the slightly 'iffy' background colour. At 42ft in length, this was by far the largest of Lydney's six signal boxes and was provided in 1904, built entirely of wood to a standard GWR design as a replacement for a much smaller cabin. As its name implied, this box controlled the junction between the GWR main line and what was, at the time it was built, the ex-Severn & Wye line operated jointly by the GW and Midland railways. The latter became a part of the LM&SR from 1923 and the Joint line agreement continued up until Nationalisation. The box also controlled the Down side goods yard, the connection into the Harbour industrial estate (first established as a Ministry of Supply salvage depot in 1941) and the relief loops either side of the main line; it worked to Lydney West Box to the south and to Awre Junction Signal Box to the north. Its original 67 lever frame was replaced in January 1939 with a new frame of 84 levers. Closed on 24th February 1969, it is believed to have been demolished soon after. Note the triple shunt signal in the foreground. IAN POPE COLLECTION

LEFT: Lydney West Box and crossing, also seen circa 1967 and looking most attractive in WR chocolate and cream. The structure seen here dated from 1918 and was again a replacement for an earlier box. Although mostly constructed of timber, it had brick walls at ground floor level at the station end and rear, and was built on a base of wrought iron girders as it straddled a limited headroom access way running directly beneath. A shade over 23ft in length, it had a 25 lever frame which was removed when it was reduced to ground frame status. The branch to the docks, which crossed the main line on the level, ran just to the right of the gates. The crossing was taken out in September 1963, a month after the docks branch closed. The girder just visible to the left of the box is part of the bridge carrying the line across the Newerne Stream, which feeds into the top end of the docks. IAN POPE COLLECTION

RIGHT: Lydney station circa 1973, looking south and showing the Down platform waiting shelter, which dated from the opening of the station on 19th September 1851. Colour light signals have arrived to replace the semaphores but the crossing gates still remain; these were replaced with lifting barriers in February 1974. In 2012, a major resignalling programme for South Wales saw new LED signals installed at Lydney, which was also brought under the control of the new Cardiff Signalling Centre. Sadly, this also saw the closure of Lydney Crossing Ground Frame, as the West Box had been renamed in March 1969, with its subsequent demolition in December 2012. Since this photograph was taken the front of the shelter has also been opened up but otherwise it is still recognisable today. In the left background, there is a glimpse of the ruined tinplate warehouse. Here, product brought down on a narrow gauge tramway from the nearby tinplate works was unloaded for shipment out via the docks. This area is today heavily overgrown but hidden somewhere deep in the undergrowth and held up largely by ivy, the remains of this historic forgotten building still just survive. NPC

Class '57XX' 0-6-0PT No. 4671, off Severn Tunnel Junction shed, shunts the old GWR transfer sidings on the Up side of the main line in September 1964. It was here that loaded wagons coming down from the Forest were sorted before despatch elsewhere, the preponderance of loaded and empty mineral wagons giving the clue as to the bulk of the traffic on offer. However, note the open wagon in the left foreground loaded with wheel sets for the wagon works, with 'WHEELS UPPER YARD SHOPS' chalked on the door. General goods were dealt with at a small yard complete with shed and cattle pens situated just out of sight to the right on the far side of the main line. Facilities here were limited because there was another goods yard at Lydney Town station, just half a mile up the S&W line, in the centre of the town. In the left distance is Lydney Junction Signal Box and on the far left are the twin S&W passenger lines, used by trains running between Lydney Town and Berkeley Road via the Severn Bridge. Following the accident of 1960 which brought down two of the bridge spans, the passenger service had ceased running, hence the tracks had become rather overgrown by the date of this view. In the far distance Otterspool Junction Signal Box can also just be made out. Lydney had quite a rail complex in steam days, at one time boasting three stations and six signal boxes, as well as an engine shed (closed March 1964), the wagon workshops, extensive sidings and the branches heading off into the Forest, down to the docks and across the Severn to Sharpness. However, as this was mostly connected with freight coming out of the Forest of Dean, certainly in later years, we will explore it all more fully in the next volume. ALAN JARVIS

Lydney...	...	1	6.0 a.m.	15	15	15	15	1½	—	86	0	Shunt Yard and Main Line Sidings, also trips to Pine End and Trading Estate, as required. To Shed 9.0 p.m. **SX**. 5.0 p.m. **SO** or as ordered.
		2	5.45 p.m. **SX**	2½	2½	2½	2½	—	—	11	15	Shunt Main Line Sidings and Goods Shed.
		3	7.15 p.m. **SO**	—	—	—	—	1½	—	1	15	Shunt when required. (Engine off 6.28 p.m. Passenger ex Berkeley Road.)

An unidentified Class '41XX' 2-6-2T hurries north along the Severn estuary with a Cardiff to Gloucester stopping service on 20th June 1964. The attractions of Gloucestershire's many branch lines, coupled with the spectacular beauty of the main line running up through the Stroud Valley, meant that some of the county's railways did not receive quite such good coverage as others. This applied particularly to the old South Wales Railway main line from Chepstow to Gloucester, with most of the stations receiving scant coverage compared to other less well used places. Coupled with this is the fact that the light along the Severn estuary was on the wrong side for photography in the mornings, as the line hugged the river closely in many of the more photogenic locations and was then blocked out in the afternoons by higher ground inland. However, Trevor Owen had here wandered out into the fields just to the south of Severn Bridge station, where the afternoon light was not shielded by the proximity of higher land behind. In the right distance, the end of Lydney pier can just be seen, marking the entrance to the harbour, whilst across the river on the left is the pier protecting the entrance to Sharpness Docks. Beyond that can be seen the twin towers of Berkeley nuclear power station. Construction of this had begun in 1956 and electricity production commenced in 1962. Equipped with two Magnox reactors with a maximum output of 276 megawatts, the power station was in production for twenty-seven years, with reactor No. 2 shut down in October 1988 and No. 1 in March 1989. The decommissioning work undertaken since has ensured the continued survival of the Sharpness Branch from Berkeley Road. *T.B. Owen*

Looking across the estuary to Sharpness Docks on an altogther hazier day in 1959, as an 'Austerity' 2-8-0 ambles past on the main line with a train of loaded iron ore hoppers. In the left foreground there is just a glimpse of the branch leading round to the Severn Bridge, off picture to the left, whilst the signal protects the approach to the 506 yards Severn Bridge Tunnel. Prominent across the river on the right is the training ship *Vindicatrix* where, between 1939 and 1966, over 70,000 boys trained to be merchant seamen. Converted from the hulk of a three-masted barque, she was moored in the old Gloucester & Sharpness Canal dock and used for training exercises. Her history will be covered more fully in a future volume. T.B. OWEN

Taken from the end of the approach viaduct to the Severn Bridge in 1959, a '43XX' Class 2-6-0 heads south with a train of empty mineral wagons. Out in the estuary, the remains of the grain freighter *Rameses II* can be seen. She grounded here whilst inbound with 7,000 tons of grain on 23rd March 1951. The panicking Egyptian crew were only just stopped from launching the lifeboats into this treacherous stretch of river by the pilot – and were then able to walk to shore when the tide went out a few hours later. She broke her back as she settled and although 6,000 tons of her cargo were salvaged she had to be cut up where she lay, an operation which took nine years to complete. Her keel is still occasionally visible at low tide. T.B. OWEN

Viewed from track level near the telegraph pole in the left foreground of the picture above, Class '25' No. D5202 trundles towards Gloucester with a train of 'Dogfish' hoppers loaded with ballast on 25th October 1972. This could be from Tintern Quarry but, equally, may have emanated from Parkend, where stone was still being loaded at Marsh Wharf, a traffic that continued until 1976. D5202 was new in to traffic in May 1963, the locomotive being renumbered as No. 25202 in February 1974; it was allocated to Bristol Bath Road from 1972 to 1976, withdrawn from Plymouth Laira in October 1980 and scrapped at Swindon by the end of that year. BILL POTTER/KRM

'Mogul' No. 6338 passes by on 10th July 1959, with the Severn Bridge as a backdrop and the driver observing the photographer. The single headlamp indicates that this is an 'ordinary passenger train', probably a Gloucester to Cardiff 'stopper'. T.B. OWEN

As already indicated, we shall explore the Severn Bridge in detail in the next volume but here is a taster of what was lost when this magnificent piece of Victorian engineering was demolished in 1967-69. The bridge was damaged when two petroleum barges missed the entrance to Sharpness Docks in fog on the night of 25th October 1960. They drifted upstream and collided with the pier supporting the fifth and sixth spans from the Lydney end (the 16th and 17th from the Sharpness end). The resulting explosion brought down both spans whilst, tragically, five of the crewmen onboard these vessels lost their lives. Although plans were quickly drawn up for a replacement span, nothing was done about it and the bridge stood abandoned whilst discussions dragged on. In the event, with railways on the decline, the Beeching Report being implemented, with the services which had used the bridge being diverted away and the Severn road bridge downstream under construction, the decision was taken to demolish it instead. The only substantial remnant of it still extant today is the round stone tower at the Sharpness end, which supported the swinging span over the Gloucester-Sharpness Canal and this only survived because it was decided that it might damage the canal bank if it was demolished. The bridge had been strengthened for use by heavier locomotives and freshly painted shortly before the accident. Looking at this picture, it is difficult to believe now that such a short sighted decision was taken to demolish such a useful asset. T.B. Owen

CHEPSTOW to GRANGE COURT JUNCTION

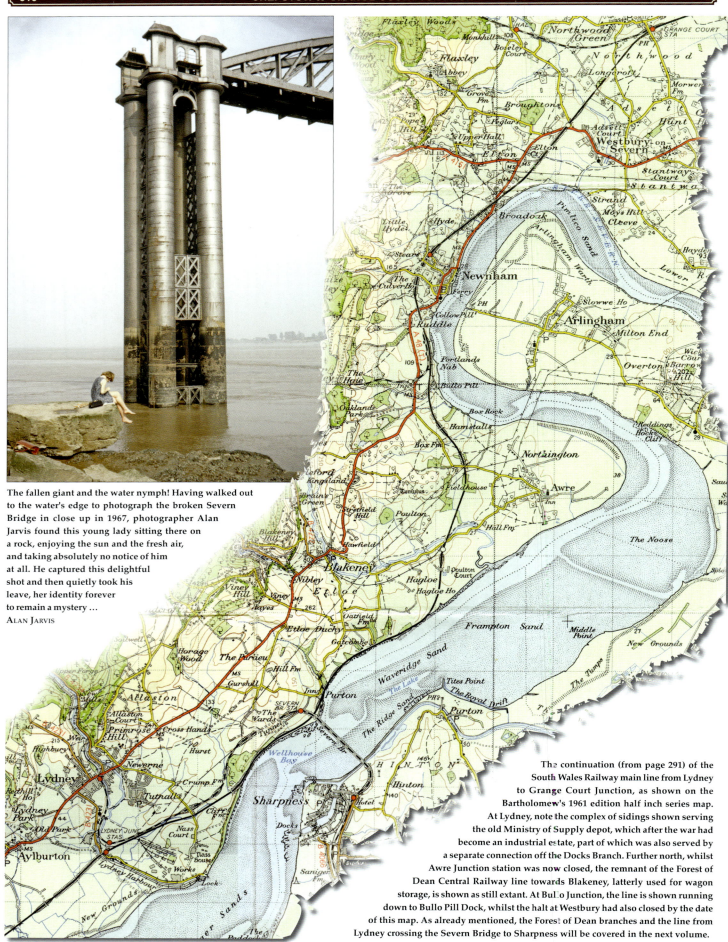

The fallen giant and the water nymph! Having walked out to the water's edge to photograph the broken Severn Bridge in close up in 1967, photographer Alan Jarvis found this young lady sitting there on a rock, enjoying the sun and the fresh air, and taking absolutely no notice of him at all. He captured this delightful shot and then quietly took his leave, her identity forever to remain a mystery …
ALAN JARVIS

The continuation (from page 291) of the South Wales Railway main line from Lydney to Grange Court Junction, as shown on the Bartholomew's 1961 edition half inch series map. At Lydney, note the complex of sidings shown serving the old Ministry of Supply depot, which after the war had become an industrial estate, part of which was also served by a separate connection off the Docks Branch. Further north, whilst Awre Junction station was now closed, the remnant of the Forest of Dean Central Railway line towards Blakeney, latterly used for wagon storage, is shown as still extant. At Bullo Junction, the line is shown running down to Bullo Pill Dock, whilst the halt at Westbury had also closed by the date of this map. As already mentioned, the Forest of Dean branches and the line from Lydney crossing the Severn Bridge to Sharpness will be covered in the next volume.

The history, later life and demolition of the Severn Bridge is covered at length in Volume 2 of this series, *Forest of Dean Lines and the Severn Bridge*. These two views by the late Alan Jarvis should really have been included therein but inadvertently got missed out. However, as they show the early days of the bridge's dismantling from the Lydney bank of the river, I felt that they could be included here as part of our journey back up the main line to Grange Court Junction. They date from late August 1967 and show the Hamburg-based floating crane *Magnus II* at work lifting the spans off the piers. As the top picture also shows, the work proved quite a draw for local people, who came out to sit on the rocks here. Jokingly referred to as 'Severn Bridge beach', this patch of muddy foreshore had been a place to come and catch some sun, have a picnic and maybe a careful paddle, for Lydney and Blakeney residents for several decades following the construction of the bridge and thanks to the proximity of Severn Bridge station. However, summer days at 'the beach' ceased following the closure of the station and the removal of the bridge. The hiring of *Magnus II*, at great expense, was not a great success and was one of the factors which was to lead to the eventual bankruptcy of the demolition company. The tidal nature of the river drastically affected the length of time when it could be used and round the clock working failed to be instigated, whilst the spans were intended to be brought down intact and resold for use, it is rumoured, in South America. In the event, those that were not damaged during the dismantling were cut up on site on the river banks, whilst nine days hire of the crane turned in to three weeks and a bill for £21,000, a colossal sum then. There are no remains to be seen on the Lydney side of the river today but, on the Sharpness side, the round stone tower on which sat the swing section over the Gloucester to Sharpness canal, along with the arch and abutment facing it across the waterway, still survive. As an aside, we held a launch for Volume 2 at the GWR Museum established in the old Coleford goods shed by Mike Rees. There, I was privileged to spend a couple of very entertaining hours in the company of Graham Morgan, fireman to driver Donald Powell (Vol. 2, page 108), who were the last footplate crew over the bridge at the head of the Lydney-Stoke Gifford goods on the night of 25th October 1960, minutes before it was hit. Graham sadly passed away a few weeks after that day and Mike Rees has also now left us, so perhaps these two pictures can also serve as a tribute to two fine Forest railwaymen. BOTH ALAN JARVIS

A spectacular view looking north from the approach arches to the Severn Bridge, towards Gatcombe Bay and Drake's house on 20th June 1964. Built of local sandstone, these arches spanned the main line but were demolished along with the rest of the bridge in the late 1960s, so this viewpoint no longer exists. A 'Grange' heads south with a trainload of steel billets. Note the other photographers in the foreground below. T.B. OWEN

ABOVE: We now begin a run of pictures taken along the short and highly picturesque stretch of line skirting the River Severn by Purton Passage and Gatcombe Bay. The majority of these were taken by Bill Potter in the blue diesel era of the early 1970s, as he searched for interesting new locations following the loss of so many of the secondary and branch lines. Whilst this gives us a chance to study an interesting range of traffic flows, some of which still remain, and rolling stock which has almost all gone, it also highlights the dearth of pictures taken along this route in the steam era in colour. From a viewpoint lower down in the field than that from where the picture on the previous page was taken, 'Peak' Co-Co diesel No. D73 hurries past with a Newcastle to Cardiff train on 5th October 1972. Later designated Class '45', this engine became No. 45111 under TOPS and was withdrawn in 1988. The remains of the Severn Bridge approach arches form a pile at the left edge of the picture. BILL POTTER/KRM

ABOVE: Class '25' No. D7614 ambles south on the main line with a train of empty coal hoppers on 5th October 1972. Viewed from the site of Severn Bridge station, the pile of rubble in the foreground was all that remained of the stone-built approach arches to the Severn Bridge. These were demolished with the use of high explosives in March 1968. New in to traffic in May 1966, D7614 was originally built for the Scottish Region and fitted with tablet catcher equipment. Gravitating south in 1968, it seems to have switched between Bescot, Toton and Crewe depots, so is well out of its area here. Later renumbered 25264, the retention of vacuum brakes saw it become an early class casualty, being withdrawn in December 1980 and cut up at Swindon in 1983.

RIGHT: A similar train from the same vantage point, although here the haulage power is being supplied by English Electric Type '3' (later Class '37') No. D6895 on 6th September 1973. The view is looking across to the hamlet of Purton on the far bank, which straddles the canal on its way north from Sharpness to Gloucester. Coincidentally, there is an even smaller hamlet by the name of Purton on this side of the river too, just to the left of the Severn Bridge station site. BOTH BILL POTTER/KRM

Another train of steel bar skirts the bay past Purton Passage as it heads towards South Wales on 20th May 1974, with Class '31' No. 31308 in charge. Dating from circa 1600, the white-painted house prominent in the distance is known as Drake's House, from an unsubstantiated story that Sir Francis Drake stayed there when visiting Sir William Wintour at Lydney. It was later an inn, possibly first known at The Gatcombe Boat but latterly called The Sloop Inn. Gatcombe had been a small but important port in earlier times, an outlet for Forest timber and salmon caught in the Severn, so it would not have been unlikely that Drake stayed here. However, its trade declined dramatically following the establishment of new docks at Lydney and Bullo Pill in the early 19th century, and was finally destroyed completely by the building of the railway, which cut if off from the river. BILL POTTER/KRM

D7095 heads towards Chepstow with an assortment of hopper wagons on 28th July 1971. The Severn, the longest river in Great Britain, is tidal to some way above Gloucester and experiences one of the highest tidal ranges in the world, with a difference of up to 28 feet between highest and lowest. As such, the construction of the South Wales Railway along its banks in the late 1840s required the provision of substantial stone walls and abutments such as this to stop the line being washed away. New in to service in late December 1963, D7095 started its career at Cardiff Canton and returned there in 1966 after a sojourn to the West Country. It was withdrawn in October 1972, having spent less than nine years in service and cut up at Swindon. BILL POTTER/KRM

These pictures clearly show why many photographers did not bother with this stretch of line, despite its visual impact. The best locations were difficult to find or involved quite a trek and there was little space between river and land to work with. The light is from the river side in the morning but is shielded from much of the track by the high ground in the afternoon and there always is the possibility of a low lying fog rolling across the Severn at any time. They also show, however, that Bill Potter's time and perseverance in searching out locations and angles paid dividends. When the conditions were right, this stretch of line could deliver superb photographic results and can still do so today, although the motive power has changed and there is much less variety in the rolling stock. On 9th September 1971, English Electric Class '3' (later Class '37') No. D6917 rumbles past Purton Passage with a train of empty 'Dogfish' hoppers, bound first to Chepstow, where the locomotive will run round before hauling them up the branch to Tintern Quarry. New to Swansea Landore depot in early 1964, No. D6917 was allocated to Cardiff Canton at the time of this view. Renumbered under TOPS as No. 37217, the locomotive was withdrawn from service by English, Welsh & Scottish Railway in 2006 and purchased by the Harry Needle Railroad Company. In 2008, it was one of four Class '37's restored for use by Network Rail on the ERTMS resignalling project on the Cambrian line. Repainted in Network Rail yellow, renumbered as No. 97034 and named *John Tiley*, the locomotive remains in use today, operating from HNRC's base at Barrow Hill and approaching its fiftieth birthday in 2014. BILL POTTER/KRM

RIGHT: Looking from Purton Passage north to Gatcombe and showing the full extent of Gatcombe Bay, as Class '37' No. 37125 motors south with a train load of steel bar on 20th May 1974. Traffic to and from the British Steel Corporation's South Wales works at Llanwern, near Newport, and Port Talbot, such as iron ore coming in and steel slab heading out, has always been quite intense, with much it using this line. Despite the contraction in the industry, which saw BSC privatised in 1988, become Corus in 1999 after merging with a Dutch steel company and finally taken over by the giant Indian company Tata Steel in 2007, steel traffic continues to pass along the line on a daily basis, heading between the South Wales plants and sites in the north east. The Class '37' became No. 37904 in April 1987 and was taken out of use in 1998. Note automatic signal UM130 is still showing red following the passage of an Up DMU, just visible near the headland. BILL POTTER/KRM

ABOVE: With a wave of acknowledgment from one of the cab crew, Class '45' No. 45101 sweeps round Gatcombe Bay and past Purton Passage on 8th August 1975. At a quick glance, this could be the South Devon coast near Teignmouth, rather than the muddy shores of the Severn Estuary in Gloucestershire. The train was unrecorded by the photographer but the reporting number 1V 88 identifies it as the 10.12am from Newcastle to Cardiff. Previously No. D96, No. 45101's career came to an end in November 1986 and it was scrapped by Berry's of Leicester in 1988. Although not a local engine, several of the class did spend time stationed at Gloucester and so were regulars on this line. BILL POTTER/KRM

LEFT: Classmate No. 45118 *The Royal Artilleryman* heads north at Gatcombe with a train of oil tanks from one of the West Wales refineries near Milford Haven. These trains still run today, albeit not as frequently due to the establishment of a nationwide network of oil pipes to carry the product around the country. Originally No. D67, this locomotive is one of eleven Class '45's saved for posterity and, at the time of writing, is undergoing restoration to working order at RVEL Derby, prior to returning to its home on the Northampton & Lamport Railway. BILL POTTER/KRM

LEFT: With the paintwork on its nose end looking rather worn, 'Peak' Class '45' diesel No. D121 heads a northbound Freightliner train past Purton Passage on 28th July 1971. The high stone retaining wall supports the garden of Purton Manor, a Grade II* listed manor house dating from 1618. Local rumour has it that Sir Walter Raleigh visited his mistress who lived here but as he was executed in the same year that the house was built, this would seem highly unlikely. The manor house can be seen in the view below. D121 later became No. 45069, under which guise its working career finished in July 1986. BILL POTTER/KRM

ABOVE & RIGHT: When British Railways finally finished with steam locomotive power in 1968, they imposed a ban on preserved steam locomotives working on their system. The only exception was *Flying Scotsman*, which had a clause in its 1963 purchase contract allowing the engine to still operate on the main line. However, the ban was lifted in 1971 and since then, the occasional steam special has traversed the Gloucester to Severn Tunnel Junction line. On 16th April 1974, ex-GWR 'Castle' Class 4-6-0 No. 4079 *Pendennis Castle* became one of the first steam engines to work this way since the end of 1965 and is seen passing Purton with a short train which Bill noted as a stock positioning movement. On the rear is ex-GER Inspection Saloon No. 1, fitted with L&NER bogies, owned by Bill McAlpine and today to be found on his private railway near Henley. The 12-wheeled red and cream liveried coach is believed to be an ex-Royal Train vehicle, again probably owned by McAlpine, as he was also part owner of *Pendennis Castle* at this time. In 1977, No. 4079 was sold to the Hamersley Iron Co. in Australia for use on their private system but was happily repatriated back from there in 2000. As of 2012, the engine was still undergoing restoration to full working order at the GWS's base at Didcot. Both BILL POTTER/KRM

At the very tail end of our period, on 27th February 1977, a Swindon 3-car Cross Country DMU crosses the steel girder span over the inlet at Purton Passage, on a Gloucester to Newport stopping service; this is the successor to the 'Prairie' hauled train (albeit working in the opposite direction) that we saw on page 306. Before the coming of the railway, Purton had been a small port and also the base for a ferry across the river to the Purton on the other side. In 1830, a scheme to build a railway, the Purton Steam Carriage Road, into the Forest of Dean got under way, and some earthworks and a 3-arch bridge were built before it all foundered. The line would have required an incline to drop down to Purton and the whole project would have been long forgotten but for the survival of the bridge, spanning a minor country lane seemingly in the middle of nowhere and which is now a Grade II listed structure. Gatcombe Wood cloaks the high ground behind. BILL POTTER/KRM

'Hymek' No. D7046 heads a mixed bag of mineral wagons south past Gatcombe on 7th October 1971. The stone embankment has a single small arch in the centre, over the inlet to the tiny port of Gatcombe, which ceased general trading after it was cut off by the building of the railway but was then from where several generations of the Baylis family still operated their stop net salmon fishing boats. The end of the roof and a chimney of their house can be seen just above the train and also appears in the distance in the top picture on page 314. BILL POTTER/KRM

RIGHT: Awre Junction station was a later opening, on 1st April 1869, as a replacement for the station at Gatcombe. It was the junction for the Forest of Dean Central Railway, an impecunious concern which built a line into the Forest in the hope of tapping into some of the lucrative coal traffic. In the event, with Crown backing initially and despite the combined opposition of the GWR and Severn & Wye Railway, the line was built but the Company's prospects quickly dwindled when the intended coal traffic failed to materialise. The line never had a passenger service and was shut north of Blakeney by the 1920s. The service to Blakeney Goods station finished in 1947 and the line was thereafter used for wagon storage. Awre Junction station was situated 2 miles from Blakeney and a mile from Awre, so was badly affected by bus competion from the 1920s and was eventually closed to passengers on 10th August 1959. Its isolated nature meant that it also saw little attention from photographers, so this view of the signal box in 1967 is all that we have. It had a 28 lever stud frame but was reduced to the status of a gate box on 2nd June 1969. However, the ground frame was taken out on 30th December 1973, although the box was manned until November 1974. It survives in use as a PW store and is now one of only four original signal boxes that remain in the county on Network Rail. IAN POPE COLLECTION

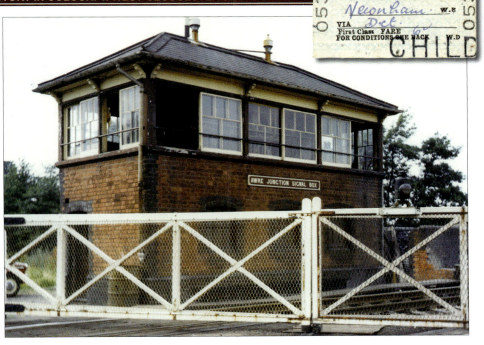

LEFT: An unusual view of the access road to Bullo Pill Dock in 1967, looking through one of the arches of the South Wales Railway viaduct, which originally spanned the Forest of Dean Tramroad when first built. This horse worked line brought coal down from the Cinderford area to the docks but was superceded by the broad gauge Forest of Dean Branch with the coming of the railway. This access road was GWR property and passed to BR on Nationalisation; it is still marked as a 'Private Road' today. In earlier years, the bridge arches were gated and were locked every night. The bracket signal carried the Up Main Home signal for Bullo West box, with the bracketed arm controlling access to the Up Goods running loop from the Up Main. Just glimpsed far left is the West box Down starter. The first West box had stood just to the left of the bracket signal, on this side of the line; it was replaced in 1898 by the box shown over the page. IAN POPE COLLECTION

RIGHT: The remains of Bullo Pill Dock in June 1966, looking east out over the River Severn. Last used for commercial coal traffic in 1926, during the 19th century it had been a busy and important outlet for Forest coal. Vessels traded downriver to the ports of the Bristol Channel, upriver to Stonebench and Elmore just below Gloucester, and across the river and up to Stroud via the Stroudwater and Thames & Severn canals to serve customers such as Stroud gas works, whilst the canal crossroads at Saul Junction also allowed Cadbury's factory alongside the Gloucester & Sharpness Canal at Frampton to be fed with coal from Eastern United Colliery prior to the First World War. The coal tip at the dock was situated where the large bush is on the left, which is obscuring the stone buttress on which it stood. It was removed circa 1950, whilst two further tips had serviced vessels from the river bank just out of picture to the right. As can be seen, the dock had silted up badly after closure, with the gates being left open. However, new gates were fitted in 1989, the dock cleaned out and today it is in use by a marine engineering company. JOHN STRANGE/NPC

Bullo Junction looking towards Lydney on 27th April 1967. On a main line peppered with interesting locations, this was perhaps the most interesting of them all. On the right, the Cinderford Branch (also known as the Forest of Dean Branch) climbs steeply away from the main line before curving away west to cross the A48 road. The main line was on a more gentle curve at this point and also on a slight rise to the junction, with goods loops on either side. In the left background is Bullo Pill West Signal Box, behind which the branch to Bullo Pill Dock made its way down to the dock. After the dock fell out of use in the 1920s, the branch remained in use to Bullo Rubber Mill, established in 1923 in the old wagon works which had closed around the time of the First World War. Goods inwards included bales of rubber delivered by rail from the docks in London, through which it had been imported, along with china clay which was used in the production process. Goods outward comprised the finished products, such as tubing, pram tyres and car hoses. Rail traffic on the branch finally ceased in 1963 and the track was lifted soon after. Thereafter, the mill was served by road and continued in production until 2007. The signalman is strolling across the track with the token for the branch, to hand to the driver of a goods train which was due to head up to Cinderford shortly after the picture was taken. Bullo Junction is another location we will be returning to in the next volume. BILL POTTER/KRM

Bullo Pill West Signal Box dated from 1898, when it was provided as a replacement for an earlier box situated further south, close by the viaduct spanning the dock access road and on the opposite side of the line. The new location certainly gave the signalmen a far better view of the line in both Up and Down directions and allowed line of sight to the East box. In 1907 it was fitted with a GWR HT 3-bar frame with 49 levers, the date suggesting that this was done in accordance with the establishment of a passenger service of railmotor trains on the Forest of Dean Branch to Cinderford, which hitherto had been goods only. A typically attractive GWR box in red and blue brick, it had two windows at the rear which were provided so that an eye could easily be kept on the Bullo Pill Dock Branch but which also gave the signalmen views across the River Severn to Arlingham and beyond. With pleasant vistas in all directions and plenty of varied traffic in the steam era on both main line and branch, there were certainly worse places to work. The box closed on 18th March 1968. IAN POPE COLLECTION

Bullo Junction as viewed from the start of the Forest of Dean Branch on 27th April 1967, three months before it closed to all traffic. The steep drop down to the junction was such that a sand drag had been installed to protect against runaways, a feature not often seen on British railway lines. The intensive coal traffic, from the Forest coupled with the motive power requirements to service it, had seen an engine shed established here from the opening of the line in 1851 and explains the generous provision of water facilities. The shed, which was a single road affair in brick, with wooden end walls and a slate roof, was sited just beyond the water tanks, with the line it straddled running right through it. Closed in 1931, it was used thereafter for wagon storage until finally demolished in the late 1950s. In the distance, just visible past the legs of the water tank, is Bullo Pill East Signal Box, with the brick offices for the Bullo Pill yard staff also in view on the extreme left. Bullo Pill East was an early style GWR box, built entirely of brick and with smaller windows, date uncertain but probably circa 1860. It was fitted with a new frame in 1898 and again in 1930 at which time it had 33 levers. It closed on 2nd June 1969. By the date of these photographs, the yard at Bullo was little used but even just a decade earlier, the sidings and loops here would have been filled with wagons for transfer and goods trains being held to keep the main lines clear. In the right distance is The Nab at Newnham, a promontory overlooking the Severn on which stands St. Peter's church. BILL POTTER/KRM

RIGHT: In the first of four views all taken at Bullo on on 1st August 1973, Brush Type '4' No. D1623 is seen passing the site of Bullo Junction. Under the TOPS scheme, the Type '4's were shortly to be redesignated as Class '47', with this locomotive being renumbered as No. 47042 in January 1974. No. D1623 was a Bescot-based engine at the time of this view, so this could be a Cardiff to Birmingham service. In April 1983, the engine was renumbered again, becoming No. 47586 and it was given the name *Northamptonshire* in a ceremony at Kettering station on 20th September 1989. The locomotive was renumbered for a fourth time in 1991, becoming No. 47676 but the nameplates were retained. Stored by Trainload Freight North East in October 1994, prior to the part re-privatisation of the railways, the nameplates were removed in 1996 and it was scrapped by Booth Roe of Rotherham in April 1998. BILL POTTER/KRM

LEFT: Looking north east across the site of the junction, with the grass grown trackbed at the bottom of the old Cinderford Branch incline on the left. The photographer was standing part way up for a raised view of Class '31' No. D5837, as it clattered past with an unusual freight working. The 'Z' in the headcode indicates that this was a Special, almost certainly an McD train, although the destination was not recorded. The nearest rail connected military site to here was RAF Caerwent, a few miles south of Chepstow but, equally, it could also have been heading all the way to West Wales, to RNAD Trecwn, near Fishguard. Both were armaments/explosives depots. D5837 was soon to become No. 31304 under TOPS and continued in service until March 1996. BILL POTTER/KRM

RIGHT: Looking south east, BR Type '4' No. D83 thunders by with a train of container wagons. The first ten of these locomotives were named after English mountains, which was how the generic term 'Peaks' came to be applied to all members of what became, under TOPS, classes '44', '45' and '46'. They had unusual 4-axle bogies, of which the front axles were unpowered, giving them a 1-Co-Co-1 wheel arrangement. As a member of Class'45', the locomotive was renumbered as No. 45142 and finished work in June 1987. In 1810, an abortive scheme was begun to tunnel under the Severn at this point and remains of the earthworks can still be made out in the fields here. Intended for use by foot passengers and the horse-drawn Forest of Dean Tramroad, if successful it would have been the first subaqueous tunnel in the world. Bill Potter/KRM

LEFT: Class '45' No. D30 heads south unusually with a trainload of coal to South Wales. The train reporting number indicates that this is a Toton to Severn Tunnel Junction working, so this is coal from the Nottinghamshire coalfield which was presumably destined for the furnaces at Llanwern steelworks. To the right of the 'Peak', the formation widens where the short branch down to Bullo Pill Dock used to run. New in to traffic on 20th May 1961, the engine became No. 45029 under TOPS and spent some time allocated to Gloucester Horton Road depot. Withdrawn in July 1987, it then spent a final twelve months at Tinsley depot, Sheffield, as the Chief Civil Engineer's locomotive, for which it became No. 97410. BILL POTTER/KRM

ABOVE: Photographed from Hyde Lane Bridge in late summer 1958, a two-coach train bound for Cinderford is just pulling away from its scheduled stop. The short bay on the right was added in 1907, for the new railmotor service to Cinderford and, from 1908, north to Drybrook Halt as well. The branch service was worked Gloucester-Cinderford in the mornings and evenings, and Newnham-Cinderford during the day but the bay was closed and the connection taken out on 24th March 1957, so for the last eighteen months of its operation was worked solely to and from Gloucester. The lettering under the station name on the board on the left reads 'CHANGE FOR CINDERFORD BRANCH'. The attractive footbridge was to a non-standard design, whilst the goods yard, with its sizeable goods shed, was at the Gloucester end, just out of sight round the curve. The station closed to all traffic on 2nd November 1964 and there is nothing left of it today. Incidentally, after decades of locals referring to it as such, the village is now called Newnham on Severn but historically it was always simply Newnham and that was the name the railway used. MICHAEL HALE

BELOW: Looking in the opposite direction, towards the 232 yards long Newnham Tunnel from an Up train circa 1964, this view provides an excellent study of the original South Wales Railway station building on the Down platform. The red brick parcels office replaced an earlier corrugated iron hut. I particularly liked this view for the two lads enjoying themselves on the platform; I wonder if anyone recognises who they are? NPC

ABOVE: Despite the somewhat isolated nature of some of the stations between Chepstow and Gloucester – Woolaston, Awre Junction and Oakle Street, in particular – the fairly regular spacing of stops on the line precluded the establishment of halts. The one exception was at Westbury on Severn, a sizeable village around 2 miles out of Newnham towards Gloucester. Here, on a stretch of embankment in the fork between the main A48 road and the lane leading to Blaisdon, the GWR opened Westbury-on-Severn Halt (with the hyphens) on 9th July 1928. This view, looking north east towards Gloucester, shows the site of the halt on 3rd July 1962, as heavyweight 2-8-2T No. 7247 clanks past with a lengthy train of empty mineral wagons heading back to South Wales. The halt must have struggled for patronage against bus competion, with many of the services running to and from the Forest of Dean using the main road thence to Gloucester and thus passing through the centre of the village. Known black & white views of the halt invariably show it without a passenger in sight but it did provide a good vantage point for photographing passing trains. It had two wooden platforms 128 feet in length, with corrugated iron waiting shelters, oil lamps and access via gates and steps from both sides of the road bridge. The remains of the entrance gates and sign boards for the Up platform can be seen here but at rail level everything had been removed completely. NPC

BELOW: Westbury-on-Severn is nationally renowned for its magnificent Dutch water garden, originally laid out by the owner of Westbury Court, Maynard Colchester II, between 1696 and 1705. These two colour photographs are themselves historic, having been taken on 10th June 1937 probably for a magazine feature. The main house (twice replaced) no longer exists and the gardens became derelict in the mid 20th century but were taken over in 1967 by the National Trust. Today, restored to their former glory and only featuring plants introduced before 1700, they are open for the public to visit. The view right shows the main canal. NPC

Completing our picturesque circular tour of the Wye Valley lines and the 'Severn Riviera', we finish up once more at Grange Court Junction, just about my favourite location and the one I would dial in to the Tardis if travelling back in time – and which I am currently recreating in model form. To stand on the bridge here and watch the constant procession of main line trains – expresses, stoppers, branch trains, freights and the occasional light engine, interspersed with the regular workings on and off the Hereford line, on a warm sunny day like this would be an enthusiast's dream. And even the fact that 'Castle' Class 4-6-0 No. 7019 *Fowey Castle* is in such filthy condition for an ex-GWR express passenger engine and on a lowly mineral working, would probably not serve to dampen the enthusiasm much. Taken on 26th September 1964, the engine still had five months of service left, being withdrawn from Wolverhampton Oxley shed on 10th February 1965. Note the rake of loaded coal wagons in the background; much use seems to have been made of this siding for storage. HUGH BALLANTYNE

A rare shot of the Up loop in use it is believed in summer 1963, showing Class '72XX' 2-8-2T No. 7203 pulling out with a train of bogie bolster wagons loaded with new track panels. The locomotive was shedded at Severn Tunnel Junction (from where it was withdrawn in December 1963), whilst the train has almost certainly originated from Radyr Pre-Assembly Depot (PAD) near Cardiff. Radyr PAD was established in 1959 for the assembly and loading of track panels, with the depot shunter being sent out with the train to shunt the wagons 'on site' – and there was no other PAD yard in South Wales – then the shunter tucked inside is PWM651, a Ruston 0-6-0 new in 1959. If Radyr was where the train had originated – and there was no other PAD yard in South Wales – then the shunter tucked inside is PWM651, a Ruston 0-6-0 new in 1959. This locomotive survived in use long enough to make it into the re-privatisation of the railways, being sold in to preservation by English, Welsh & Scottish Railway in 1996; it now resides on the Strathspey Railway in Scotland. Where the track panels were desinted for, however, is not known. In the centre distance, the lack of wagons in the storage siding on this occasion means that Church Road crossing and its attendant cottage can be seen, with the crossing gates closed across the line. Incidentally, the siding was referred to in the WTT as Walmer Siding and the points leading to it were kept chained and padlocked in favour of the running line. If it needed shunting, the porter had to get the key to unlock it from the Grange Court Junction signalman. BILL POTTER/KRM

Two views of the junction taken moments apart, with 2-8-0 No. 3812 approaching on the main line with a train of laden coke hoppers; this is the same train shown passing through the platforms seconds later on page 92. Note the Home signal for the station was positioned 'wrong side', on the inside of the curve, for siting purposes. There had also been a trailing crossover between the two running lines at this point, which was removed on 28th August 1961 after having been out of use for several years. Although very similar, I have included both pictures because whilst the train is much closer in the bottom view, that above shows the wagons parked in Walmer Siding in more detail. This siding, which had a capacity for eighty wagons, was used for additional storage when the Up loops were occupied, which involved a lengthy reverse shunt through the Hereford line platforms. T.B. OWEN

CHEPSTOW to GRANGE COURT JUNCTION

LEFT: A short train of 'Dogfish' wagons loaded with ballast heads to Gloucester yard from Whitecliff Quarry, in the Forest of Dean, in January 1965. The fireman of '57XX' Class 0-6-0PT No. 8745 acknowledges the photographer with a grin. Travelling into the Forest via Lydney Junction, with a reversal at Coleford Junction to gain the old Severn & Wye branch to Coleford and finally down the last mile of the old GWR branch from Coleford to Monmouth to reach the quarry, this would have been a picturesque and enjoyable turn for the train crew. As the pannier continues on its way to Gloucester, we shall end our tour of west Gloucestershire here, facing towards the '*fair hills of Dean*', which we shall be exploring in detail in the next volume. JOHN STRANGE/NPC

BELOW: The end. T.B. OWEN

In the days of steam and pounds, shillings and pence, every station had a cash bag, a leather pouch in which would be placed the day's takings, accompanied by a copy of the receipts. On busy lines these would be collected on a daily basis but on other routes possibly just once a week. They would be given to the guard of the last train of the day and taken to a central point for emptying by the accounts department. They would then be delivered back out to each station by the first train of the day following, or on a Monday morning if on a weekly collection on a line with no Sunday service. The Hereford-Ross-Gloucester line bags would all have been returned to Gloucester for emptying and the bags were all identical apart from the different brass name tags for each station. As there was generally only one for each station, they are now highly sought after items of railwayana. IAN POPE COLLECTION

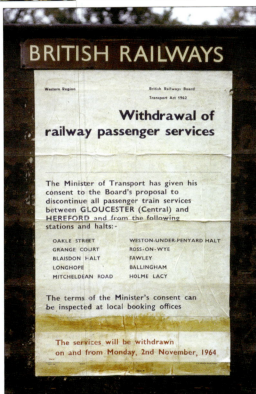

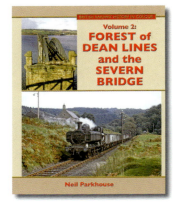

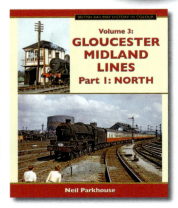

VOL. 2: FOREST OF DEAN LINES AND THE SEVERN BRIDGE. 328 pages. ISBN: 9781899889 98 3. Price £30.00 + £4.00 p&p.

VOL. 3: GLOUCESTER MIDLAND LINES PART 1: NORTH. 280 pages. ISBN: 9781911038 18 4. Price £30.00 + £4.00 p&p.

Visit the Lightmoor Press website to order: www.lightmoor.co.uk

COLOUR IMAGES WANTED FOR THIS SERIES

There are still locations that I have little or nothing of for the planned further volumes in this series, whilst I am always interested in finding images for my collection from anywhere in the county. Anyone with colour slides or photographs of Gloucestershire railways that they would like to share with a wider audience and that I could possibly use in future volumes is invited to contact me directly at the Lightmoor office address at the bottom of the Contents page or by email: neil@lightmoor.co.uk